The Spatial Organisation of Multinational Corporations

The Spatial Organisation of Multinational Corporations

IAN M. CLARKE

ST. MARTIN'S PRESS
New York

Library of Congress Cataloging in Publication Data

Clarke, Ian M.
    The spacial organisation of multinational corporations.

    Bibliography: p.
    Includes index.
    1. International business enterprises. 2. Industrial
management. 3. Chemical industry. 4. Imperial Chemical
Industries, Ltd. I. Title.
HD62.4.C52   1985   338.8'8   85-2265
ISBN 0-312-75028-5

Contents

List of Figures

Figures

List of Tables

Tables

For Jude

Preface

The purpose of this volume is to examine, through case studies, the spatial structure and the geographical implications of modern multinational corporations. An ability to conceptualise the spatial form of the apparently new types of *global* rather than merely multinational business organisations is critical to an understanding of their effects on the space economy. Hence, the forthcoming chapters focus on aspects of the complex organisation of corporate structures — by surveying relevant sections of the theoretical literature and using original empirical material — in an attempt to provide a preliminary framework within which the processes of corporate reorganisation in space can be described and evaluated. However, because of the rather uncertain nature of the relationships between corporate structure and the various stages involved in the internationalisation of production, the book prefers to concentrate on elucidating these relationships and highlighting some of their ramifications, regarding this as an ample and important area of analysis in its own right. Consequently, no attempt is made to address the imperatives of capital accumulation and circulation in corporations directly from a theoretical perspective, although it is inevitable that they will be referred to in the course of discussion. Rather, the aim is to focus on the form of the 'cart' before addressing the mechanics of the 'horse', which can be assessed in later studies. Thus, by providing a conceptual framework within which the activities of business organisations can be described and evaluated, it is anticipated that this volume will be of direct use to the large number of disciplines concerned with multinational corporations' role in the world economy, including economists, organisation theorists and regional scientists, as well as geographers.

The chosen theoretical perspective requires that a framework be established which provides a means of linking macro- and micro-scale processes operating in space, integrating propositions relating to the organisation and spatial structure of corporations. The business organisation itself, therefore, is taken as the appropriate unit of analysis to gain insights into the position particular geographical events occupy within *corporate* space. Consequently, the analytical framework is derived from theories concerning the structure of business organisations.

The argument is conducted within the context of business organisations operating in the chemicals industry between 1970 and 1980, special attention being given to one corporation, ICI. In particular, several conceptual problems of corporate structure are identified and addressed, concerning differentiation between and within organisations, and the role space plays in establishing, maintaining and increasing structural inequalities. The analysis expands these general arguments but also underlines the importance of historical patterns of corporate development which are embodied in organisational structures. Furthermore, the analysis both clarifies and exposes factors influencing the creation of a changing international spatial division of labour in the 1970s and 1980s by emphasising the need to address processes operating inside individual plant locations, as well as inside different types of business organisation.

The material included in the study represents the outcome of three years of postgraduate research at the Australian National University in Canberra. I would, therefore, like to acknowledge with gratitude the help provided by several organisations and many individuals, to whom I am indebted for information, encouragement and ideas. The university, which awarded me a scholarship, and especially the Department of Human Geography in the Research School of Pacific Studies, which financed my fieldwork, deserve special thanks for supporting the research and ideas which emerged from the work.

I am particularly grateful to Michael Taylor and Nigel Thrift, who supervised my research and were constant sounding boards in the formulation of ideas and in dealing with practical and theoretical problems. Both Peter Rimmer, who acted in the capacity of advisor, together with Dean Forbes, assisted during my early months in Canberra and helped initiate and maintain the study. I am grateful too for the many ways in which other members of the Department of Human Geography contributed to the creation of this work. Lio Pancino and Keith Mitchell helped in the preparation of some of the early diagrams and Ken Lockwood was always helpful with constant technical advice and cheery comments. Furthermore, I would like to thank Elizabeth Lawrence, Carol McKenzie and Pauline Faulkner for their consistent help with the typing. I am indebted to Suzy Jeffcoat for completing the diagrams, Carol McKenzie for typing much of the initial manuscript and subsequent revisions and Norma Chin for producing the tables. I am also grateful to Croom Helm for allowing me to reproduce material published elsewhere, particularly that contained in Chapters 4 and 6. I warmly acknowledge the constructive comments of the anonymous examiners of the thesis on which this book is based, comments which must undoubtedly form part of an ongoing research agenda. I am also grateful to many individuals working for ICI who assisted during my visits and who were valuable sources of information. Equally, I would like to extend my gratitude to those innumerable site managers who found time to search out information and complete a questionnaire for yet another researcher.

Many other intangibles aided the process of writing, not the least of which were Rory's amusing canine antics, which kept me sane, fit and smiling during a cold Canberra winter. Undoubtedly too, the warmth and charm of the Australian landscape were a constant source of inspiration. Finally, I thank Jude for her love and support, for keeping my feet on the ground and for helping me maintain a realistic perspective on the task I had set myself. This book is dedicated to her.

1 Introduction

Having exposed the tremendous magnitude of the task of formulating a theory of space economy, Weigmann stops for breath. How to
locate the basic form? How to represent as an empirical Gestalt unit
the multitude of interlaced, mutually related individual markets,
market strata, and market densities? (Walter Isard, 1956, *Location
and Space Economy*, p. 39.)

The rate of industrial restructuring has quickened markedly in the
world economy during the 1970s and early 1980s and one of the most
potent vehicles of change is said to be the multinational corporation,
a form of capitalist enterprise with an unprecedented scale and scope
of operations. Geographers, economists and regional scientists
alike have gradually awoken to 'the plain fact . . . that national economies no longer are "isolated states" of the kind originally hypothesised in location analysis by von Thünen' (Holland, 1976a, p. 39),
dominated and interlaced as they are, to a greater or lesser extent, by
large multi-locational, multi-product, multi-divisional organisations.
These trends need little elaboration. Hymer's (1960) classic study of
the international operations of international firms was followed by
other works on the implications of multinational corporations for
uneven development (e.g. Hymer, 1972; Palloix, 1977, Holland, 1976b)
and, more specifically, on their role in regional crisis formation (Mandel, 1978; Wallerstein, 1979; Carney, Hudson and Lewis, 1980). In
geography alone, a succession of recent publications have offered
insights into the structure, workings and effects of these large corporations at regional, national and international levels (e.g. Massey and
Meegan, 1979b, 1982, Watts, 1980a; Townsend, 1982b; Taylor and
Thrift, 1982d), with the changing geography of employment being a
prominent focus of these studies.

The publication in English of *The New International Division of
Labour* (Fröbel, Heinrichs and Kreye, 1980) has acted as an analytical
benchmark and as a fulcrum for research in this respect by providing

an overall explanation of the simultaneous occurrence of growing structural unemployment in industrialised countries and industrialisation in developing countries. The continued success of most large companies amidst economic, social and political problems in western industrialised countries, formed the backcloth for Fröbel *et al.*'s thesis, which argued that there had been a fundamental change in the structure of the world economy in the second half of the twentieth century, resulting in the creation of a 'new' international division of labour, as opposed to the 'old' international division of labour which had been a characteristic of the first half of the twentieth century. A radical shift in the spatial organisation of production in the world economy is integral to this change: from an old division of labour which was largely the outcome of the preponderance of wage labour as the basis of manufacturing in the industrial centres of Europe, USA and Japan, and coupled with a peculiar form of wage labour as the basis for the extraction and production of raw materials for export to world markets in the enclaves of Latin America, Africa and Asia; to a new division of labour resulting from a substantial growth in the orientation of industrialisation of the developing countries to world markets. The latter phase has been enabled by the creation of an almost inexhaustible supply of disposable labour in the developing countries, the division and subdivision of the production process to allow manufacturing to be performed with minimum levels of skill and the development of techniques of transport and communication allowing production to be located at almost any site in the world. According to Fröbel *et al.* (1980, p. 13), the coincidence of these three preconditions:

> has brought into existence a world market for labour and a real world industrial reserve army of workers, together with a world market for production sites. Workers in the already established countries are now placed in a world-wide labour market and forced to compete for their jobs with their fellow workers in the developing countries.

An important corollary of this argument is that companies wishing to survive in the new operating environment of the world economy are forced to initiate a transnational reorganisation of production (Fröbel, Heinrichs and Kreye, 1980). However, a critical weakness of the perspective is that it treats the company simply as a *reactive* element in the restructuring process, and fails to give adequate emphasis to the opportunities companies may have to initiate restructuring of the space economy. The difficulty here is in providing an analytical framework within which the concept of the new international division of labour can be operationalised, explained and assessed. In part, the weakness stems from an inability to show as well as to realise that 'globally organised production must logically be tackled from a global perspective, otherwise we will fail to understand the subtle reorganisations taking place' (Forbes, 1982, p. 107).

Thus, although the concept of a new international division of labour was quickly embraced by industrial geographers, it has remained a catchword, even though it has the potential to unite otherwise separate research emphases. This failing is made evident in a review of the field by Wood (1980) which catalogued five main foci of research in industrial geography: measures of regional economic change; prediction and policy evaluation; 'components of change' studies; the growing dependence of regional economies on outside control; and the implications of multinational activity for regional policy. Although these areas of study are valuable in their own right, no adequate link has yet been forged between them. As a means to uncover this link and to tie together facets of a new international division of labour, three approaches within industrial geography can be considered.

The broadest of the approaches is the 'industrial systems' framework advocated by Hamilton and Linge (1979), which examines the enterprise itself and its environment, as well as relationships between the two. In a recent comment on the state of industrial geography, Malecki (1982, p. 1572) noted that this framework:

> is perhaps best described simply as a very large umbrella, since it concerns nearly any topic concerning firms to be within its purview; however, it does not provide an explicit structure for analysis.

The second approach which may offer an integrative framework is the 'structuralist' form of analysis expounded by Massey and Meegan (1979b). In this methodology, the authors detail three analytical steps which they regard as necessary to understand changes in the structure of industry: an analysis of national and international economic trends; an examination of the implications of these trends for each firm; and an evaluation of how these affect the form of production and hence employment. Marshall's (1982) assessment of the structuralist framework is that it argues against adopting 'functionalist' concepts (especially from the organisational sciences) because these are conservative in their own right, and he advances that 'firms are grouped on the basis of their experience of economic change, rather than in terms of their organisational characteristics' (Marshall, 1982, p. 1675).

These industrial systems and structuralist approaches differ in the amount of emphasis they place on studying the individual business organisation. Whilst possibly overstating the case, Wood's (1981, p. 416) comment that 'if we must study the whole economic order as a prelude to the explanation of any specific location problem it may not result in very much progress in the field', holds some truth with respect to these approaches. Thus, while the two approaches act to integrate material and analysis at a number of levels, particularly that of political economy, with factors which directly affect the organisation, they fail to provide a central, identifiable and tangible analytical focus for the separate elements of industrial geography.

A third framework in industrial geography which might help provide a mechanism to link the aspects of a new international division of labour is the 'enterprise approach'. Pioneered by McNee's (1958; 1960) work over two decades ago, and followed by a stream of articles by a number of authors (e.g. Krümme, 1969, 1981; Watts, 1974, 1978, 1982; Steed, 1971; Dicken, 1976; Rees, 1972), the enterprise approach takes as its main focus the behaviour and spatial ramifications of corporate activity. With regard to the five main research foci of industrial geography outlined above, therefore, the enterprise approach provides a central theme of investigation by focusing on the corporation as the main agent of spatial change. However, even the enterprise approach as it stands has made only limited inroads into understanding the principles of corporate organisation, and in establishing possible causal effects, for example, on employment at an international level.

It can be asserted that these three main approaches are limited in their capacity to develop deeper insights into the causes of the changing spatial division of labour, either because they fail to situate the business organisation as a principal mechanism creating and altering spatial structures, or because of an overly regional emphasis. Thus, although the object of this study is the multinational corporation, the organisations approach which is adopted to study it seeks to explain spatial change through the structural characteristics and behaviour of individual business organisations. A business organisation framework operates on the assumption that the individual enterprise is the most tangible and fundamental unit of the economy, the nexus or crucible in which macro- and micro-scale processes are played out (Baran and Bielby,

1980; Taylor and Thrift, 1983), and it attempts to establish principles the spatial and organisational structure of these enterprises, as well as their behaviour. In this respect, the approach is much wider than that of the 'enterprise school', which has tended to focus largely on firm behaviour. Consequently, the aim of this book is to sketch, in a preliminary way, some of the main organisational dimensions of corporate space, into which otherwise disparate and disaggregated spatial events can be integrated. By using an organisations approach, the aim is to examine the effects of the organisational structure of the multinational corporation on the new and changing international division of labour.

This brief introductory chapter therefore has a threefold purpose. The first objective is to examine some of the principal features of multinational corporations in order to see how they might affect the spatial division of labour. A second objective is to describe some of the more recent trends which are emerging in organisational structures and thereby to identify some of the more problematic areas which require attention. These two objectives will be discussed in the first two sections of the chapter. In the final section, the objective is to draw together these basic tenets and to outline the aims and organisation of the book.

Multinational Enterprise and the Changing Spatial Division of Labour

The growth of the multinational form of enterprise has increased in a series of quantum leaps from the late 1960s for several reasons, including developments in manufacturing technology and communications, the formation of trading blocs (such as the EEC and ASEAN) and the opening up of financial, resource and labour markets on a world scale, a form of 'global sourcing' by the multinational corporation (Palloix, 1977). As a direct result of these trends, the opportunities for large corporations to spread their geographical production networks have increased dramatically. A useful indicator of this trend is the sudden increase in the level of foreign investment in manufacturing production in the 1970s, which grew by 82 per cent between 1971 and 1976 (UNESCO, 1978). Most of this growth was controlled by slightly more than 400 large multinational corporations operating at a global level (Stopford, Dunning and Haberich, 1980). It is not surprising, therefore, that the multinational corporation has become a focus of study in its own right in disciplines as diverse as geography, economics and sociology, and central to the work in each of these disciplines has been a search for an overarching theoretical explanation of present international industrial trends.

In geography, for example, attention has concentrated on the expanded use of space on a global scale as an integral part of a multinational's organisation. This process has forced dramatic alterations in the spatial organisation of production, as centres of capital and administration have become separated from nodes of production on a global scale (see Forbes, 1982). The so-called 'internationalisation' thesis (Gibson, 1980; Fagan, 1980) has emphasised labour (e.g. Clark and Massey, 1982; Storper and Walker, 1983), capital (e.g. Walker and Storper, 1981) and resources (e.g. Forbes, 1982; Geddicks, 1977) as the main generating forces in this, the latest stage of international capitalist development.

A review of the economics literature on multinationals is beyond the scope of this discussion and, in any case, one has already been compiled by Caves (1983), albeit from a very specific viewpoint. Nevertheless, it is useful to note that modern economic theory on multinational enterprise has shifted somewhat from the established neo-classical theories of foreign direct investment and notions of comparative advantage, because of flaws which had appeared in the theory. One of the more interesting schools of thought to be developed in economics is represented by the broadly termed internalisation thesis (e.g. Buckley and Casson, 1976; Rugman, 1982). According to this theory, which implicitly parallels the geographic theory of internationalistion, multinational corporations are encouraged to *internalise* their activities and technologies because of market failures, regulations and tariff structures imposed by governments. Dunning (1979) has proposed his own 'eclectic' theory of the growth of multinationals, but it is only an amalgam of ideas which can be inserted under the internalisation banner. The eclectic theory points out that firms will tend to undertake foreign direct investment when two basic conditions are met: whether or not the firm will benefit from internalising its overseas activities, compared to exporting goods or licensing production to foreign firms; and whether or not the firm has any locational and ownership advantages over other firms to enable it to achieve internalisation.

In sociology, very few researchers have taken the multinational corporation as the explicit object of study, although a valuable contribution has been made towards understanding the structure of firms by organisation theorists. This omission has been bemoaned by Evans

(1981) in his review of sociological research on multinational corporations. Even so, he does point out the considerable wealth of research sources available within the discipline, ranging from theories of the firm and product life-cycle theory (e.g. Vernon, 1979), to the work of the dependency theorists (e.g. Frank, 1967; Cardoso, 1972; Kahl, 1976; Duvall *et al*., 1981) who consider multinationals to be an active force in generating dependent development on an international scale. The main division in the discipline is between approaches which study multinationals as organisations based on class relations, and those which take a functional approach, based on the perspective of the organisational sciences (e.g. Hickson *et al*., 1971; Pugh *et al*., 1968) Few conclusions have been made, however, which relate explicitly to the multinational corporation.

Despite the certain amount of common ground in studies of multinational corporations in each of these disciplines, it is pertinent to note the limitations of each approach. On the one hand, geographical studies have paid little regard to the internal workings of multinationals, preferring instead to concentrate on their interactions with other organisations (for example, in the study of plant linkages) and their spatial effects. On the other hand, the organisational school in sociology is confusing and uses ambiguous terminology, and does not include spatial structure as a basic feature of the organisation. A similar criticism can be made of the economics literature. But as McDermott and Taylor (1982) have profitably shown, a fusion of geographical and organisational theories in particular can resolve some of these fundamental contradictions. Furthermore, many of the studies of the 'firm' in economics and sociology are usually only able to infer conclusions from analyses of sectoral rather than organisational data (e.g. in economics see Dunning, 1979; Thirwall, 1982; Singh, 1977; and in sociology see Oster, 1979; and Kaufman, Hodson and Fligstein, 1981).

In this light, the enterprise approach in industrial geography, seen in its broadest terms, is well placed to understand the causes and effects of corporate restructuring through its emphasis on the business organisation itself, and with reference to space as a basic element of multinational corporate structure. However, the 'business organisation' perspective is preferred to the 'enterprise approach' because of the explicit emphasis it places on structure. Before such work can be carried out, it is useful to examine some of the findings of previous work, in order to establish new research emphases and to point to areas of the organisations literature which need to be examined.

A major feature of the geographical research on multinational corporations is the wide range of spatial effects they can induce. For example, plants belonging to multinationals have been shown to produce both stabilising effects on local economies (e.g. McAleese and Counahan, 1979) and destabilising effects (e.g. Smith, 1979) in relation to employment and industrial structure caused by the types of technology they introduce (e.g. Ashcroft and Ingham, 1979).

Such conflicting evidence is also present when the spatial dynamics of the operations of multinational corporations are evaluated. During the present global recession, rationalisation of the facilities of multinationals has affected many areas such as the United States (e.g. Bluestone and Harrison, 1982), Ireland (e.g. Perrons, 1981) and Scotland (e.g. Hood and Young, 1982; Firn, 1975; Dicken and Lloyd, 1976). In other regions, the expansion of investment by multinational corporations has been shown to produce distinct benefits. Examples from Australia (e.g. Fagan, 1981; Utrecht, 1978; Alford, 1979), Austria (e.g. Sinclair and Walker, 1983) and the United States (e.g. Håkanson, 1979), point towards some of the potential benefits when it has proven possible to attract such investment. Thus, in some circumstances, the expansion of multinational investment can have a distinct multiplier effect on the local economy, whilst in others, rationalisation or simply the plain failure of their ventures (e.g. Grunberg, 1981) may act as a reverse multiplier or 'contraction pole' (e.g. Rabey, 1977, Van den Bulcke *et al.*, 1979). So much depends on the characteristics of the corporation, the region, the nature of the venture and the establishment itself, that it is difficult to draw any firm conclusions on the spatial effects of multinational corporations from studies of this kind.

In order to explain the employment effects of the changing international division of labour as induced by multinational and other large business organisations in any single national economy -- for example, those illustrated for the United Kingdom in Table 1.1 – it is necessary to examine a number of factors together. First, each case must be placed in the context of the overall adjustments in the worldwide operations of the individual corporations (e.g. Chapman, 1974; Perrons, 1981). Second, this means understanding the interaction between locational changes (e.g. Rees, 1972), and changes in the production process (e.g. Carmichael, 1977) within the business organisation. Although some authors have stressed that the production or 'labour' process is at the heart of the changing spatial division of labour (e.g. Clarke, 1981; Clark and Massey, 1982; Walker and Storper, 1981), the problem lies more in articulating this interaction within the first two sets of forces of corporate adjustment and locational change. As Olle and Schoeller (1982, p. 57) have noted specifically in this respect:

> It is the historically unique *combination* of innovations in site, products and processes in a phase of world economic stagflation, which constitutes the substance of the reorganisation of the world economy over the last ten years.

So far, industrial geography, and especially the enterprise approach, has made little progress in understanding the causes of this changing international division of labour. This failure arises out of the inability to place micro-level changes within the worldwide adjustments being made by individual corporations. In this respect, an important study by Teulings (1984) on the Dutch group Philips shows the way. As Teulings (1984, p. 612) points out:

> The international capital movement of the 1970s is not the involuntary result of a multitude of uncoordinated and anomalous employers' decisions, but is directed, to an important degree, by a limited number of mutually highly interwoven dominant enterprises, which give the internationalisation process its organised character.

Teulings's study examined movements of capital between the main continental divisions of the company, as reflected in interdivisional employment changes, thereby demonstrating the relative ease with which multinational corporations can restructure their production. The implicit consensus from the few studies which have adopted or modified Teulings's approach, for example, on the West German and British multinational chemical corporations Hoechst (Watts, 1982) and ICI (Clarke, 1982), is that the methodology builds on the existing enterprise literature in geography by emphasising its main weak spot: a lack of appreciation of even the most fundamental aspects of internal organisational structure. It can be concluded that it is vital to understand the form of organisation peculiar to the corporation before the spatial effects can be evalued.

Integral to this weakness is the difficulty which is encountered in conceptualising the relationship between changes in organisational structure and the internationalisation process within multinational corporations. A review of industrial geography by McConnell (1982, p. 1636), stressed that most studies 'do not provide an explicit meaning of the. . .[internationalisation]. . .process. They do not clearly

Table 1.1: Large Corporations and Employment Change: United Kingdom, 1973-81

	NUMBERS EMPLOYED IN UNITED KINGDOM			PERCENTAGE CHANGE IN EMPLOYMENT			COMMENTS
	1981	1977	1973	1973-77	1977-81	1973-81	
GEC	157,000	156,000	170,000	-8.2	+0.6	-7.6	
Br. Steel	109,600	209,000	229,000	-8.7	-47.6	-52.1	
BL	104,000	171,943	171,296	+0.4	-39.5	-39.3	
Thorn-EMI	90,894	74,661	78,568	-5.0	+21.7	+15.7	Merger EMI 1980
Br. Aerospace	79,000	66,000	71,000	-7.0	+19.7	+11.3	
Unilever	79,148†	91,923	88,544	+3.8	-13.9†	-10.6†	
Courtaulds	77,405	112,009	125,000	-10.4	-30.9	-36.1	
ICI	74,000	95,000	104,000	-8.7	-22.0	-28.8	1973 excludes IMI
Ford	70,000	73,333	70,143	+4.3	-4.5	-0.2	
Br. Shpbldrs	67,500	-	-	-	-22.1*	-	Post-nationalisation figures
Hawker-Sidd.	55,000	50,900	82,400	-38.2	+8.0	-33.3	From 1975 excludes BAe subsid.
Lucas	55,000	68,778	71,330	-3.6	-20.0	-22.9	
GKN	51,000	73,196	78,351	-6.6	-30.3	-34.9	
Rolls-Royce	55,000	56,646	61,446	-7.8	-2.9	-10.5	
Tube Inv.	50,300	51,490	53,813	-4.3	-2.3	-6.5	
BAT Ind.	47,450†	36,388	36,782	-1.1	+30.4†	+29.0†	Major UK retailing expansion
BP	39,000	33,708	26,072	+29.3	+15.7	+49.6	Shell Mex. BP split Jan. 1976
Northern Eng.	36,000	33,673	-	-	+6.9	-	New group 1977
BICC	32,100	32,200	36,200	-11.0	-0.3	-11.3	
Dunlop	32,000	48,000	52,000	-7.7	-33.3	-38.5	
S. Pearson	31,322†	28,946	27,282	+6.1	+8.2†	+14.8†	
Philips	30,000§	N/A	61,339	-4.1	-34.4†	-51.1	
Vickers	29,425†	27,095	29,724	-8.8	+8.6†	-1.0†	Rolls-Royce Motors merger 1980

Burmah	28,000	31,900	38,700	−17.6	−12.2	−27.7	
IMI	22,255	26,664	28,173	−5.4	−16.5	−21.0	
Vauxhall	21,000	30,180	34,141	−11.6	−30.4	−38.5	
Shell UK	20,035	19,767	–	–	+1.3	–	Shell Mex. BP split Jan. 1976
Babcock Int.	19,238	22,521	20,716	+8.7	−14.5	−7.1	Name change in 1979
Distillers	18,943	19,156	19,300	−0.7	−1.1	−1.8	
Michelin	17,500	18,658	17,274	+8.0	−6.2	+1.3	
Dowty	16,635	13,886	13,222	+5.0	+19.8	+25.8	Acquired Ultra in 1977
Massey-Ferg.	15,870	21,486	18,907	+13.6	−26.1	−16.1	
IBM	14,741	15,488	12,428	+24.7	−4.9	+18.6	
Racal	14,135	5,373	3,533	+52.1	+163.1	+300.1	Merger Decca 1980
Glaxo	13,725	15,944	16,568	−3.7	−13.9	−17.1	
Rank Xerox	12,520	11,615	10,762	+7.9	+7.8	+16.3	
Eng. China C.	11,795†	10,977	10,900	+0.7	+7.4†	+8.2†	
Kodak	10,496†	11,364	12,768	−11.0	−7.4†	−17.8†	
Talbot/Chrys.	10,000	22,800	30,283	−26.2	−56.1	−67.6	
CIBa-Geigy	9,234	10,933	7,465	46.5	−15.5	+23.7	Takeover Ilford 1975
Davy	9,113§	5,929	4,938	+20.1	+53.7	+86.5	
Esso Petroleum	8,614†	8,666	10,026	−13.6	−0.6†	−14.1†	
Rothmans Int.	8,057	6,349	5,956	+6.6	+26.9	+35.3	
Inco Europe	6,400	7,552	4,187	+80.4	−15.3	+52.8	Acquired Daniel Doncaster 1975
Cummins Eng.	6,109	3,760	3,389	+10.9	+62.8	+80.3	
Johnson Matthey	5,888	5,635	5,748	−2.0	+4.5	+2.4	
Caterpillar	4,812	5,114	4,655	+9.9	−5.9	+3.4	
Intl. Harvester	3,500	6,430	5,829	+10.3	−45.6	−40.0	Acquired Seddon Atkinson 1974
Mobil	2,477†	2,342	N/A	–	+5.8†	–	
Conoco	2,299	2,259	1,724	+31.0	+1.8	+33.3	

Notes: † 1980 figure used.   * 1978-81.
§ Floated Cambridge Instruments 1981, taking about 5,000 Philips jobs.
ξ Acquired Herbert Morris and British Testing in 1978.
Source: *Financial Times* (1981, p. 35).

specify the dependent variable, which is necessary if the transformation is to be modelled.' In this respect, some geographers have gone to considerable lengths to synthesise models of the stages in the spatial evolution of large corporations (e.g. Hayter and Watts, 1983, p. 169; Taylor and Thrift, 1982a, p. 27), frequently at an international level. These efforts are based on the same premise that corporate behaviour and spatial form are intimately related, and there is often an implicit assumption that a comprehensive general theory of international business behaviour can be developed (e.g. McConnell, 1982, p. 1638). By implication, this assumption presupposes there is uniformity in all organisational structures.

Spatial Change and Changing Structures

Even if this relationship between behaviour and spatial form could have been proven at one time, an increasing amount of circumstantial evidence has been accumulated in the 1970s and 1980s which suggests the emergence of new forms of multinational corporations radically different from earlier types. These forms are in complete contrast to the multinationals of the 1960s, which were dominated by overseas investment originating from the United States and corporate structures of a mother-daughter type of relationship (Franko, 1976; Stopford and Wells, 1972). Consequently, at least two forms of multinational enterprise have been suggested. The first form, of course, is the classic multinational corporation. Quite clearly, however, international investment by a second form of multinational corporation has undergone a fundamental change (Stopford, Dunning and Haberich, 1980). The characteristics of this new form of corporation, particularly its organisational and geographical structure, has led to the coining of the name 'global' corporation (e.g. Dicken, 1977; Vernon, 1979; Davidson and Haspeslagh, 1982; Hout, Porter and Rudden, 1982; Taylor and Thrift, 1982a). According to Vernon (1979), two changes have led towards the emergence of these new global structures. The first has been a profound change in the investment environment and income levels of industrialised countries. The second change has been in the expanded geographical scope of multinational corporations (see Table 1.2). To quote Dunning's (1979), pp. 271-2) assessment of this change:

As the extent of the multinationality of MNCs [multinational corporations] has widened, the nature of international production has undergone a distinct transformation. From investing overseas primarily to exploit natural resources for export, or to supply local markets with a particular product similar to those produced at home, MNCs have increasingly engaged in regional or *global process* [emphasis added] and product specialisation, to take advantage of differential resource endowments, scale economies or integrated markets.

Table 1.2: The Foreign Manufacturing Subsidiary Networks of 315 Large Multinational Corporations in 1950 and 1970

NUMBER OF ENTERPRISES WITH SUBSIDIARY NETWORKS INCLUDING:	180 US-BASED MNCs		135 MNCs BASED IN THE UK AND EUROPE	
	1950	1970	1950	1970
6 countries	138	9	116	31
6–20 countries	43	128	16	75
20 countries	0	44	3	29

Source: Vernon (1979, p. 258).

The problem of the geographical literature, therefore, is that it makes little attempt to recognise that there are different types of organisation and that they will have varied spatial effects. This weakness is particularly evident in the stereotyped view of the multinational corporation which has been taken as a single undifferentiated unit (Yannopoulos and Dunning, 1976; Dicken and Hewings, 1982). The apparent emergence of a global corporation, therefore, only exacerbates the theoretical void within the discipline. In fact the distinction between the global and multinational types of corporation has never been demonstrated empirically in a clear way. What is clear, however, is that if the global form of corporation does exist, there is a firm case for establishing models of organisations which are bounded in space and time (Taylor and Thrift, 1982a). In other words, the sequence of steps in organisational development towards a global structure, as modelled by Stopford and Wells (1972) in Figure 1.1, must be inserted into a historical context, as shown in Figure 1.2. Thus, there are a number of possible routes of corporate development which need not end in the same structural format. As a result of this hypothesis, industrial geography cannot hope to produce a universal theory of the international behaviour of business organisations because of the existence of a 'dual' or 'segmented' economy which has been firmly demonstrated in the organisational and related geographical literature (e.g. Oster, 1979; Kaufman, Hodson and Fligstein, 1981, Taylor and Thrift, 1982c).

Figure 1.1: Sequences of Structural Change in Large Corporations

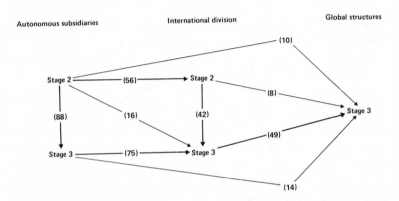

Note: The numbers in the arrows indicate the number of firms out of 170 that had undertaken the structural change by the end of 1968. Six cases of structural change in directions opposite to those shown are excluded. The term 'global structures' includes all the area division, worldwide product division, mixed and grid forms.

Source: Stopford and Wells (1972), p. 28).

Consequently, the main task for industrial geography and for the enterprise approach in particular is to conceptualise these different forms of corporate organisation. Inevitably, this will mean borrowing and modifying ideas from the organisation theory and management science literature, which is something many researchers have been loath to do. Such an organisation's perspective of industrial geography is based on the supposition that the relationship between corporate behaviour and spatial form is *mediated* by organisational structure, and that this should form one of the dependent variables which McConnell (1982) stressed geographical studies did not specify. In fact if McConnell had looked closer at his own examples, he would have discovered that many of them were concerned with organisational structure, but more often than not he failed to recognise this fact. Marshall (1982, p. 1674) pinpointed the problem when he noted:

Figure 1.2: The Historical Emergence of the Global Corporation

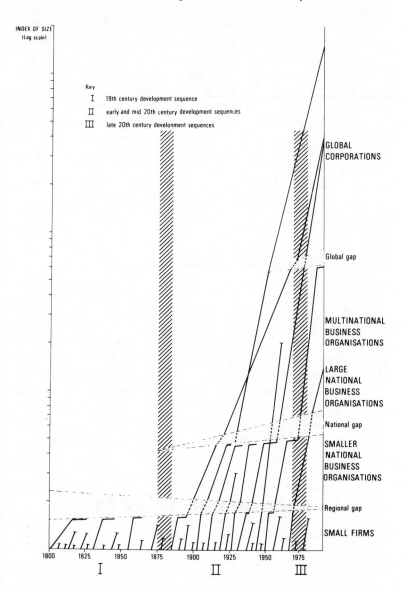

Source: Taylor and Thrift (1982a, p. 24).

With respect to organisational structure, industrial geographers have with few exceptions (see McDermott, 1977) adopted a small number of contextual variables such as operations technology, employment size, and plant status as surrogates for differences in organisational tasks. The only actual measure of structure regularly examined in industrial location is nonproduction employment (Crum and Gudgin, 1977; Marshall, 1979a). This is unsatisfactory because the Aston studies clearly show that organisational structure is a multidimensional concept which cannot be encapsulated in one single measure. In addition, in functionalist work the significance of individual organisational determinants of structure are unclear. . . Since individual aspects of structure are affected by different variables (Child and Mansfield, 1972; Hickson *et al.*, 1969), geographers need to be more sophisticated in their analysis of organisational structure.

Objectives of the Study and Organisation of the Book

The basic thrust of this book is, therefore, to discuss and develop, at least in a preliminary way, some of the neglected aspects of corporate structure — particularly corporate space — by adopting an organisations perspective as a basis for analysis (see for instance, Wood, 1978; McDermott and Taylor, 1982; Taylor and Thrift, 1981a). This small but growing area of interest within industrial geography has emerged from a dissatisfaction with other approaches to industrial change. This book begins to address the void in the theory in this area of industrial geography. Three key questions have emerged from the initial discussion and are addressed in the chapters which follow:

1. Does organisational structure differ between corporations, and what part does space play within this structure?
2. Are there any organisational regularities in the multi-site operations of large corporations (i.e. at the plant level)?
3. How does the multi-plant structure of large corporations relate to their organisational structure?

A central theme running through the study is the relationship of the changing international division of labour with corporate organisation and the internationalisation of production. The structure of the study is aimed specifically at highlighting the role of the business organisation which underlies the formation of a new international division of labour at a number of levels within the corporation. Organisations involved in the multinational chemicals industry between 1970 and 1980 are taken as an analytical case study. Several chapters are based on work carried out on a single business organisation, ICI, a multinational chemicals corporation with its headquarters in Britain. Despite this concentration on one organisation, however, the aim is not to add a further example to the growing number of 'enterprise' studies, but rather to focus on several aspects of the organisation of corporate space and thereby to make a contribution to the reduction of the 'chaotic conceptions' (Sayer, 1980) which are such a feature of the geographical work on organisations.

The relationship between the three aspects of organisational structure, the internationalisation of production and the changing spatial division of labour are, therefore, the core of this book. The aim is to address these relationships at a number of levels, gradually narrowing down the empirical focus in successive chapters from the industry and business organisation, to individual plants. To address this aim, of developing a basic understanding of several dimensions of the organisation of corporate space, Chapter 2 highlights the main features of the existing theoretical literature from geography and the organisational sciences on the internal organisation and plant structure of business organisations, and underlines a number of key issues which have been either underplayed or ignored. These issues are then pursued in subsequent chapters.

In Chapter 3, the central issue raised is whether or not multinational corporations can be differentiated into distinct groups. A cluster analysis of the top 79 business organisations operating in the chemicals industry in 1980 is used to categorise the companies and corporations according to their internal organisation, geographical structure, production and performance. Some of the implications of the organisational groups which are revealed in the analysis are also discussed within a segmentation framework, particularly their interrelations and possible processes of transition between the groups.

The geographical significance of the emergent global type of corporation is discussed in Chapter 4, which examines the restructuring process which has taken place within one corporation, ICI. This case study of ICI first examines the internal financial and product reorganisation within the corporation as a prelude to a discussion of the geographical-cum-organisational changes which have taken place within the business organisation. These changes have had profound spatial effects which are discussed in relation to the changing international division of labour within ICI. The discussion serves to throw some light on the processes enabling corporate transformation which were discussed in Chapter 3.

The major theme in Chapter 5 is the strength of ownership linkages within and between corporations. This topic is discussed with reference to the multi-plant network which is a characteristic of the modern corporation. The main objective of the chapter is to operationalise the two concepts of intra-organisational and environmental 'centrality' in order to model the position of each plant. This is attempted through a case study of the plants which belong to the paints division of ICI. In Chapter 6, the significance of the position of each plant is discussed with reference to labour dynamics. Using multiple regression techniques, the effects of the plant position on the changing labour structure of each establishment are evaluated. Chapter 7 provides a qualitative expansion of the structure of production inside four plants, to illustrate the technological basis of peripherality inside the business organisation.

Finally, Chapter 8 draws together some of the findings of the study and emphasises certain aspects of the organisation of corporate space. In particular, the conclusions emphasise the insights gained into the new international division of labour by viewing the corporation as a principal agent of change, from an organisation down to a plant level.

2 The Organisation of Corporate Space

The introductory chapter has indicated the inadequate way in which the structure of business organisations has been conceptualised in industrial geography. This weakness was attributed to three problems: the relationship between organisational and spatial structure at a broad level; the structure of multi-plant operations at a specific level; and the interaction between these two macro- and micro-scales of analysis. This chapter addresses these problems and attempts to resolve the absence of a detailed conceptualisation of intra-organisational structure in space by examining and integrating some of the more useful areas of literature in organisation theory and industrial geography.

In adopting this very specific approach, certain limitations to the discussion must be recognised. To begin with, the argument does not attempt a comprehensive review of all the geographic and organisational literature. Instead, the approach taken is to include literature which helps to throw light on the three problem areas of the structure of business organisations which have been reiterated above. By doing this, it is hoped to highlight certain contentious problem areas of corporate organisation which exist and about which little is known. Furthermore, because of the overt emphasis on structure it must be realised that the discussion holds the external environment of the business organisation constant most of the time, and does not purport to examine the effects of environmental dynamics, such as periodic regional and global recessions.

What is certain is that although the structure of business organisations has been more thoroughly conceptualised in organisation theory than in industrial geography, organisation theory itself is not without its problems. Indeed, this chapter attempts to show that ideas on corporate structure derived from the two disciplines can be profitably merged. The discussion is divided into three main sections. In the first section, particular attention is paid to the conceptualisation of corporate structure within the structural contingency model of organisations. Aspects of the spatial structure of business organisations are then discussed in the second section, which examines the limited geographical literature on corporate organisation. The concluding discussion attempts an integration of the two sets of ideas in order to formulate a tentative model of the spatial and organisational structure of large business organisations.

Intra-organisational Structure in the Structural Contingency Model of Organisations

Conceptualisation of corporate structure within organisation theory is bound up with the position of the business organisation within the environment, with which it interacts. This open systems view of the organisation is embodied most clearly in the structural contingency model developed by Petit (1967) and elaborated more recently by McDermott and Taylor (1982). As is the case with most of this literature, the environment is held to influence the structure and performance of the business organisation through its rate of change (Jurkovich, 1974), and complexity (Harrison, 1978). Conversely, it is also contended that, through feedback mechanisms, it is possible for the organisation to regulate the forces of the environment which most closely impinge upon it, thereby forming its own representation of the environment. This 'enacted' environment (Pfeffer and Salancik, 1978) brings about a certain amount of stability to the context of the firm (Katz and Kahn, 1966), thereby reducing operational uncertainty.

The way in which the organisation 'filters' its environment in this way is important, as these representations impinge most closely upon the operation of the organisation. Conceptually, therefore, it is possible to distinguish several 'levels' of environment, the broadest of which are the global and societal environments. The societal environment consists of cultural, technological, educational, political, legal, natural resources, demographic, sociological and economic forces (Kast and Rosenweig, 1974). Difficulties associated with operationalising the level of the societal environment and, more importantly, of determining how it influences the structure of the organisation, have resulted in more concise definitions of the organisations' enacted environment using the concept of the domain and task environment (Figure 2.1). Prompted by the work of Levine and White (1961), Thompson (1967, p. 27) emphasised that business organisations establish an environmental 'domain' which 'identifies the points at which the organisation is dependent on inputs from the environment. The composition of that

Figure 2.1: Conceptualisation of the Environment of the Business Organisation

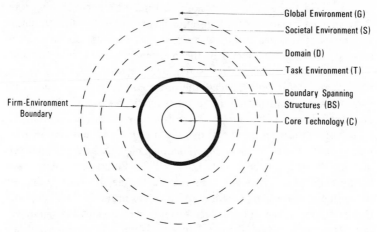

Source: McDermott and Taylor (1982, p. 78).

environment, the location within it of capacities, in turn determines upon whom the organisation is dependent.' Essentially, the domain represents the potential environment of the organisation. In addition, Dill (1958) provided an even more detailed specification of an organisations environment when he advocated the concept of the 'task' environment, which is composed of four main groups:

1. customers (users and distributors);
2. suppliers (of materials, capital and labour, equipment and work space);
3. competitors (for markets and resources); and
4. regulatory groups.

The task environment describes the organisation 'set' outlined by Evan (1963) and it highlights the main points at which an organisation is dependent upon its immediate operational environment (Jacobs, 1974), with the consequence that no two organisations' environments can be the same (Thompson, 1967). The environmental domain and task environment of the organisation are principal features of the structural contingency model and they provide a realistic means of conceptualising how the forces of the environment impinge upon the organisation.

The importance of the concepts of the domain and task environments within the structural contingency model lies in the fact that they are held to be prime causes of structural differences within organisations. The creation of organisational structures by differentiation and integration arises from the need for the business organisation to serve homogeneous segments of the environment, particularly through *horizontal differentiation* by establishing departments. In addition, *vertical differentiation* divides the organisation into various levels and spans of control to form a bureaucratic hierarchy. The various departments and levels within the organisation thus play a vital role in the simplification of the firm's dealings with its environment. In this respect, boundary-spanning functions such as sales and marketing are particularly important (Dill, 1958). Conversely, these basic building blocks of organisational structure also need to be coordinated if the organisation is to function and perform properly. This coordination is known in the literature as the process of organisational *integration*. The two opposing forces of differentiation and integration in the organisational structure are a vital feature of the structural contingency model. Indeed, they raise important questions as to why different organisational forms should be created. Consequently, the next section turns to an examination of these concepts in greater detail.

Structural Differentiation and Integration

The most ambitious empirical study of differentiation in organisations was undertaken by Blau (1970) who attempted to develop a formal theory based on a survey of 1,500 organisations and organisational sub-units. Although he put forward a number of propositions, these can be collapsed into two general propositions. First, any increase in the overall size of an organisation has the effect of generating structural differentiation along various dimensions at decelerating rates. Second, structural differentiation tends to enlarge the administrative component in organisations. However, these findings tell us little about the processes involved in forming organisational structures.

Within the structural contingency model the boundary-spanning sub-systems which relate the firm to its task environment are dependent on the qualities of the environment itself. Burns and Stalker's (1961) classic study of the electronics industry in Scotland and England represented an important turning point in academic thought because it recognised the effect of environmental conditions on management systems. The authors established that structural differentiation is no more than an outgrowth of the division of labour in performing the total task which the organisation undertakes. Burns and Stalker concluded that variations in the environmental characteristics of the individual organisations they studied had created two divergent management systems as end points on a continuum of management practice. Where stable environments were present, this allowed the organisation to develop a 'mechanistic' type of management to break down the overall task into specialisms. In contrast, the 'organic' systems were adaptations to unstable conditions 'when problems and requirements for action arise which cannot be broken down and distributed among specialist roles within a clearly defined hierarchy' (Burns and Stalker, 1961, pp. 5-6). The characteristics of the mechanistic and organic forms of organisation as put forward by Burns and Stalker are set out in Table 2.1.

Thompson (1967) provided a more detailed explanation of this relationship and he regarded the mechanistic structure of a business organisation as an indication of a stable, relatively certain environment. In these circumstances, it is possible to divide up the task and to operate a hierarchically and horizontally divided system of management by establishing rules which lay down roles and by giving instructions. This imposes a structure of 'ordered superiority' in the organisation. Organic systems, typical of business organisations operating in uncertain environments, had structures which were less distinct, with fewer levels in the hierarchy and greater lateral interaction. As well as the distinction between the two forms of organisation, on the grounds of internal divisions, Burns and Stalker (1961) also recognised the existence of stratification, even in organic structures. The difference between the two structures lies in the basis for stratification. In mechanistic systems, this is based on a concentration of knowledge at the top of the hierarchy, whereas in organic systems it is based on the expertise of individual members. A second difference is the wider scope of the commitment of personnel inherent in organic structures and a third is in the common beliefs and values which are held by their members. More than any single factor then, mechanistic or highly structured organisations are determined by the twofold principle of 'definition and dependence' (Burns and Stalker, 1961, p. 123).

The structure of an organisation, according to this early work, is both a reflection, and in part a cause, of environmental differences. This explanation is, however, tautological and deterministic, and it is indicative of the search within organisation theory for direct and dependent relationships between facets of the organisation. In particular, causal relationships have been established in organisation theory

Table 2.1: Management System Characteristics of Mechanistic and Organic Structures

MECHANISTIC STRUCTURES	ORGANIC STRUCTURES
(1) Specialised differentiation of functional tasks	(1) Common tasks
(2) Abstract nature of task	(2) Realistic nature of task
(3) Reconciliation of task and performance at each hierarchical level to superiors	(3) Continual adjustment and redefinition of tasks through interaction
(4) Precise definition of each role and limited responsibility	(4) Overall responsibility
(5) Translation of role into a functional position	(5) Spread of commitment
(6) Hierarchical structure of control, authority and communication	(6) Network structure of control, authority and communication
(7) Concentration of knowledge towards the top of the hierarchy	(7) Spread of knowledge throughout the network with *ad hoc* centres of control
(8) Vertical interaction between members	(8) Lateral interaction between members
(9) Operations and behaviour governed by instructions and decisions issued from superiors	(9) Communication of information and advice
(10) Loyalty and obedience to superiors	(10) Commitment to organisation and its tasks
(11) Importance of internal or local knowledge, experience and skill	(11) Importance of external affiliations and experience

Source: Compiled from Burns and Stalker (1961, pp. 119-22).

between structure and the environment, technology and the environment and technology and structure (and the reciprocals of each), depending basically on the aims and interests of the author in each case. To a certain extent, the assumption that one-way dependent relationships can be established is naive. The advantage associated with the structural contingency model is that it highlights the two-way nature of these relationships. Even so, structure itself as seen in the model is primarily the outcome of a combination of task, technological and environmental forces.

Concern over this mode of explanation led Hower and Lorsch (1967) to investigate the effects of inputs to the organisation. The study had two important findings. First, following Fiedler's (1965) work, they concluded that the relationship between task and organisational structure might be mediated by social and interpersonal factors. The injection of behavioural considerations complicates the relationship considerably and as Hower and Lorsch (1967, p. 168) pointed out:

> it is evident that there is no automatic adjustment of structure and procedure to external variables. The key to the differences in the two systems [mechanistic and organic] seems to be mainly in the behaviour of top management — in its ability to establish and maintain a pattern of readiness for change.

Hower and Lorsch termed this mediating influence 'leadership style'. A second conclusion, which complicates a straightforward view of organisational structure, is the realisation that internal as well as external environments of organisations are not homogeneous, or, in their own words 'different parts of the environment may be more or less certain than others' (Hower and Lorsch, 1967, p. 170).

The consequence of the two major conclusions of Hower and Lorsch's work is that mechanistic and organic structures can arise within the same business organisation simultaneously. Thus, Table 2.2 demonstrates measures of differentiation in three types of department: research, sales and production. In research departments, structuring of activities is kept to a minimum, and primary orientation towards scientific matters requires not only the long-term orientation of personnel, but also close contact between workers. Evidently, organic structures enable the rapid dissemination of information within organisations, a fact demonstrated by Allen and Cohen's (1969) and Allen's (1977) work on research and development laboratories.

Alternatively, production departments with an orientation towards the plant have increasingly mechanistic structures, because they are separated from the wider environment by 'buffers' in the form of boundary-spanning departments, like sales departments with an orientation towards the market, and research and development departments. In other words, the characteristics which are typical of mechanistic

Table 2.2: Intra-organisational Differentiation

DEPARTMENT	PRIMARY ENVIRONMENTAL ORIENTATION	PRIMARY TIME ORIENTATION	ORIENTATION TOWARDS CO-WORKERS	DEGREE OF FORMALITY IN DEPARTMENTAL STRUCTURE
Research	science	long	permissive	low
Sales	market	short	permissive	medium
Production	plant	short	directive	high

Source: Hower and Lorsch (1967), p. 171)

and organic structures identified by Hower and Lorsch (Table 2.3) can themselves be applied *within* organisational departments as well as within whole organisations.

The problem of differentiation and integration within organisational structures was approached in a more detailed way by Lawrence and Lorsch (1967), in their study of six business organisations operating in the chemicals processing industry. The industry was chosen specifically because it was characterised by rapid technical change, innovation and product modification, requiring a high degree of differentiation and integration in organisation structures. The study reaffirmed the work of Hower and Lorsch (1967) in its belief that whole organisations segment their structures into sub-systems to deal with variations in the environment. The degree of structure in these sub-systems is a function of the degree of *control* over their task environment, which is greatest in production and least in research. Importantly, Lawrence and Lorsch note that in dealing with a non-homogeneous environment by creating differentiation in their own structures, organisations were, at the same time, forced to reconcile specialisation with a need for coordination. To integrate differential structures, and following on from Litterer's (1965) work, Lawrence and Lorsch established there are three systems of integration:

1. through the *hierarchy*;
2. through *administrative* or *control systems*;
3. through *voluntary activities*.

Consequently, the organisation's capacity to cope with a disaggregated environment is a function of the effectiveness of structural ties in

Table 2.3: Structural Characteristics of Organic and Mechanistic Organisations

ORGANISATIONAL CHARACTERISTICS INDEX	TYPES OF ORGANISATION STRUCTURE	
	ORGANIC	MECHANISTIC
Span of control	Wide	Narrow
Number of levels of authority	Few	Many
Ratio of administrative to production personnel	High	Low
Range of time span over which an employee can commit resources	Long	Short
Degree of centralisation in decision making	Low	High
Proportion of persons in one unit having opportunity to interact with persons in other units	High	Low
Quantity of formal rules	Low	High
Specificity of job goals	Low	High
Specificity of required activities	Low	High
Content of communications	Advice and information	Instructions and decisions
Range of compensation	Narrow	Wide
Range of skill levels	Narrow	Wide
Knowledge-based authority	High	Low
Position-based authority	Low	High

Source: Hower and Lorsch (1967, p. 168).

the differentiated structure of the organisation, as well as the activities of personnel.

The most thorough exposition of the integration aspect of organisational structure is that by Thompson (1967). Thompson established the concept of 'internal interdependence' within organisations, and illustrated clearly how different forms of organisational structure could be used to meet varying contingencies in the task environment of the organisation, that is, to unify a necessarily differentiated structure. The importance of the *hierarchical* configuration of organisational structure was stressed explicitly. Consequently, the degree of inter-dependence between organisational sub-units can be dealt with by alternative structures ranging from organic to mechanistic.

The basis for a conceptual connection between structure and inter-dependence lies in the need to coordinate the organisational com-ponents or sub-systems to cope with the task set by the environment. In Thompson's proposition, a distinction is made between three types of interdependence which can be related to an empirical tendency to create three different forms of structure (Table 2.4).

Where differentiated sub-units are related simply on the basis that if they do not perform adequately, the total organisation may be jeopardised, this is said to constitute *pooled interdependence*. In a stable environment, the organisation differentiates its activities into 'technical-core' and 'boundary-spanning functions', which can be isolated from one another. These sub-units, in a mechanistic structure, can be coordinated by standardised methods of communication in a rigid hierarchy which promotes centralised control. In real terms, Thompson points out that centralised, mechanistic structures tend to translate into organisational structures based on *functional* divisions, such as marketing, production and research.

Sequential interdependence is Thompson's second category. In this case, each sub-unit in the organisation must readjust if one alters, so coordination needs to be planned. The organisation is structured to reflect the need to cope with unique tasks, by basing specialists in homogeneous groups. Theoretically, this leads to a separation of technical-core and boundary-spanning functions while maintaining links, in a structure in which there is a balance between horizontal and vertical differentiation and, hence, forces of centralisation and decentralisation. By implication, such organisations tend to be charac-terised by *divisions* in practical terms, placing them somewhere between the theoretical mechanistic and organic extremes.

Reciprocal interdependence is Thompson's final category. In organ-isations of this type, actions of any one sub-unit must be adjusted to all others in the organisation, so there is a policy of mutual adjust-ment. Thompson stressed that when reciprocal interdependence is extensive, sufficient to overtax the communications mechanisms, organisations tend to rank order the interdependent positions in terms of the amount of contingency each poses for others, so that 'those with the greatest intercontingency form a group, and the resulting groups are then clustered into an overarching second-order group' (Thompson, 1967, p. 59). In effect, technical-core and boundary-

Table 2.4: Relationship between Interdependence and Structure in Organisations

THEORETICAL STRUCTURES	INTERDEPENDENCE	COORDINATION	RELATIONS BETWEEN TECHNICAL-CORE AND BOUNDARY SPANNING FUNCTIONS	NO. OF LEVELS IN HIERARCHY	ORGANISATIONAL FORCES	ACTUAL STRUCTURES
Mechanistic	Pooled	Standardised	Separated	High	Centralised	Functional
Intermediate	Sequential	Planned	Linked	Medium	Centralised/Decentralised	Divisional
Organic	Reciprocal	Mutual Adjustment	Clustered	Low	Decentralised	Area

Source: Compiled from Thompson (1967).

spanning functions are segmented in these cases, but clustered, with relatively few levels in an organic hierarchy. Such clustering and decentralisation is analogous to grouping by *geographic areas*, with each 'cluster' constituting a self-sufficient unit, equipped with resources to meet any contingencies which may arise.

According to Thompson, then, organisational structures are differentiated to adjust to a non-homogeneous environment. However, the structures which are ultimately adopted and the degree to which they are integrated relate to the requirements of the task which the organisation has been set. Thus, because environmental constraints affecting the organisation vary in their sources and in their nature, there is, by definition, no one best way to structure the organisation. As Thompson (1967, p. 57) summarises:

> The question is not which criteria to use for grouping, but rather in which *priority* [emphasis added] are the several criteria to be exercised. That priority, we suggest, is determined by the nature and location of interdependency, which is a function of both technology and task environment.

The preceding discussion regarding the processes of differentiation and integration within organisational structures has emphasised the importance of the task environment within the structural contingency model of organisations. Interaction between the task and the stability of the organisation's environment influences the division of labour within the organisation and produces a differentiated structure. In the case of a stable environment, mechanistic structures arise which have a larger number of levels in the managerial hierarchy. Conversely, unstable environments tend to produce organic structures. It was also hypothesised that because environments are not homogeneous, the processes of creating differentiated and integrated structures are unequal, which means that both mechanistic and organic structures might appear simultaneously within the organisation as a series of organisational sub-systems, or sub-units.

A crucial question which arose from this discussion was how the organisational sub-units are integrated within the structure. The work of Thompson (1967), especially, pointed out that internal dependence is manifest in the form of the structure (hierarchy and control systems), voluntary or behavioural activities, and their relationship with the task environment of the organisation. Finally, it was concluded that there is no ultimate structural form, because of variations in the task and the environment of each organisation. In the end, the literature on the structural contingency model pointed towards the priorities which the organisation set itself, rather than simply a straightforward interaction with the environment, as a principal influence in the determination of intra-organisational structure.

This explanation of intra-organisational structure is not entirely satisfactory. Although inequalities within the organisation are discussed in the structural contingency model, they are not given enough consideration. A basic feature of the model is the division of the 'task' into a number of components, which are then structured within the organisation. Consequently, not only the environment, but also the task (or component of it) of each sub-unit will vary. By implication, it can be assumed that sub-units will not all carry equal weight within the organisation. The structural contingency model, as it stands, fails to deal with inequalities in intra-organisational structure, apart from establishing a few basic first principles on the effects of the environment. To address this question fully, it is necessary to examine one related but distinct school of thought within the organisational literature.

Centrality, Power and Dependence

Several problems can be identified with the bulk of the literature relating to organisational structure. The two most notable problems are the confused terminologies and the failure to explain which level of the organisation is being evaluated. With regard to the confusion of terms, technology, environment and structure have not been rigorously defined and so there is some confusion over their effects. The level of analysis is a second major problem. Some studies examine organisational wholes, whilst others only study sub-units of organisations. Failure to distinguish between these levels raises many doubts as to the validity of some of the conclusions. Noting these weaknesses, Comstock and Scott (1977, p. 178) feel it would be appropriate to:

> conceive of organisational structure as an overarching framework of relations linking sub-units of considerable diversity, and to attempt to develop measures that capture the distinctive characteristics of this supra-structure.

As a result, the problem which needs to be conceptualised in the structural contingency model, is how to distinguish between parts of the same organisation. In this respect, the relationship between the structural contingency model is how to distinguish between parts of been addressed almost exclusively by a group of researchers based at the Industrial Administration Research Unit in the University of Aston, Birmingham.

Initially, the main concern of the Aston group was to derive several descriptive dimensions of organisational structure. The features which were isolated were the degree of specialisation, standardisation, formalisation, configuration and centralisation in the organisational structure (see Pugh *et al.*, 1968). The *specialisation* dimension was concerned with the division of labour within the organisation. Procedures were the second category and this was measured in terms of their *standardisation*. The third dimension, *formalisation*, denoted the extent to which rules, instructions, procedures and communications through the structure were written down. *Configuration* was the fourth dimension and this measured the 'shape' of the role structure in the organisation, such as the vertical span of control (height), and the administrative ratio (width) of the hierarchical structure. Finally, the *centralisation* dimension of structure was concerned with identifying the locus of authority for decision-making within the organisation. The centralisation dimension is the most important aspect of the Aston studies in relation to this discussion, because it is the only aspect of organisational structure which is not covered in one form or another in the existing literature.

In fact, the interests of the Aston group gradually focused on centralisation, as their changing research emphases indicated. A theoretical framework was eventually established to explain inequalities in intra-organisational structure and intra-organisational relations. However, before the concept of centralisation is discussed in greater depth, some cautionary comments are required.

Child (1972a), for example, has noted the Aston studies make some critical oversimplifications in respect of certain concepts. Notably, the group failed to recognise the distinction made by Max Weber when they adopted the use of his two, originally separate, aspects of authority:

1. the level to which decision-making is *delegated* within the organisation; and
2. the original *source* of the authority.

The failure to distinguish between these concepts leads directly to Child's second criticism, which is the use of organisations of different status within the group's sample. In fact, the sample included not only organisations, but also their branches and subsidiary elements (organisational sub-units). The upshot of these weaknesses has been an undoubted effect on the centralisation scores of some organisations

(Donaldson, Child and Aldrich, 1975). Given these shortcomings, the concepts and the empirical findings of the Aston group deserve closer attention.

Beginning with the work of Hickson *et al.* (1971), the Aston group attempted to operationalise the centralisation concept as a means to explain inequalities within the structure of organisations. The concept of centralisation couches the importance of any single sub-unit relative to others in the organisation in terms of 'power' relations. The concepts and findings of the Aston group, therefore, differ markedly from those of other structural contingency theorists because the technology, environment and structure of the organisation are all allowed to vary independently. Consequently, the theory of intra-organisational power relations which emerged from this work (Hickson *et al.*, 1971; Hinings *et al.*, 1974) is to be distinguished from other theories which are concerned with inter-organisational relations. The two theories diverge in their explanation of the source of power. Inter-organisational power has been defined as the ability of one organisation to control the resources necessary for the functioning of another (Pfeffer and Salancik, 1978; Aldrich and Mindlin, 1978). In contrast, intra-organisational power is derived, at least at first, by the 'charter' (role) granted to the sub-unit of the organisation, on the authority of the parent organisation. The power of a sub-unit, therefore, 'might be represented by the formally specified range of activities they are officially required to undertake and, therefore, to decide upon' (Hickson *et al.*, 1971, p. 218).

To a certain extent, the emphasis on activities merges neatly with the central role of task, which is used in explaining differentiation and integration in the structure of business organisations. The distribution of tasks is synonymous with the differentiation into sub-units. The Aston group, however, develop more fully their theory of intra-organisational structure. The theoretical extension is made by the distribution of tasks, which produces inequalities within the structure of the organisation. The concept of power as seen by Hickson *et al.* (1971) is derived from four main features of the task set for any single sub-unit:

1. the ability of the sub-unit to cope with *uncertainty*;
2. the degree to which the activities of each sub-unit are *substitutable* by the organisation;
3. the extent to which the work performed by the sub-unit is *central* to the organisation. This consists of two components:

a. *pervasiveness* — the degree to which the sub-unit's workflow is linked to that of the other sub-units in the organisation;

b. *immediacy* — the speed and severity with which the workflow affects the final outputs of the organisation; and

4. the ability of the sub-unit to control *contingencies* arising within the organisation.

Some of the variables and operationalised sub-variables used by the group are shown in Table 2.5. It is important to note the element of the task each sub-unit undertakes is referred to as workflow, so that it describes the degree to which the activities of the sub-unit are linked with those of other sub-units in the organisation. This is the crux of the concept of centrality.

Accordingly, the difficulty and variability of the task the sub-unit is required to carry out determines its importance in a power-relations network inside the organisation (Van de Ven and Delbecq, 1974). As the dependent variable, Kaplan (1964) pointed out sub-unit power has three distinct dimensions: weight (the degree to which it will affect other sub-units); domain (the number of sub-units whose behaviour it determines); and scope (the range of behaviours of each sub-unit it determines). As a result, some sub-units within an organisation's structure are more powerful than others, and, therefore, more central to the organisation. The implication of this theory is that a system of dependency relations is invoked within the organisation.

The centrality framework developed by the Aston group provides the most robust explanation available of inequalities in organisational structures. Nevertheless, several criticisms are warranted. First, the distribution of tasks is not the only important factor in determining the initial power of an organisational sub-unit. The form of ownership and the position of the sub-unit in the organisation will also affect these relations. It has been suggested by Evans (1975) and again by Franklin (1975) that sub-units which are lower down the organisational hierarchy are more remote from the hub of the organisation and are less powerful. As Evans (1975, p. 258), succinctly pointed out:

The *structure* [emphasis added] of multiple hierarchies may well be more critical in determining organisational effectiveness than spans of control or the number of levels in the hierarchy. Furthermore, multiple hierarchies present a new set of structural variables with which to explain the distribution of power among positions within the organisation.

Table 2.5: Variables and Operationalised Sub-variables Used by the Aston Group to Define the Concepts of Power and Centrality in Intra-organisational Structure

POWER (weight, domain, scope)

    Positional power (authority)

    Participation power

    Perceived power

    Preferred power

UNCERTAINTY

    Variability of organisational inputs

    Feedback on subunit performance

      Speed

      Specificity

    Structuring of subunit activites

COPING WITH UNCERTAINTY, classified as:

    By prevention (forestalling uncertainty)

    By information (forecasting)

    By absorption (action after the event)

SUBSTITUTABILITY

    Availability of alternatives

    Replaceability of personnel

CENTRALITY

    Pervasiveness of workflows

    Immediacy of workflows

Source: Hickson et al., (1971, p. 219).

Indeed, Franklin observed a lagged effect when information and orders are passed down the hierarchical structure of the organisation and, in a related discussion, Ouchi (1977) demonstrated this filtering process can create a position in which direct control over the sub-unit is lost. Thus, even though some plants can be central to the organisation in relation to the task they carry out, in ownership terms they can be peripheral. In order to control these sub-units, an organisation may have to exert new methods of monitoring (Ouchi and Maguire, 1975). While the Aston studies placed considerable emphasis on the organisation being able to maintain control, other findings have demonstrated that centrality can also be determined by how influential a sub-unit is, ownership remoteness being no real barrier (Mizruchi and Bunting, 1981).

For example, Negandhi and Reimann's (1973) study of 30 manufacturing firms in India illustrated that decentralisation within an organisation's structure can allow the more peripheral sub-units to be more effective. In other words, as the authors go on to establish, the performance of a sub-unit may also be influenced by the wider environment, as well as the organisational or task environment. Alternatively, Hirsch's (1975) comparative study of companies involved in the pharmaceutical and record industries in the United States demonstrated how important the position of a sub-unit within the organisation might be in relation to performance. Despite many environmental similarities, the profitability of those companies operating in the pharmaceuticals industry grew more rapidly than those in the record industry, because the sub-units had been able to exercise control over their institutional environment by means of patents, distributional practices and control over wholesale prices. Indicators suggest that the issues of ownership and the position of each sub-unit within the organisation will be important in the creation of inequalities in organisational structure. These aspects of centrality are not approached in the Aston studies.

A second related criticism is the failure of the Aston studies to appreciate historical factors. How do power relations change over time within the structure of the organisation? According to the Aston model, the power of a sub-unit is determined by the charter (task) granted to it in the first instance by the organisation. In reality, a number of other processes affect this structure and these are not considered by the Aston group. For instance, an organisation is often restructured for administrative reasons, or sub-units may be added to or subtracted from the structure by acquisition, or closure. These processes might have a significant effect on the balance of power relations within the structure of the organisation.

A final criticism of the Aston model of intra-organisational relations is its failure to include space as an integral element of structure. Unwittingly, Child (1972a) noted that there is a process of differentiation of tasks within the organisation away from core functions and between sub-units, and this pattern may have geographical corollaries. A geographical perspective of organisational structure may help explain why, for example, the effects of technology have been found to be strongest close to the primary or central work locations within the organisation (e.g. Comstock and Scott, 1977).

Summary

This section has examined some of the principal dimensions of organisational structure, beginning with the structural contingency model of organisations and looking in detail at the reasons for and processes behind the creation of different types of organisational structures. The level of debate in the organisation theory literature concerning the processes of differentiation and integration, coupled with an understanding of how inequalities are created by an unequal distribution of authority between organisational sub-units, is a marked improvement over the simple and sometimes absent notions of organisational structure in industrial geography.

Notwithstanding the conceptual and operational shortcomings of the organisational literature with regard to structure, this conceptualisation might be profitably transferred to industrial geography, to gain an improved understanding of the structure of business organisations in space. However, it is first necessary to establish precisely what generalisations can be extracted from industrial geography on the spatial and structural dimensions of business organisations.

The Spatial Structure of Business Organisations

In comparison with theories of the structure of business organisations in organisation theory, the geographical literature is *ad hoc* (McDermott and Taylor, 1982) and consequently only partial in its treatment of corporate structure (Hayter and Watts, 1983). However, two distinct themes do emerge from the literature and these are used as a framework for discussion in this section. The first theme revolves around the interest of a number of industrial geographers in the evolution of business organisations. The present discussion concentrates on the literature which deals directly with larger business organisations and does not address the smaller firm. Furthermore, in keeping with the discussion in Chapter 1, particular attention is paid to how corporate organisation and spatial structure change during the stages of the internationalisation of production in large business organisations. The second theme relates to the multi-plant structures which are a characteristic of the corporation.

The Internationalisation Process and Corporate Structure

Conceptualisation of the structural metamorphosis associated with the internationalisation process in business organisations was initially modelled in a four-stage development sequence by Chandler (1962) and later by Ansoff (1965). The four stages are market penetration, product development, market development and diversification, and these can be applied in a general sense at both a national and multinational level (see Taylor and Thrift, 1982a). A more extensive treatment of the geographical and structural implications of corporate development was given in the landmark study by Stopford and Wells (1972). As this is one of the four studies which has considered the transition from a national level of operations to a multinational level in anything approaching a comprehensive way, it deserves a brief outline.

Stopford and Wells (1972) held that multinational business organisations had three strategic options for development open to them: *structural*, *product* and *area* or geographic, or indeed, combinations of each. The model outlined a pattern of structural changes in 187 American business organisations selected from the *Fortune* list of companies in 1963 and 1964. Together with examples of relevant geographical literature which will be discussed below, the stages and structures advanced by Stopford and Wells, and others which have subsequently been added, are summarised in Figure 2.2.

At a strictly sub-national level of operation, the sequence by which small firms grow into large business organisations, first locally and then at an inter-regional scale by a risk-minimising diffusionist strategy, has been described by Taylor (1975) and Watts (1980a). Growth from a single-product, single-plant establishment, to a larger business organisation, usually results in a structure which is organised around functional divisions (Figure 2.3a), such as production, marketing and research. Increasingly, however, the processes by which small firms snowball into larger ones is becoming restricted by government policies and by an inability to gain access to capital for expansion (see Taylor

Figure 2.2: The Internationalisation Process and Corporate Structure

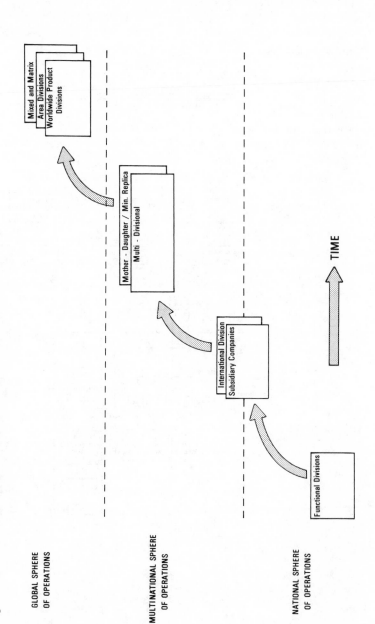

Figure 2.3: Forms of Corporate Organisation Associated with Stages in the Internationalisation Process

(A) FUNCTIONAL DIVISIONS

(B) INTERNATIONAL DIVISIONS

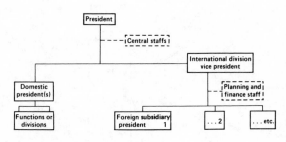

(C) MOTHER-DAUGHTER STRUCTURE

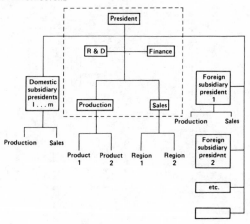

(D) WORLDWIDE PRODUCT DIVISIONS

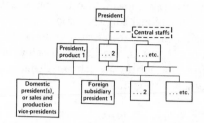

(E) AREA DIVISIONS

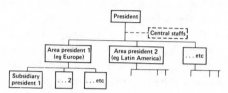

(F) MIXED STRUCTURE

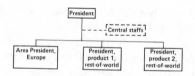

(G) MATRIX STRUCTURE

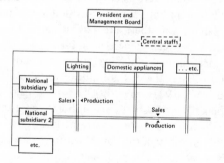

Sources: Franko (1976, pp. 187, 194-6); Stopford and Wells (1972, p. 116).

and Thrift, 1981; 1983). Thus, given that some firms were able to grow, the concern of the argument here is how organisations transcend the barrier between national and international operations, and then expand multinationally. In fact, for discussion purposes, it is possible to refer to three broad stages in the internationalisation process – national, multinational and global – which are characterised by an expanding geographical scope of operations.

The National Sphere of Operations. Decisions by business organisations to expand abroad are generally made haphazardly at first, with the organisation going through an initial period when all foreign subsidiaries which are set up are tied together only by loose financial links, often through a holding company. Although expansion of the product range tends to accompany overseas expansion, overseas activities are predominantly concerned with development of markets for existing products. The important turning point comes when overseas interests are sufficient to establish new priorities for the organisation. The need to manage subsidiary overseas operations, at least in the early days of corporate growth, is met through the formation of an international division (Figure 2.3b).

Stopford and Wells (1972) referred to the international division as an 'umbrella' which is able to coordinate the activities of otherwise disparate subsidiaries, and to raise the performance of each above the level which would have been possible if they behaved autonomously. Events within the international division are seldom closely monitored by the parent, and there are few attempts to establish strong links and controls between domestic and foreign activities 'due to the central office's lack of understanding when international problems arise. . . short of a disaster there is no immediate cause for interference' (Stopford and Wells, 1971, pp. 22-3). In part, a major reason for the parent not stepping in and establishing elaborate controls is because the division is still too small, the 'centre of gravity' of the corporation still lying predominantly in the home country.

Studies by a number of authors have established geographical regularities which can be associated with the preliminary stages of the internationalisation process in corporations. For example, there is a tendency for business organisations to expand first into areas which are geographically contiguous to the nation in which the corporate headquarters are based. Franko (1976) showed that European organisations in their formative stages established facilities in other European countries and especially the more developed nations. British companies, however, preferred to invest in countries which were affiliated to Britain as colonies or dominions. Similarly, Watts (1979; 1980a) has noted the locational preferences of a variety of national sub-sets of organisations (British, American, French and German). Hayter (1982) also underlined the strong patterns of American investment in Canada; Japanese investment in South East Asia; and British firms in Commonwealth countries. At a more specific level, Blackbourn's (1974) study of American investment in Europe found that Britain and the Benelux countries received a disproportionate amount of the investment.

The precise reasons for these patterns of expansion along the lines of geographical, linguistic or cultural affinity − often in countries bordering the domestic headquarters and with a preference for, and concentration in, certain core regions inside these countries − can be summarised as possible attempts to reduce the uncertainty inherent in international expansion. Blackbourn (1982) has made a review of these tendencies, but there are strong indications from the geographic literature that expansion is oriented to host counties with certain types of characteristics.

Franko (1976) is one of the few authors to have attempted to explain the structural contexts of these growth processes, in a comparison of European and American corporations. European corporations were apparently able to maintain simple structural relations between the parent and the overseas subsidiary in a mother-daughter type of structure (Figure 2.3c). This form of organisation is often referred to as a 'miniature-replica' structure because of the similarity of the parent and subsidiary structures. The reasons for the success of this form of organisation, in European enterprises at least, are, according to Franko, the existence of management structures based on kinship ties, the short geographic distances involved in European expansion, avoidance of joint ventures (which allowed subsidiaries to operate independently) and a separation of markets. The first steps in the internationalisation process in American corporations had an entirely different sequence, with international divisions disappearing much earlier and president-president relationships emerging more rapidly. When European enterprises expanded into America at a later stage, typically 'American' structures were rapidly adopted, seemingly reaffirming the conclusion that certain types of organisational structure are unsuited to operate on an enlarged international scale. Quite clearly, the early stages of corporate growth and internationalisation are characterised by geographical expansion along certain lines of orientation and are accompanied by uncomplicated organisational structures.

The Multinational Sphere of Operations. Enlargements of the geographical sphere of operations of a largely national corporation into a number of countries, resulting in a significant shift in the organisation's centre of balance, is generally held to be the major factor involved in the transition to a multinational corporation. Apart from official definitions of what constitutes a multinational corporation (e.g. UNESCO, 1978) there is no clear-cut consensus on the structural implications of this change.

Rees (1978) and Thomas (1980) have attempted to explain the multinational stage in the internationalisation process in terms of Vernon's (1966) product cycle and the oligopoly model (Hymer, 1960; Knickerbocker, 1973). The argument is that in order to survive and grow, the organisation continues to introduce existing products to foreign markets so as to elongate the 'standardisation' phase of the product and to allow time for research and development on new products. The primary characteristic which apparently differentiates the multinational from the national phase of organisation is this emphasis on product diversification, as well as market development overseas. In other words, the 'development', 'growth' and 'mature' phases in the product life cycle which were identified by Thomas (1980) have direct spatial corollaries.

A second characteristic of the multinational stage of development is the tendency for organisations to behave in an oligopolistic fashion. In a study of large American rubber and tyre companies, Rees (1978) identified a 'follow-the-leader' behaviour, in which companies sometimes responded with a counter-move to the expansion of a competitor. In other cases, the companies expanded in such a way as to avoid conflict, with the largest organisations concentrating their attention on European markets, whereas the smaller organisations opted for direct development in the remoter and less secure markets, such as South America. Within this development sequence, there is a relative prominence of standardised products in overseas markets, and research and development establishments are concentrated in the core countries and urban centres; low-cost production is located in peripheral regions and countries (Rees, 1978). This implicit spatial structure of the multinational stage of development apparently still continues to follow an orientation towards locations and host countries with certain types of characteristics. These patterns are especially evident in the case of the research and development establishments, as Rees and others have noted (e.g. Le Heron, 1978; Malecki, 1979, 1980b; Crum and Gudgin, 1978).

Thus, the natural growth and decay of each product within the multinational corporation takes place unevenly, in staggered sequences over time and space. This characteristic is reflected in the structure of the organisation in the form of subsidiary companies producing different products, some of which are at the leading edge as product innovators, whilst others are producing mature products and are less innovative. Consequently, the structure of the multinational corporation is such as to enable it to *simulate* the product life-cycle (Vernon, 1966; Taylor and Thrift, 1983).

An important facet of the multinational phase of development which has been given scant attention in industrial geography is the relationship between product and market development and corporate structure. Håkanson (1979) has addressed this problem by noting three types of product diversification an organisation can adopt — horizontal, vertical and concentric (or conglomerate). These forms of organisation can aid in multinational expansion. For example, Håkanson has pointed out that vertical integration, 'by extending the firm's authority to adjacent sectors of the corporate environment, increases the scope for planning, co-ordination and control and enhances the effectiveness of expansion strategies' (Håkanson, 1979, p. 136). Håkanson (1979, p. 34) also notes that 'frequently. . .foreign subsidiaries are established through the acquisition of former agents in which case their location. . . then determines the initial locus of foreign expansion'. One conclusion which emerges from this point is the importance of the historical sequence of events, in the determination of corporate structure. Thus, although the organisation may expand first by a diffusionist strategy, this can act as a basis for takeover in the future. This phenomenon has been illustrated by Watts's (1980b) reference to the expansion of Philips's activities in south east England.

Precisely what structural features are characteristic of a corporation in a multinational stage of development are unclear. Geographically, business organisations continue to follow initiatives set at earlier stages, but this is also modified by a certain amount of oligopolistic behaviour and a more extensive base over which the product cycle can be simulated. Taylor and Thrift (1983) have gone so far as to label this stage of corporate development as 'multi-divisional', because of the apparent tendency for business organisations operating at a multinational scale to adopt organisational forms based on regional or product divisions. But in fact there is a complex mixture of organisational forms at the multinational scale, and further research is evidently required to answer this point.

The Global Sphere of Operations. The forms of organisation adopted by established multinational corporations, according to Stopford and Wells (1972), vary considerably, but three main types are discernible: worldwide product divisions (Figure 2.3d), area divisions (Figure 2.3e) and mixed and matrix structures (Figures 2.3f and 2.3g). As with the previous stages of development, the authors emphasise there is an increasing need to adopt these new forms of organisation as a 'stress boundary' is approached, the boundary consisting of a change from the domestic priorities of products, to the international priority of areas (Table 2.6).

Table 2.6: Priority Changes Associated with Corporate Growth

DOMESTIC PRIORITIES	INTERNATIONAL PRIORITIES
Products	Areas
Functions	Products
Areas	Functions

Source: Davis (1979, p. 234).

Such a radical change in priorities seems to require two factors. First, a substantial shift in the geographical centre of gravity of the corporation so that it rests overseas. For the first time, domestic interests form only a small proportion of the organisation's total concerns. Second, and complementing this change, the growth of subsidiary components of the organisation to approach, equal or even rival the domestic centre of operations. Alternative structures which embody these priorities needs to be 'capable of "de-coupling" some of the communication and coordination linkages. Decoupling may be achieved by building subsystems composed of units that have strong interactions and by reducing the number of links needed to connect such subsystems' (Stopford and Wells, 1972, p. 15). It is important to note that the alternative global 'subsystems' which Stopford and Wells refer to were only just emerging when their study was made. In fact no clear distinction was made between multinational and global structures. Events over the past 15 years or so, as described in Chapter 1, have led to the emergence of distinctly new forms of global corporations to rival those of established multinationals, and an enlarged geographical scope is a key element in this structure.

According to the limited literature available on this most recent stage in the internationalisation process, the global corporation has a number of distinctive characteristics, the most significant of which is a global strategy. It sees the world as one market, not, like the multinational corporation, as a collection of national markets, and operates a long-term strategy, orchestrating and integrating the strategies of a diverse web of local subsidiaries. The global corporation also has only a tentative affiliation to the home country.

In addition, it has been suggested that the attitudes displayed by the management of the global corporation are very different from those of the multinational corporation. The top management at least, must develop a 'geocentric' attitude (Perlmutter, 1969). At a practical level, such an attitude requires a number of different and possibly unconventional managerial practices to be adopted. For example, in pursuit of a global strategy, it may be necessary to accept projects with low returns on investment simply because of their competitive payoff; to accept a diversity of performance targets for different subsidiaries; to embark on the construction of production facilities in both high- and low-cost labour countries; and to promote in some markets product lines which are intentionally underpriced or over-designed (Hout, Porter and Rudden, 1982).

Several processes are behind this structural change. The importance of behavioural considerations was pointed out by Davidson and Haspeslagh (1982) when they noted that 32 per cent of the 180 organisations included in the Harvard Multinational Enterprise project had, by their definition, switched to a global product structure by 1980. Corporate perception (in other words a continuation of oligopolistic behaviour) of the need to follow the moves of other corporations was particularly stressed as a process characteristic of global corporations. Finance and timing are two additional processes in the emergence of global corporations. The willingness and ability of a multinational corporation to obtain capital and commit itself to investment are crucial in creating growth potential, but successful timing of such a change, for example, allowing full use to be made of a production or a cost advantage as a leverage point on the market, if made before anyone else, can potentially increase cash-flows and inhibit competition. The belief is that only a few business organisations can make the transition from a multinational to a global structure and orientation, thereby preventing the growth of others (Taylor and Thrift, 1982a).

The way in which these processes of growth are played out over space is less clearly understood. In an interpretation of Wertheimer's (1971) scheme of corporate expansion, Taylor and Thrift (1982a, p. 28) propose that 'the foreign subsidiary may well embark upon. . . [the]. . .same risk-minimising diffusionist sequence which had brought about its own creation by its parent'. In a practical example, Taylor and Thrift (1981b) also describe how CRA, the Australian subsidiary of the British mining house Rio Tinto Zinc, had grown to such an extent that it formed a substantial proportion of the group's interests. Growth of CRA had involved substantial overseas expansion in the Pacific and even back into Britain. These and other examples give some clues to an essential geographical feature of the structure of business corporations at a global level. The most significant change is the growth of a multi-nodal structure, usually based on area divisions. In a study of the spatial structure of the business organisations involved in the automotive industry, Bloomfield (1981) has illustrated the decentralised structure of one such global corporation, General Motors. This structure compares with that of Toyota which is centralised and involves exporting, and Volkswagen which is less centralised and utilises some foreign assembly.

Only a handful of studies have addressed the processes behind the changing spatial structure of global corporations. Teulings's (1984) study of the Dutch electronics giant Philips was able to demonstrate a 'double movement' of capital within the organisation, the spatial effects of which could be tied down. The latest stage of internationalisation in Philips during the 1970s had involved a move out of the Netherlands and a simultaneous concentration of capital in the central areas of industrialised countries.

Rimmer and Black's (1983) description of the emergence of global financiers, consultants and contractors in the South West Pacific since 1970 focuses on particular global corporations like the Bechtel group from the United States. Rimmer and Black base their definition of a global corporation on one factor, the percentage of billings in terms of new contracts from foreign sources, and their explanation of the success of Bechtel is couched in these terms. However, no attempt is made to draw the link between spatial and organisational structure and the performance of organisations like Bechtel. In fact, the Bechtel Corporation is one business organisation which has used a matrix form of organisation (Davis, 1979a), and even though Bechtel has performed well, considerable doubt has now been cast on the success of the matrix structure in corporate organisation, because even though it implied that 'managers with conflicting views or overlapping responsibilities communicate problems and confront and resolve differences. . .barriers of distance, language, and culture impeded this vital process' (Bartlett, 1983, p. 139). To highlight the relationship between organisational and spatial structure further, Clarke (1982) has, therefore, made a preliminary attempt to explain the emergence of Imperial Chemical Industries as a global corporation in the 1970s by relating processes of rationalisation and expansion in Britain to the growth of certain area and product divisions elsewhere within the organisation.

The discussion of the evolution of business organisations in relation to stages in the internationalisation process has highlighted several regularities in corporate spatial structure and organisation. First, specific types of organisational structures were shown to be best suited to certain geographical scales of operation. For example, functional and international divisions tend to be used when the international operations are small in relation to the size of the corporation. Product divisions, although normally developed for the domestic market, are continued as foreign operations expand from exporting to foreign production in the multinational phase of growth. A mixture of structures, often with area divisions, is apparently the most suitable form of organisation for the largest corporations in the global phase of development. These regularities follow similar conclusions by Brooke and Remmers (1970) and Blackbourn (1974), but overall, the geographical literature only considers organisational structure as a secondary factor.

A second regularity stressed in the discussion was that business organisations at different stages in the internationalisation process have differing degrees of orientation towards the home country, the level of centralisation decreasing as the corporations expand. The so-called global corporation is spatially the most decentralised form and is characterised by a nodal spatial structure. Even so, there is conjecture over whether or not the organisational structure of such corporations promotes centralised control, and, if so, to what degree.

Third, corporations show a preference for expanding along lines of least resistance, at least in the earliest stages of development. Very definite orientations towards host countries with specific types of characteristics (language, cultural or political affinity), and towards certain locations inside these countries, appear to represent ways of reducing uncertainty in corporate growth, at least in the earliest stages of international expansion.

Fourth, the internationalisation process embodies a subtle change of organisational priorities, and although there is no straightforward relationship between strategy and structure, there is a general trend for priorities at least to shift from products to areas or markets. This change in priorities is often reflected in the adoption of more suitable structures as outlined in the first point.

In short, although relationships between spatial behaviour and organisational structure have been described only in a qualitative way, these are sufficient to warrant further research in this direction. So far, it can be concluded that the major pitfall stems from the fact that 'little or no effort has been put into interpreting the selected indices in terms of organisational structures, notwithstanding evidence which shows that at least in large corporations, internal structure has considerable locational and operational significance' (McDermott and Taylor, 1982, p. 59).

Multi-plant Structures

Another aspect of corporate spatial organisation which is a major theme in industrial geography is the structural characteristics of the multi-plant network which is typical of the large corporation. This section briefly considers the most significant elements of multi-plant structures insofar as they add to an understanding of corporate spatial organisation.

The predilection of geographers and regional scientists to studying the plant, office, warehouse, or simply establishment, can perhaps be traced to early work on the location problem in which the single-plant firm was usually the centre of attention. However, the multi-plant corporation has fundamentally altered this situation, posing new questions, although it is still argued by Dicken (1977, p. 142) that 'there is no reason why least cost location theory should not form a *part* of such a theory'. The problem with this conventional wisdom is that it diverts attention away from possible effects of organisational structure in the modern multi-plant corporation, often resulting in examining plant location simply through the characteristics of place (e.g. Norcliffe, 1975). In a large business organisation, the interplay between three sets of forces — the number of sites, the products produced and the magnitude of acitivities at each site (Watts, 1974) — acts to distort the neo-classical view of location to a considerable extent. When combined, these forces determine the functional characteristics of each site in a network of plants. Schmenner's (1982) empirical work in the United States used these factors as a basis for classifying plants within the corporation as:

1. *product* plants — producing only one product;
2. *market* plants — serving one market with an array of products;
3. *process* plants — vertically integrated with other plants and performing only a part of the production process; and
4. *general purpose* plants — for flexible use.

A functional view of the plant of this kind is a first step in recognising the existence of a structure within the corporate plant network, and it redresses the imbalance caused by a perspective which is strictly locational. Even the array of plant linkage studies in industrial geography has, with few exceptions (e.g. McDermott, 1976; McDermott and Taylor, 1982), concentrated on establishing the material and information linkages between a plant and its environment, rather than with its parent business organisation. The importance of McDermott's (1976) study lies in the fact that it stressed the importance of intra-organisational linkages, a point also stressed by Chapman (1973) and Steed (1970).

Overbearing attempts to understand plant-environment relations have, therefore, only exacerbated the conceptual gap which exists between the plant and its corporate context. For pragmatic reasons, the majority of plant studies only use samples of establishments which, because of their inherent tendency to focus on specific regions, can, at best, only be a partial representation of the multi-regional structure of most multi-plant corporations. This is unsatisfactory because as Watts (1980a, p. 52) has argued:

> The spatial arrangement and inter-relationships of plants within an enterprise's plant structure is an almost unexplored topic in the geographical literature, yet Krümme has argued that the 'spatial structure of a corporation, as well as its size. . .[is a]. . .factor of great significance with respect to a firm's ability to adjust to and generate change'. What is more, Steed believes there is a great need for locational analysis 'to place a given plant within its own corporate environment'.

Only recently has there been any response to this argument, with emphasis on the ownership aspect of a plant's position within its corporate structure.

Ownership Structures. The ownership structure of a plant is a critical variable because not only will plants owned by different corporations have contrasting characteristics, but also their importance to each respective parent business organisation will change over time as the corporation itself evolves (Dicken, 1976). For example, Healey's (1982) recent work on the textile and clothing industry in Britain, concluded that plants belonging to multi-plant corporations were more likely to close than other plants which did not, and that some plants were more at risk than others. But by concentrating on the effects of ownership structure only as it relates to plant closure, Healey may have missed other important ramifications. Massey and Meegan's (1979b) work on the electrical engineering and electronics industry in Britain examined the problem of ownership in a wider sense, and showed that plant openings, closures and capacity changes, in different combinations, were characteristic of plants owned by specific types of corporation. Indeed, the ownership 'position' of a plant within the parent corporation has been suggested as a possible rule of thumb in determining the potential viability of an establishment (e.g. McDermott, 1976; Yannopoulos and Dunning, 1976; Massey and Meegan, 1982; Mason, 1982; Marshall, 1979). Even so, most of these studies have examined the ownership issue only in passing.

Recent research on the iron foundry industry in the United Kingdom has examined the structure of plant ownership explicitly. Smith and Taylor's (1983) study of establishment openings, closures and takeovers showed that over half of the plants were controlled by multi-plant groups in the 1970s, compared to only a quarter in 1967. What is more, the increased incidence of multi-plant ownership has tended to distort the simple economic rationale of firm failure and plant closure. A primary conclusion of the study was the need for research to investigate the internal workings of each plant, as previous work has only inferred these processes, and how they may relate directly to ownership structure.

Additionally, Taylor and Thrift's (1982b; 1982c) work on the iron foundry industry in the West Midlands also evaluated the effects of ownership structures on plant performance. The study showed that plants could be 'segmented' on the basis of their ownership and performance, into four groups ranging from 'leading' through 'intermediate' to 'laggard' and 'support'. More importantly, the segmentation framework, by incorporating an understanding of ownership structure in plant networks, provides an effective backcloth against which plant dynamics can be evaluated. In particular, the function of the plant, together with its 'point of onset' (i.e. when it was established or taken over) as part of the multi-plant structure was shown to affect the performance of the plant and, possibly, its future. Consequently, 'the degree of peripherality and centrality needs to be considered *within* [emphasis added] as well as between enterprises' (Taylor and Thrift, 1982c, p. 1631).

From the limited evidence available, it can, therefore, be hypothesised that ownership is a significant element in multi-plant structures, but there still remains a need to conceptualise the position of the plant within the structure of a business organisation as discussed in the previous section. This aspect of corporate structure has received very little attention, but one constructive lead is given by the work of Törnqvist (1968; 1970; 1979).

Törnqvist's proposition began by considering the diffusion of information and innovation. Using concepts derived from systems analysis, and expanding early work on control models, Törnqvist formulated a framework for representing the spatial structure of organisations. As he noted:

> Small organisations usually consist of one place of work. Large organisations often have a hierarchical structure. They are divided into units, which in turn are subdivided into smaller units, and these are again subdivided and so on. Very large organisations may be divided into many individual places of work. Thus the organisations may be divided into many separate places of work. Thus they are called, for example, the head office, the regional office and district office. The names of units vary from one organisation to another (Törnqvist, 1970, p. 121).

Törnqvist's explicitly spatial model of organisational structure is illustrated in Figure 2.4. The primary division within this structure is between productive units and administrative units, the first of which receives, processes and issues materials, the second information. In addition, based on the degree of contact, Törnqvist was able to identify a number of levels of adminstrative activity. At the first and second levels, decision-making is non-programmed and personal contacts are high. At the third level, decisions are programmed and there is no personal contact whatsoever. In manufacturing organisations, the administrative and production units can be separated or combined in the same location. The advantages of Törnqvist's representation of organisational structure are not only its inclusion of space, but also that administrative and productive units can be combined or separated. The model also differentiates between different levels in the organisation. Finally, the model allows the size or capacity of each unit to be represented. As Törnqvist noted, this representation of ownership structures has realistic implications because 'most of the contacts seem to be channelled via the head office of the organisation' (Törnqvist, 1970, p. 86), at least in small organisations and the earliest stages of development in large corporations.

Figure 2.4: Personal Contacts and Organisational Structure

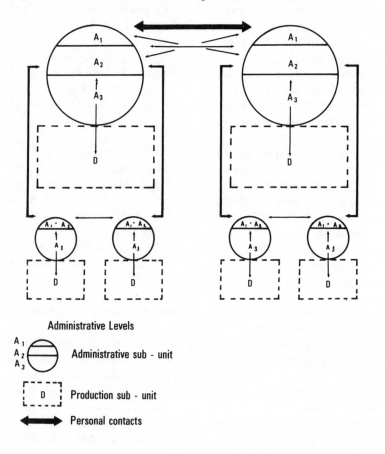

Source: Törnqvist (1970, p. 85).

Summary

This section has extracted some of the main structural and spatial dimensions of business organisations from industrial geography. Bar one or two exceptions (e.g. Dicken, 1976) geographical work has not attempted to integrate concepts derived from organisation theory with a spatial model of the *internal* structure of large corporations. The discipline, however, has been able to make some useful contributions to such a conceptual model, specifically through its appreciation of problems involved in the coordination of organisational structures over space, and through an understanding of the apparent locational orientations of corporations at an international scale.

Concluding Discussion

This chapter has highlighted some of the principal dimensions of the organisational and spatial structure of large business organisations, particularly those which operate at an international level. The generalisations from organisation theory, discussed in the first section of this chapter, can be integrated with the generalisations from industrial geography, discussed in the second section, to form a conceptualised model of the organisation of corporate space. It is now important to illustrate the complementary nature of these two sets of generalisations.

A review of organisation theory showed, with reference to the structural contingency model, that the most useful level at which to examine a business organisation is within its operational domain and task environment. An essential feature of the contingency model is the differentiation and integration which take place in organisational structures in order that the business organisation is able to deal with varying degrees of uncertainty in elements of its domain and task environment. To this end, 'organic' structures are a reflection of unstable environments, whereas 'mechanistic' structures are a response to stable environments. However, differentiation of the structure of a business organisation also brings with it the problem of how to coordinate the separate parts. The main agent for tying together structural sub-units is reckoned to be the configuration of the organisation, especially the structure of its hierarchy. To understand inequalities within the structure, it was considered necessary to discuss the distribution of authority by the organisation as a basis for the evolution of sub-unit power. In short, the creation of an intra-organisational power network was considered to be a function not only of the distribution of tasks, and linkages within the organisation, but also of the ability of each sub-unit to deal with uncertainty.

Studies in industrial geography have focused on different problems, particularly the spatial aspects of behaviour and the evolution of business organisations. Business organisations at different stages of development were shown to adopt contrasting structures, seemingly because of problems associated with coordination over progressively larger geographical areas of operation. At the early stages of growth, business organisations displayed a tendency to expand along lines of least resistance, with locational preferences and contiguous development apparently representing ways of dealing with environmental uncertainty. As the centre of gravity of the business organisation shifts to lie outside the home area, 'leap-frogging' development becomes characteristic and consequently coordination of the organisation becomes a problem as decentralisation and the geographical scope (multinationality) increases. The structure of the multi-plant network was also examined and function, scale and ownership structure were stressed as indicators of the viability and position of each plant within the organisation.

Two questions emerge from these discussions which are critical to a developed understanding of the organisation of the corporate space economy: how do different forms of organisational structure relate to the spatial characteristics of a business organisation; and how is the process of differentiation of a business organisation into sub-units to be represented in space? These two questions are addressed in turn.

With regard to conceptualising structure, organisation theory has been most successful in tackling the vertical dimension, that is, the *hierarchical arrangement*. The division of tasks is seen, first and foremost, as a division of labour between sub-units arranged vertically, and so *horizontal differentiation* has received less attention. A geographical perspective on the same subject emphasises the *spatial* aspect of the division of labour, which is, by definition, horizontal. Thus, a fusion of ideas relating to horizontal differentiation from industrial geography with those on vertical differentiation from organisation theory would draw a direct link between the structure and spatial form of the business organisation.

The division of business organisations into sub-units considerably complicates this theoretical scheme. Instead of a clear division of the organisational 'pyramid' into levels, a complex network of levels and units is revealed. On the one hand, the notion of *centrality* from organisation theory offers a framework for understanding inequalities in this structure by emphasising the sub-unit as a dynamic and indeed semi-autonomous element of the organisation, either able or unable to deal with contingencies in its task environment. Industrial geography, on the other hand, has recently begun to stress *ownership structure* as the legal confines of the sub-unit — often the division, but frequently the plant. If these two notions are combined, it is possible to begin to make a direct link between macro- and micro-level forces and scales within the business organisation. In addition, geography has also emphasised the *locational* aspect of sub-unit structure. A combination of these three components should allow a differentiated business organisation to be represented in space.

To illustrate these two contentions, it is possible to formulate a simplified model of the principal dimensions of organisational structure in corporate space (Figure 2.5). In the model of a two-product business organisation, organisational and spatial structure are illustrated simultaneously. Hierarchical differentiation is represented within the business organisation as a *whole* — for example, each level of administrative or office establishments — as well as within each sub-unit *location*. The latter might include staff performing administrative or boundary-spanning functions, such as marketing, in each plant. Ownership linkages between sub-units are also shown. The allocation of tasks by the parent business organisation to individual sub-units, such as the type and quantity of each of the two products to be produced, can also be represented, and the spatial structure is shown when the locations of sub-units are mapped. From this viewpoint, each location has a separate task environment. At head office level the task is broad and strategic. At the subsidiary office or plant level, lower down the hierarchy, tasks are defined more specifically by the parent firms.

The model is also divided into domestic and overseas operations. This deliberately broad distinction emphasises the structure of 'branches' within organisations. The overseas operations might represent an international division covering operations in a number of countries, or simply an area-based subsidiary company. What this means is that non-homogeneity in the environment of the business organisation is likely to bring about structural differentiation. Thus, additional uncertainty associated in overseas operations might produce a subsidiary structure which has fewer levels in the hierarchy, and therefore represents an organic structure. Domestic operations are less uncertain, possibly resulting in a mechanistic structure.

Of course, it is to be expected that this structure will change as the business organisation itself evolves. A business organisation operat-

Figure 2.5: A Model of the Organisation of Corporate Space

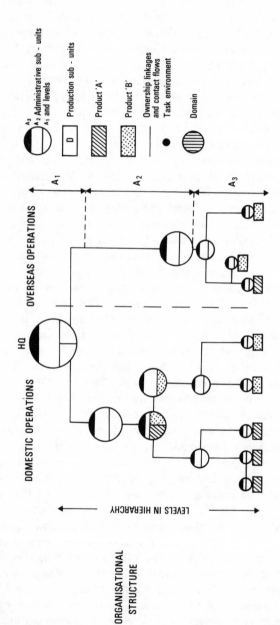

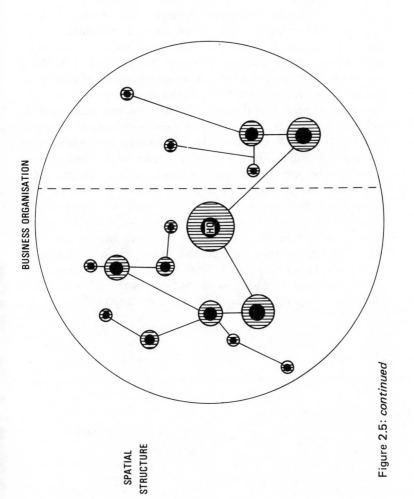

Figure 2.5: *continued*

ing primarily at a national level, with high interdependence between sub-units, might have a mechanistic structure based on product or functional divisions. As the overseas operations gain significance, a typical response is to establish a subsidiary company or an international division. Extensive multinational or even global operations further increase uncertainties, and the need to differentiate the structure is accompanied by a need for integration. In these cases, a number of organic or area-based divisions might result through a need for structural decentralisation.

This simplified model of the organisation of corporate space based on a fusion of ideas from industrial geography and organisation theory emphasises the main dimensions of the structure of business organisations. However, as the opening discussion stressed, the argument has preferred to concentrate on the issue of structure and, in so doing, any conclusions which have been drawn do not evaluate the effects of changes in the environment of the business organisation, for example. Thus, the unequal spatial impact of recession may mean that the external environment of a sub-unit can become more or less uncertain over time, as well as over space. Notwithstanding these deliberations, this theoretical discussion has raised a number of poignant questions which will be addressed in the following chapters. First, it must be emphasised this is only an *a priori* model. Whether or not such organisational structures can be identified empirically is a major question which is tackled in this study (Chapter 3). A second problem which needs to be addressed is how large business organisations evolve over space (Chapter 4). Third, it is possible to identify the main elements of the structural and environmental contexts of organisational sub-units (Chapter 5), and what implications do these positions hold for the operational characteristics of each sub-unit (Chapters 6 and 7)?

3 The Structure of Business Organisations in the Chemicals Industry

The purpose of this chapter is to make an exploratory analysis of the alternative structural forms which business organisations have adopted, using an empirical case study of the enterprises involved in the chemicals industry between 1970 and 1980. The aim of the exercise is to clarify and specify more fully the internal organisational attributes of chemical enterprises, and to gain some insight into the overall organisational structure of the chemicals industry. As only large business organisations are studied, the conclusions that can be drawn from the analysis are restricted in scope. Also, it will be necessary to take into account considerations other than the structural and spatial aspects of enterprises, such as organisational performance and production.

It is useful to bear in mind the performance of a business organisation as an integral aspect of structure, because as Kanter and Brinkerhoff (1981, p. 334) have pointed out:

> sets of organizational characteristics, whether involving structure or process, can only be correlated roughly with an organization's overall effectiveness, including productivity or output. . .but they are not irrelevant for that reason. They can be useful "state of the systems" indicators for managerial decisions. It is important from a scientific standpoint to determine the essential correlates of effectiveness in different types of organizations. If, as in the goal-centered approach, we look only at outputs and outcomes and not at structures and processes, we never learn *why* something works.

No attempt is made at this stage to establish the 'effectiveness' of different organisational structures (see for example, Coulter, 1979; Friedlander and Pickle, 1968; Goodman *et al.*, 1977; Hirsch, 1975; Negandhi and Reimann, 1973; Pennings, 1975; Pfeffer and Salancik, 1978). Instead, some measures of organisational performance are included to act as an 'internal index of an enterprise's success' (Mc-Dermott and Taylor, 1982, p. 115). Measures of performance will be particularly important in an industry such as chemicals, which is traditionally capital intensive, and closely linked to the business cycle through its intimate relationship with other industries. Measures of production are also obviously vital to a study of industrial business organisations even though they can only be expressed in a general way for the enterprise as a whole.

An attempt is, therefore, made to evaluate the performance, production and structural characteristics of 79 business organisations operating in the chemicals industry using a multivariate approach based on 36 attributes. The argument is developed in three parts: the introduction of the concept of segmentation as a means to conceptualise different types of business organisation; the operationalisation of selected dimensions of corporate organisation with the aid of a multivariate grouping procedure to highlight distinct types of business organisation; and the evaluation of the results and their ramifications for business organisation segmentation in the chemicals industry.

The Concept of Organisational Segmentation

The idea of defining and describing homogeneous clusters in the structure of economies is not new, despite the recent emphasis on categorising different forms of business organisation within a spatial context. Marx (1967), for example, noted the unevenness of technical change and capital accumulation involved in the development of business organisations and, in particular, made a distinction between the factory and joint stock organisation. The existence of dual or segmented economy is now generally accepted (Averitt, 1968; Tolbert, Horan and Beck, 1980). A variety of terms have been coined to distinguish the components of organisational structures, including planned and market economies (Galbraith, 1972), monopoly and competitive capital (Friedman, 1977a), core and peripheral sectors (Averitt, 1968; Friedman, 1977a) and leading and laggard firms (Taylor and Thrift, 1981a, 1982b). This so-called segmentation framework has, however, been applied at a number of levels, as these and other cases testify. Applications range from types of economies and business organisations, through labour markets, to industries and occupations (Taylor and Thrift, 1983). The interpretation of segmentation used here relates to business organisations, with the belief that the *organisation* is a primary cause of patterns of segmentation at other levels of analysis.

Definite patterns of business organisation segmentation are held to relate to homogeneity in the characteristics of a number of organisations, sufficient to differentiate them from other coherent groups of enterprises. The dual economy is, in fact, 'lumpy' and is 'composed of heterogeneous institutions and values and...structures...[which] ...are discontinuous and segmental' (Berger and Piore, 1980, pp. 147-8). To constitute a distinct pattern of segmentation Taylor and Thrift (1983) have stressed structural integrity must be maintained over some minimal period of time, with the understanding that a balance must be struck between economic flux and stability. Like Marx, Berger and Piore (1980) explain patterns of segmentation by the impact of flux and uncertainty in the economic system on business organisations, but they also argue that Marxist theory is insufficient in its explanation: not only because it pre-empts categories which are grounded in established modes of production, but also because it implies a convergence of social structures as industrialisation proceeds.

Segmentation is, therefore, a variant of the classic 'chicken and egg' problem, and brings with it the criticism of circularity. Unevenness in environments can cause the emergence of different forms of business organisation, just as the reverse may be true. This same criticism has been levied at the structural contingency model, which views the organisation as a semi-open system able to act on, and react to, its environment. This argument can, however, be countered by an understanding of inter-organisational power relations (e.g. Benson, 1975; Taylor and Thrift, 1981a) which, as defined initially by Dahl (1957), are a set of relationships between social actors, in which one can pressure another to behave as it would not otherwise have done. The concept of power has economic, social and political facets. One consequence of uneven environmental uncertainty is to initiate a power network between business organisations, after which growth processes and structures are themselves uneven and cannot return to a position of equilibrium. As a result, it has been asserted that certain types of organisation use characteristic processes (Aldrich and Mindlin, 1978), so, in the long run, the differences between business organisation segments serves to perpetuate their existence. Mergers between business organisations, for example, can be used to reduce competitiveness, or act as a means for diversification for the enterprises concerned (Pfeffer, 1972). They can also act to diminish the chances of smaller firms growing because they are a process which tends to be used by the larger organisations. One of the practical upshots of this conclusion is that 'some of the large business organisations remain, in the first instance, determinedly national, whilst others become multinational early on' (Taylor and Thrift, 1982a, p. 23). Of course, organisational power is a difficult concept to describe exactly. Pfeffer (1981, p. 4) has noted these difficulties associated with measuring and operationalising the concept, as it is necessary to estimate:

1. what would have happened in the absence of the exercise of power;
2. the intentions of the actor attempting to exercise power; and
3. the effects of actions taken by the actor on the probability that what was desired would actually occur.

Segmentation conceptualises differences in organisational structure and hypothesises how these might change over time, especially when the notion of power is introduced, because it accomodates historical factors. The few studies that have tried to test the proposition of a dual or segmented economy empirically, such as the work of Oster (1979) and Kaufman, Hodson and Fligstein (1981), have adopted a sectoral approach and, therefore, can only infer the existence of different types of business organisation. This approach is highly contentious and the results are questionable on a number of counts with respect to organisations: it is likely that differences peculiar to business organisations will be masked using sectoral data because the dimensions of organisation are not measured directly; it is doubtful if conclusions can hold across industry sectors, or even within a single industry sector; it is impossible to assess the precise balance of power of individual business organisation's segments from tests which use sectoral data; and it is not possible to assume that the rate of change of various features of sectoral groupings can be translated directly to business organisation segments.

To sum up, sectoral approaches to segmentation are not equipped to make inferences on the structure of business organisations. There is a need to adopt an organisational approach to segmentation to substantiate (or reject) claims about the structure of business organisations. The test in this study lies in operationalising some of the principal dimensions of organisations. This emphasis will act to check and enrich the previously established *a priori* model of corporate space.

Operational Dimensions of Business Organisation

The generalisations on geographical and organisational structure (Chapter 2), together with production and performance, provide the basis for devising a number of operational variables to depict the configuration of an enterprise. These are listed in Table 3.1. The geographical dimension of corporate organisation has three intrinsic features. The geographical scope or *multinationality* of a business organisation can be measured quite simply as the number of countries in which a business organisation operates, as the term multinational corporation is used generally to refer to an enterprise with representation in four or more countries. The ratio of domestic to overseas subsidiary companies owned by the organisation is a measure of the geographical *centrality* of its structure. Finally, *host country characteristics* of geographical structure can be gauged by measuring the number of countries of various income levels in which the organisation operates. Taken together, these three variables effectively describe the scope, weight and qualitative characteristics of the geographical structure of a business organisation.

In discussing the organisational structure of business enterprises, four pertinent features stood out and can be evaluated. The *differentiation* of the organisation into subsidiary components is measured in terms of the number of area and product divisions into which an organisation subdivides its activities and reports sales figures. The *integration* of the structure in terms of backward and forward linkages is determined by allocating the sales of each consolidated product division of a business organisation to one of four categories of activities — extractive-cum-feedstock; core chemical; chemical derivatives, and non-chemical interests. The *scale of activities* is an important measure of the size of an organisation, indicated by the total number of subsidiary companies operating as part of the organisation. The *ownership structure*, which indicates the potential control exerted over sub-units in the organisation, can be operationalised by evaluating the proportion of all subsidiaries which are owned by the business organisation, as opposed to those companies which are only associated or affiliated indirectly. Thus, these four features of organisational structure — differentiation, integration, scale of activities and ownership structure — are summary measures of the format and size of a business organisation.

To measure aspects of business organisation production, three main variables were developed. The *size of the workforce* of each business organisation is an initial attribute of production. The ratio of the assets of the organisation to the size of the workforce also provides a measure of the degree of *capital intensity* of production. Finally, the *turnover per employee* expresses the rate at which assets are turned over in relation to the total volume of sales made by the organisation, per employee.

Table 3.1: Dimensions and Operational Variables of Business Organisation

DIMENSION		OPERATIONAL VARIABLES
GEOGRAPHICAL STRUCTURE	Multinationality	*Scope of activities of the business organisation, measured by the total number of countries in which it operates
	Centrality	*Proportion of total operations of the business organisation represented by domestic subsidiaries
	Host Country Characteristics	Percentage of the number of countries the business organisation operates in which can be classified as: * (i) High income countries (World Bank definitions * (ii) Medium income countries based on GNP) * (iii) Low income countries
ORGANISATIONAL STRUCTURE	Differentiation	*Number of product and area divisions reporting sales
	Integration	Product divisions allocated to one of four categories: * (i) Extractive/feedstock (Percentage of total * (ii) Core chemicals sales in each category) * (iii) Chemical derivatives * (iv) Non-chemical This key represents the range and integration of the activities of each business organisation and demonstrates the degree of backward and forward integration from the area of 'core' chemicals (e.g. agricultural chemicals, etc.). Backward integration is into 'feedstock' and 'extractive' activities (mining, petrochemicals, etc.). Forward integration is into chemical 'derivatives', or products derived from 'core' chemicals (e.g. textiles and fibres, pharmaceuticals, paints, explosives, etc.) and also into 'non-chemical' activities (e.g. metals, finance, etc.)

	Scale of Activities	*Total number of operating subsidiary companies
	Ownership Structure	*Percentage of all subsidiary companies which are directly owned and not as affiliate or associate companies
PRODUCTION	Size of Workforce	*Total employment figures *Δ employment figures
	Capital Intensity	*Percentage ratio of assets against employment *Δ percentage ratio of assets against employment
	Turnover per Employee	*Turnover (sales/assets) per employee *Δ turnover (sales/assets) per employee)
PERFORMANCE	Capital base	**Assets, and Δ assets **Stockholders equity and Δ stockholders equity
	Business Indicators	*Sales and Δ sales **Turnover (sales/assets) and Δ turnover **Sales per employee and Δ sales per employee
	Return	**Net profits and Δ net profits (after tax, dividends, etc., have been paid) **Net profit ratio and Δ net profit ratio (net profits as percentage of sales) **Capital return and Δ capital return (net profits as a percentage of stockholders equity capital) **Profitability and Δ profitability (net profits as a percentage of assets)

Notes: * Variables to be utilised.
Δ Annual rate of change.

As annual rate of change figures for 1970 to 1980 were calculated for each attribute, the number of variables was doubled.

Business organisation performance is operationalised using a range of standard accounting measures. The first set of measures describe the capital base of the business organisation which acts as a benchmark for evaluating performance by including total assets and stockholders' equity capital. A second set of measures were used as business indicators to such matters as total sales, turnover and sales per employee. Finally, several variables, such as net profits, net profit ratios, capital return and profitability, were used to evaluate the return on capital investment in the organisation. Annual rate of change figures were also calculated to measure changes in performance over time.

The Structure of Business Organisations in the Chemicals Industry

To explore the structural dimensions of business organisations in the chemicals industry, information was gathered on the 36 operationalised variables from a number of sources. By undertaking a cross-sectional study of the industry in one year, 1980, the principal objective was to test whether or not distinct types of structures existed. Business organisations were included in the analysis if they were present on the *Fortune* lists of companies for most of the period between 1970 and 1980. Using *Fortune*'s definitions, the selection was restricted to organisations involved in the chemicals industry. Two lists were used: the first covering business organisations incorporated in the United States; the second covering business organisations incorporated in other countries. The final list of 79 business organisations fitting these requirements effectively represented the world's top chemical enterprises, ranked in terms of sales. A variety of secondary data sources were then used to generate the 36 variables outlined in Table 3.1. Several of the organisations which were included in the analysis were subsidiary companies of large corporations, but with significant operations in their own right. The distinction between the corporations and their subsidiary companies has been retained as far as possible in the data set, and linkages between business organisations are indicated.

A multivariate approach was used to assimilate the data and to distinguish homogeneous group of enterprises, or organisational segments. In selecting the appropriate test procedure, care was taken to avoid problems which have been associated with multivariate techniques of data analysis, such as geographical and temporal autocorrelation.

Just as important are the varied assumptions which different multi-variate techniques use as these have been shown to produce widely different results (Poole and O'Farrell, 1971; Boehm, Menkhaus and Penn, 1976; Longley, 1967). The cluster analysis technique which was selected avoids some of these pitfalls, principally because the 'clustan' version (Wishart, 1975) uses several procedures congruently to produce the groups. This method has the advantage of being able to choose the set of results which best reflects the consistency shown between each of the alternative procedures.

Cluster analysis uses a Q-mode or variable-by-variable principal components analysis to arrange respondents on axes reflecting differences in their structural attributes. The main dimensions of the data set are known as factors. Table 3.2 shows that the first ten factors explained over 81 per cent of the variance in the data on the 69 organisations which were included in the cluster analysis (the remaining ten organisations, with marginally incomplete data, were inserted into the appropriate groups after the analysis was completed). Inter-organisation distances were then computed from the factor scores and were used as an input to a hierarchical clustering procedure. The clustering method utilised is known as Ward's method, but in addition, relocations were performed at each level of clustering so as to optimise the clusters, thereby producing several comparable sets of results. Ward's method of clustering minimises the total error sum of squares by which clusters of cases are defined, and, therefore, represents the sum of the within-cluster error sum of squares: the sum of the squared distance of each cluster element (business organisation) from the centroid of the cluster. At the start of the procedure, each business organisation is given the status of a separate cluster and the two clusters with greatest similarity, in terms of a minimal increase in the total error sum of squares, are then fused together. The fusion process is continued in a step-like manner until a specified minimum number of clusters has been reached.

In short, each business organisation is measured against every other case in the data set, using a similarity matrix and linkage list. Cluster analysis gradually assigns and reassigns individual cases to groups based on their similarities and contrasting features, aiming to minimise intra-group variance and maximise inter-group variance. Thus, each level of aggregation or grouping incurs a loss of organisation-specific information, reflected in the information statistic shown in Table 3.3, but with increased contrast between the groups. The most revealing number of clusters is, therefore, indicated by jointly considering the loss of specific information, coupled with the added degree of

Table 3.2: Eigenvalue and Percentage of Variance Explained by the First Ten Factors

FACTOR	EIGENVALUE	CUMULATIVE PERCENTAGE OF VARIANCE EXPLAINED
1	7.74	21.49
2	4.51	34.02
3	3.85	44.72
4	2.64	52.07
5	2.30	58.44
6	2.14	64.38
7	1.85	69.52
8	1.60	73.96
9	1.41	77.87
10	1.29	81.45

Table 3.3 Change in the Information Explained at Different Clustering Levels

NUMBER OF CLUSTERS	INFORMATION STATISTIC
10	3.683
9	4.337
8	4.919
7	5.175
6	5.444
5	5.473
4	5.960
3	10.208
2	10.244
1	17.460

explanation which becomes possible through generalisation at each consecutive clustering level. The results from each of the procedures employed were compared and the most consistent set of results was chosen.

Results

The results of the analysis indicated four clusters was an appropriate level at which to stop the grouping procedure. The reason for choosing this number of clusters is the significant jump in the information statistic at the third level in the hierarchy, emphasising a marked loss of explanation through the fusion of two clusters which were different to that point (Table 3.3). Mean values for each of the 36 variables describing the four resultant groups are shown in Table 3.4 and the individual business organisations which were assigned to the segments by the grouping procedure are shown in Table 3.5, where the enterprises have been ranked, for convenience purposes, in terms of their sales in 1980. The discreteness of the four clusters is best illustrated graphically as in Figure 3.1, using the first three factors from the principal components analysis as three-dimensional vectors of difference. Business organisations in each of the clusters have a distinct archetypal profile, and these are outlined in turn below.

Cluster 1. The nine business organisations in this group have an extensive geographical structure and a high degree of multinationality, operating in between 31 and 55 countries. In addition, their geographical structure is highly decentralised with, on average, only 26 per cent of subsidiary companies located domestically in the country in which the organisation is incorporated. Host country characteristics of these business organisations differ from those in other clusters in respect of their orientation towards countries with high income levels (47 per cent of activities), and also in respect of their strong orientation towards host countries with medium income levels (43 per cent of activities). The suggestion is that although they have an extensive and decentralised multinational network, these business organisations have a structure which is concentrated on the more developed countries.

The organisational structure of business organisations in the first cluster is highly differentiated, with an average of 7.6 product and/or regional divisions. Activities are concentrated on the production of 'core' chemicals (59.7 per cent of total sales) and derivative products (21.8 per cent), indicating that while production is proportionately less vertically integrated compared to organisations in other clusters,

Table 3.4: Characteristics of Organisational Clusters

DIMENSION	OPERATIONAL VARIABLES	CLUSTERS			
		I	II	III	IV
GEOGRAPHICAL STRUCTURE[4]	Multinationality	43	40	17	7
	Centrality, %	26.7	40.8	42.9	74.6
	Host Country Characteristics:[2]				
	(i) high income countries, %	46.8	47.6	61.1	51.6
	(ii) medium income countries, %	43.4	38.8	30.8	44.3
	(iii) low income countries, %	9.8	13.6	8.1	4.1
ORGANISATIONAL STRUCTURE[4]	Differentiation:	7.6	8.6	5.6	4.8
	Integration:[6]				
	(i) extractive/feedstock, %	6.7	7.0	2.8	29.5
	(ii) core chemicals, %	59.7	46.8	34.4	48.3
	(iii) chemical derivatives, %	21.8	16.2	30.7	12.0
	Scale of Activities	167	209	55	42
	Ownership Structure	84.4	79.6	75.2	48.0
PRODUCTION[1,2,3,4]	Size of Workforce	114,281	89,644	19,532	13,113
	Δ "	2,525	-3,177	46	78
	Capital Intensity, %	2.43	2.04	2.97	7.79
	Δ "	-0.09	-0.05	-0.08	0.11
	Turnover per Employee	0.12	0.20	0.79	1.35
	Δ "	0.06	0.82	-0.16	7.35

PERFORMANCE[1 2 3 4]

Capital Base				
Assets, $m	9,538	7,399	1,927	3,013
Δ "	-38	-92	-9	1
Stockholders equity, $m	3,848	2,226	703	419
Δ "	-30	-65	-5	-4
Business Indicators				
Sales, $m	11,300	7,535	2,075	3,990
Δ "	45	-33	-2	56
Turnover ratio	1.20	1.11	1.15	1.25
Δ "	0.031	0.026	0.031	0.059
Sales per employee, $m	0.027	0.022	0.031	0.070
Δ "	-0.178	-0.020	-0.087	2.118
Return				
Net profits, $m	426	-197	70	33
Δ "	0.53	-23.38	-0.37	-0.31
Net profit ratio	4.03	-1.72	3.23	1.27
Δ "	0.01	-1.33	-0.03	-0.10
Capital return, %	11.2	-12.7	10.7	22.1
Δ "	0.35	-3.69	0.29	0.68
Profitability, %	4.6	-1.6	3.4	1.3
Δ "	0.12	-1.37	573.16	-0.03

Notes:
1. Figures in $m are in United States dollars.
2. Figures in $m for 1980 are at 1980 rates.
3. Figures in $m for 1980 are deflated to base year level when calculating Δ.
4. Except where stated Δ figures are for 1980.
5. Operational variables are defined fully in Table 3.1.
6. Percentage figures do not necessarily add to unity (i.e. 100 per cent) because each category was treated as a separate variable and the figures shown are means.
Δ Annual rate of change. Wherever possible, base year is 1970. Terminal year is 1980.

Source: *Fortune Magazine* (1970, 1980); Dun and Bradstreet (1981); *The Japanese Economic Yearbook* (1981); *Diamond Company Handbook* (1981); Stopford, Dunning and Haberich (1980).

Table 3.5: Business Organisations by Segment and Country of Incorporation

SEGMENT I

BUSINESS ORGANISATION	SALES, 1980 ($US million)	COUNTRY OF INCORPORATION
Hoechst	16,481	West Germany
Bayer	15,881	West Germany
BASF	15,277	West Germany
Du Pont	13,652	USA
Dow	10,626	USA
Union Carbide	9,994	USA
Ciba-Geigy	7,113	Switzerland
Monsanto	6,574	USA
W.R. Grace	6,101	USA
TOTAL SALES	101,699	

SEGMENT II

BUSINESS ORGANISATION	SALES, 1980 ($US million)	COUNTRY OF INCORPORATION
ICI	13,290	United Kingdom
Montedison	9,104	Italy
Rhône-Poulenc	7,155	France
Akzo	6,272	Netherlands
Flick*	4,643	West Germany
TOTAL SALES	40,464	

SEGMENT III

BUSINESS ORGANISATION	SALES, 1980 ($US million)	COUNTRY OF INCORPORATION	BUSINESS ORGANISATION	SALES, 1980 ($US million)	COUNTRY OF INCORPORATION
Degussa	4,857	West Germany	Enterprise Miniere et Chimique*	1,767	France
Solvay	4,742	Belgium	National Distillers & Chemicals	1,765	USA
Roche-Sapac	3,496	Switzerland	Ethyl	1,741	USA
American Cyanide	3,454	USA	Toyobo	1,726	Japan
Celanese	3,348	USA	Rohm and Haas	1,725	USA
PPG Industries	3,158	USA	Stauffer Chemical	1,695	USA
Asahi Chemicals	3,103	Japan	Teijin	1,690	Japan
Norsk Hydro*	2,836	Norway	Dianippon Ink & Chemicals	1,604	Japan
BOC International	2,710	United Kingdom	Turner & Newall	1,476	United Kingdom
Chemische Werke Huls*[4]	2,678	West Germany	Air Products & Chemicals	1,421	USA
Toray	2,644	Japan	Sekisui Chemicals	1,395	Japan
L'air Liquide	2,614	France	Sherwin-Williams	1,264	USA
Hercules	2,485	USA	Freudenberg*	1,237	West Germany
CSR	2,482	Australia	Boehringer*	1,148	West Germany

BUSINESS ORGANISATION	SALES, 1980 ($US million)	COUNTRY OF INCORPORATION
Asahi Glass	2,303	Japan
Ube Industries	2,269	Japan
NL Industries	2,188	USA
Henkel*	2,170	West Germany
Williams Industries*	2,073	USA
Fuji Photo	1,947	Japan
Koppers	1,929	USA
SCM	1,892	USA
Johnson & Matthey	1,888	United Kingdom
Olin	1,853	USA
Snia Viscosa	1,826	Italy
International Minerals & Chemicals	1,790	USA
Schering	1,774	West Germany
Aga*	1,094	Sweden
Kyowa	1,089	Japan
Kuraray	1,057	Japan
Akzona[2]	1,054	USA
Toya Soda	952	Japan
Fisons	927	United Kingdom
Mitsubishi Gas Chemical[1]	921	Japan
Reichold*	885	USA
Morton-Norwich*	847	USA
Thiokol	675	USA
Nalco*	617	USA
TOTAL SALES	102,281	

SEGMENT IV

BUSINESS ORGANISATION	SALES, 1980 ($US million)	COUNTRY OF INCORPORATION
Veba	9,646	West Germany
DSM	7,514	Netherlands
Charbonnages de France*	4,959	France
Mitsubishi Chemical Industries[1]	4,127	Japan
Sumitomo	3,181	Japan
Mitsui Toatsu	2,537	Japan
Showa Denko	2,191	Japan
Union Explosives Kio Tinto*	1,938	Spain
Mitsubishi Petrochemical*	1,791	Japan
Rutgerswerke*	1,275	West Germany
Mitsubishi Rayon[1]	933	Japan
Du Pont Canada[3]	851	Canada
Insilco*	642	USA
TOTAL SALES	41,585	

Notes: * Business organisation not included in the data analysis because of incomplete data, but has been inserted into the appropriate group using available data.

1. Mitsubishi group firms with chemical interests, judged as members of the Mitsubishi Enterprise Group through interlocking shareholding and other linkages.
2. Subsidiary company of Akzo, group II.
3. Subsidiary company of Du Pont, group I.
4. Subsidiary company of Veba, group IV.

Figure 3.1: Organisational Clusters Plotted on Factors 1 to 3

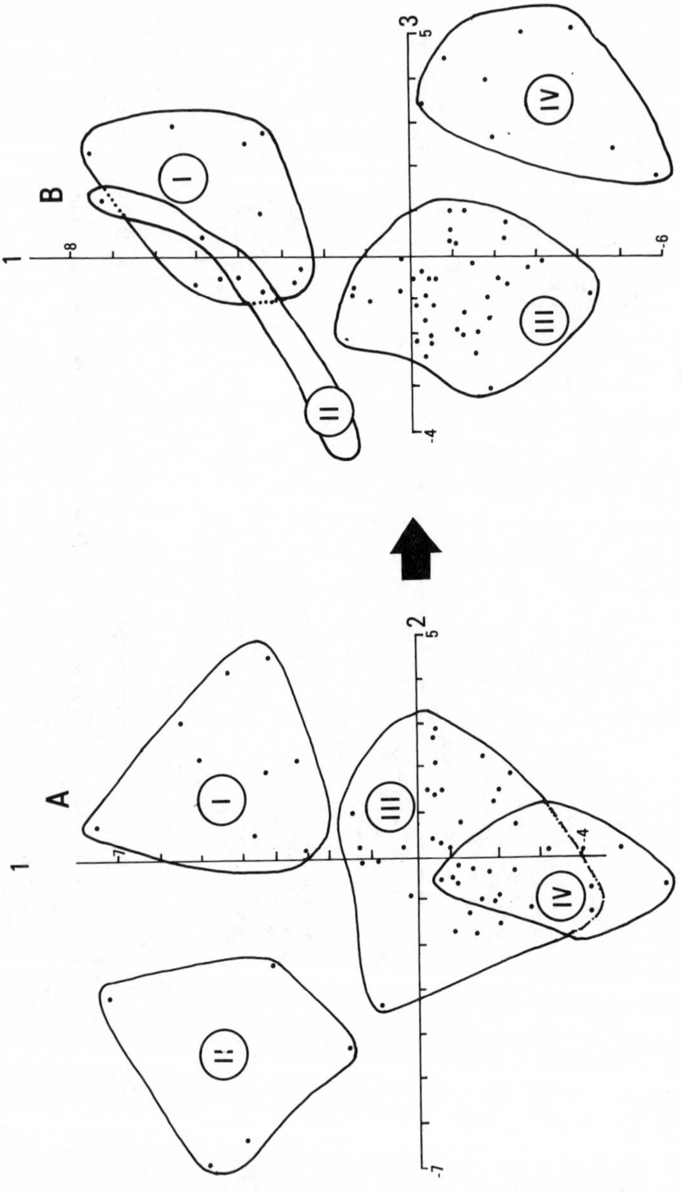

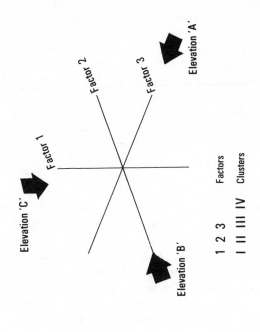

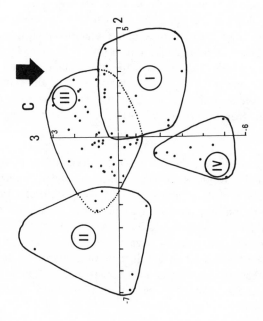

the administrative structure is highly integrated because of the smaller spread of activities. This conclusion is strengthened by the fact that over 84 per cent of the large number of subsidiary companies (between 76 and 258) are directly owned.

In terms of production, these business organisations are also massive employers. In 1980, the average size of their workforces was over 114,000, with an annual growth rate of 2,525 jobs. Production was moderately capital intensive (2.43), but was decreasing annually. Furthermore, turnover per employee was relatively low (0.12) and slightly increasing, suggesting either a concentration on products of high added value or a relative inefficiency in production.

Performance of business organisations in the first cluster must be seen in relation to their substantial capital base. Average assets and stockholders' equity capital represented $9,538m and $3,848m, for example. Though each of these capital sources is decreasing at a rate greater than $30m per annum, the financial strength of these organisations is plain. The average sales figures are approximately $11,300m, increasing rapidly at over $45m per annum. In fact, all the business indicators point towards a degree of certainty in the operational environment. As a measure of performance, the returns on business are appropriate indicators. Average profits in 1980 were $426m and these are growing at over $0.5m annually. Net profit ratios (i.e. profits as a percentage of sales) at over 4 per cent, are also higher than in the other three clusters, and this is the only cluster with an annual increase in the ratio. The return on stockholders' equity capital is over 11 per cent, exceeded only by organisations in Cluster IV. Profitability levels (i.e. return on assets) are perhaps the most telling indicators of the steady performance of business organisations in this cluster. This figure was, on average, 4.6 per cent, which is over one percentage point higher than in any other cluster, and there is a steady annual increase.

Cluster II. Structurally, the five business organisations in this cluster are very similar to those in Cluster I, in particular in their level of multinationality, scale of activities and huge workforces. In contrast, they are geographically more centralised with over 40 per cent of their subsidiaries located in the country in which they are incorporated. Furthermore, these business organisations have more subsidiaries located in host countries of low income than any other cluster (13.6 per cent). Their organisational structure is more differentiated, with an average of 8.6 product or regional divisions, and is less integrated.

There is, however, a greater level of downstream diversification, especially into chemical derivatives (16.2 per cent) and non-chemical activities (21.2 per cent). One important difference is in the ownership structure, which at 79.6 per cent of subsidiaries directly owned, is almost 5 per cent less than the same feature of Cluster I.

The structure of production also contrasts with that of business organisations in Cluster I. The average size of the workforce (89,646), is significantly smaller and there has been a heavy shedding of jobs annually (3,177). Capital intensity of production is also lower (2.04) and, coupled with the higher turnover per employee, this indicates a greater concentration on products of lower added value.

The main feature distinguishing these business organisations from those in Cluster I, however, is their performance. Not only is their capital base smaller (assets $7,399m; stockholders' equity $2,226m), but it is also becoming more restricted, with rapid annual declines in each of these sources. Part of the reason for this is the vitality of business. In 1980, sales were 67 per cent of the average for Cluster I and they are declining rapidly at an average of $33m per annum. Turnover (i.e. sales/assets) is lower than for any of the segments, and is increasing most slowly. Similarly, sales per employee are also comparatively low. The return on business indicators all consistently show bad performance: net profits ($-197m); net profit ratio (-1.72 per cent); capital return (-12.7 per cent) and profitability (-1.6 per cent).

Cluster III. Relative to the first two clusters, the 52 business organisations in this cluster possess a modest multinational structure, operating in between 6 and 28 countries. There is also a reasonable degree of centrality in the geographical structure (42.9 per cent average), most of the subsidiary companies being located in host countries of high income (61.1 per cent) and medium income (30.8 per cent). Organisational structure is less differentiated, with 5.6 divisions as an average, and is less integrated: over 30 per cent of sales take place in each of the areas of core chemicals, chemical derivatives and non-chemical activities. This feature implies a shift away from activities centred on the chemicals industry *per se*, not only into downstream chemicals, but also into non-chemical activities. The scale of activities is smaller than the first two clusters, with an average of 55 subsidiary companies, and fewer subsidiaries are directly owned (75.2 per cent).

All of the production indicators suggest a decrease in the overall scale of business organisations in this group. The average workforce (19,532) is 20-25 per cent of the size of typical workforces in the first two clusters, and is increasing modestly at 46 jobs annually. Capital intensity of production (2.97) and turnover per employee (0.79) are, however, much higher.

The performance of business organisations in this cluster is based on a smaller capital starting point, with average assets of $1,927m and stockholders' equity of $703m. Each of these is declining slightly each year. Business indicators show that sales volume ($2,075m) represents between 18 and 25 per cent of that carried on by business organisations in the first two clusters, despite the larger number of organisations. Although sales are dropping, turnover is still increasing because of the drop in assets. Net profits ratios are quite high, with a 3.23 per cent return on sales, being second only to the first segment. The profitability measure of performance, which highlights the return on equity capital, displays the same pattern.

Cluster IV. The geographical structure of the 13 business organisations in the final cluster is much more restricted. The level of multinationality is on average only seven countries, but this varies from one extreme of over thirteen countries to the other extreme in which the activities of some organisations are wholly national. This structure is, therefore, highly centralised, with a mean value of 74.6 per cent subsidiary companies being located in the country of incorporation. As with the other clusters, these organisations are primarily located in high income and medium income host countries.

The organisational structure is less differentiated than the other clusters, with only 4.8 divisions. The orientation towards core chemicals and extractive/feedstock activities indicates an emphasis on upstream diversification and a tightly integrated structure. The scale of activities is relatively small (42 subsidiaries) and the level of direct ownership of subsidiaries (48 per cent) is the smallest of the four clusters. What this suggests is that over half of the subsidiaries are indirectly owned.

The average size of the workforce of business organisations in this cluster is 13,113, and the modest annual increase of 78 jobs reflects this comparatively small scale of activities. However, production is extremely capital intensive (7.79 per cent) and it is the only cluster in which it is increasing. As a result, turnover per employee is very high (1.35), in comparison with Clusters I-III.

Though business organisations in this cluster are structurally and geographically smaller than those in Cluster III, they differ in their much larger asset base ($3,013m), which is unique in its tendency to increase; and also in sales volume ($3,990m). Annual sales are increasing faster in these business organisations than in any other cluster ($56m), as too is turnover and sales per employee. The implications of these factors are a high return on capital (22 per cent), the low profits possibly indicating growth which is based on the retention of earnings.

The Pattern of Segmentation

Cluster analysis, applied to organisations rather than industry sectors, has demonstrated a distinct pattern of segmentation in the chemicals industry. Four discrete clusters were revealed. Although no attempt was made to prove the assertion, there does seem to be at least a tentative relationship between corporate organisation and performance. A brief synopsis of some of the principal dimensions of the clusters derived from the analysis is set out in Table 3.6. The purpose of this section is to summarise this pattern of segmentation.

Business organisations in Cluster I are geographically extensive and decentralised with a wide multinational sphere of operations (the bulk of which is in the more developed countries). They also possess: a substantial number of subsidiary companies; a large number of structural divisions concentrated in the core of the chemicals industry; a large and growing workforce; a strong capital base and a growing business environment. Quite clearly, these business organisations, which include names such as Dow, Du Pont, Hoechst, Bayer and BASF, are too big and qualitatively too different to fit the general conception of a multinational corporation. Rather, they would seem to represent the group of emerging *global corporations* mentioned in Chapters 1 and 2. This set of enterprises is the most successful of all the business organisations which were analysed.

Cluster II contains business organisations very similar to those in Cluster I, the major difference being that they stand out on the basis of their poor performance and rapidly contracting workforces — caused by rationalisation. As a result of these structural similarities, coupled with performance dissimilarities, this group of business organisations has been termed *global restructuring corporations* and includes organisations such as ICI, Rhône-Poulenc and Akzo.

By far the largest group of enterprises is represented by Cluster III. This segment includes an array of 52 corporations and companies, operating on a modest multinational scale but with a primary orientation to the country in which the organisations are incorporated. In addition, they have fewer subsidiary companies and are more diversified downstream. These features, together with comparative business and employment stability, point towards this cluster as representing

Table 3.6: Principal Dimensions of Business Organisation Segments Derived from the Cluster Analysis

CLUSTER	GEOGRAPHICAL STRUCTURE	ORGANISATIONAL STRUCTURE	PRODUCTION	PERFORMANCE
I	Extensive multinational operations with a decentralised network. Tendency to concentrate major proportion of activities on developed (high and medium income) countries.	Highly differentiated and strongly integrated, with concentration of activities in mainstream chemicals. Large number of subsidiary companies most of which are directly owned.	Large, expanding workforce. Medium capital intensity.	Large capital base. Rapid growth in business and substantial capital returns.
II	Extensive multinational operations but more centralised network than I. Greater emphasis on low income host countries as well as developed locations.	Highly differentiated, more so than I and less integrated. Primary activities in mainstream chemicals but greater downstream diversity than I. Larger network of susidiary companies than I, fewer directly owned.	Large, contracting workforce. Low capital intensity.	Large but declining capital base. Rapid business contraction and negative capital returns.
III	Modest multinational scale of operations compared to I and II and a centralised network. Activities primarily concentrated in developed countries.	Less differentiated structures with extensive downstream diversity compared to I and II. Fewer subsidiaries and less directly owned than II.	Medium, stable workforce. Medium capital intensity.	Small capital base in slow decline. Slight growth in business, and reasonable returns.
IV	Small multinational scale of operations and strongly centralised network. Very little emphasis on low income host countries.	Highly integrated structures with little differentiation. Substantial backward integration. Small network of subsidiary companies and especially affiliated companies.	Small, stable workforce. Very high capital intensity.	Medium capital base and growth in business. High return but low profits.

the stereotyped *multinational corporations and companies*.

At the other extreme to Cluster I, Cluster IV contained the enterprises with the smallest multinational sphere of operations, strongly centralised on their own domestic economy. These business organisations are substantially backward-integrated and have only a relatively small number of subsidiary companies. Also, the organisations in this cluster are expanding seemingly by retaining business profits and by employing small workforces with capital-intensive methods of production. Several of these characteristics are hallmarks of the typically *large national business organisation* which may, or may not, operate multinationally. Business organisations which fit this description include the large state-controlled corporations such as Charbonnages de France, DSM and Veba. Subsidiary companies of global corporations, such as Du Pont Canada and Union Explosives Rio Tinto, a subsidiary of Rio Tinto Zinc, are also members of the group.

The number of Japanese business organisations in this cluster requires some explanation. In particular, Mitsubishi Chemical Industries, Mitsubishi Petrochemicals and Mitsubishi Rayon are related to each other by interlocking directorates through the Mitsubishi Enterprise Group. Japanese enterprise groups do not, however, present consolidated accounts, and they are not directly comparable with western-style holding companies. The importance of this set of enterprises may, therefore, be understated in the analysis. Whether or not this comparatively loose membership of companies to larger enterprise groups affects performance and, indeed, whether they have their western equivalent, is an unresolved and continuing debate (see for instance, Nakase, 1981).

Ramifications of Business Organisation Segmentation

Whereas the discussion so far has concentrated on describing the organisation of enterprises operating in the chemicals industry, this section aims to broaden the discussion to examine some of the ramifications of business organisation segmentation. In particular, three questions need to be addressed. First, what are the central themes linking these distinct forms of business organisations? Second, which are the most powerful business organisation segments? Finally, how do these structural characteristics and positions of power affect the dynamics of corporate organisation?

Forms of Business Organisation: Some Central Themes

The description of the four broad types of business organisation operating in the chemicals industry illustrates the different forms of organisation which accompany an expansion in the geographical scope of corporate space. At least four themes can be referred to which both reaffirm and extrapolate some of the tentative conclusions drawn from Chapter 2 in several respects.

Decentralisation. Growth in the multinationality of business organisations carries with it a tendency to decentralise activities out of the country in which the enterprise first began its operations. This feature is most strongly developed in the global and global restructuring forms of corporations and least evident in the large national business organisations. As subsidiary companies of global and multinational types of corporation are included in this latter group, it is important to point out that geographical decentralisation is relative to the level of organisational analysis.

Host country characteristics. These are an integral part of business organisation, and appear to change as the organisation develops. For example, the large national business organisations have concentrated their activities primarily in the high- and medium-income countries. In the business organisations with a broader spatial spread of activities, such as the multinational, global and global restructuring corporations, investment in medium and low income locations takes on a greater relative and absolute importance. As global and global restructuring types of corporation may have upwards of two hundred subsidiary companies, their potential impact is expected to be far greater in all locations.

Organisational structure. A subtle change in organisational structure also takes place with geographical expansion. The cluster analysis suggested that not only does the number of subsidiary companies increase, but also there is a concentration of ownership (fewer jointly owned companies) within the business organisation. There may be a variety of reasons for this feature. The most apparent is the need to integrate operations which are often disparate, geographically and functionally. For instance, the percentage of directly owned subsidiaries almost doubles between large national and global corporations, thereby exacerbating this problem of integrating disparate sub-units. Functionally, multinational corporations are the most diversified form of business organisation, so if it is hypothesised that global corporations grow out of multinationals, then their structure of activities must undergo a distinct transformation. The fact that global corporations derive the majority of their sales from the core chemicals industry, more than any other form of business organisation, may, therefore, be a further indication of the concentration of activities and structure which accompanies geographical decentralisation. In addition, structural differentiation also increases with geographical decentralisation, being highest in the global forms of organisation. This decision by global corporations to divide up their activities may be a mechanism for coping with their large scale of operations, geographical spread and a more complex business environment. Concentration on the core part of the chemicals industry by global corporations was, presumably, because it is the area in which they feel that they can perform most effectively.

Employment. Underlying these different forms of business organisation in the chemicals industry were variations in the scale and dynamics of employment. Not only did the average size of the workforce grow markedly with different forms of organisation, but also the rate at which employment changed altered. These features are undoubtedly due, in part, to the scale of activities, but they are also due to the performance of the business organisation. In this sense, the highly profitable global corporations have large and rapidly growing workforces, whereas global restructuring corporations which are performing badly are consistently shedding jobs.

These four main themes – decentralisation, host country characteristics, organisational structure and employment – help understand the nature of linkages between the segments of business organisations, as well as enabling the conceptualisation of some of the possible spatial effects which may arise from, or as part of, the characteristics of these distinct forms of organisation. What is less certain, in terms of the discussion at the beginning of this chapter, is the overall significance of the pattern of segmentation which has been revealed and, in particular, the power of individual business organisations and segments.

Segment Power

To establish the relative importance of the different types of business organisation, it is necessary to take an aggregate view of organisational segmentation. For example, Table 3.7, which summarises the total sales for each of the segments, illustrates that the global corporations

Table 3.7: Chemical Business Organisations: Sales by Segment, 1980

SEGMENT	NO.	TOTAL 1980 SALES ($USm)	PER CENT
I. Global Corporations	9	101,699	35.6
II. Global Restructuring Corporations	5	40,464	14.1
III. Multinational Corporations & Companies	52	102,281	35.8
IV. Large National Business Organisations	13	41,585	14.5
Total	79	286,029	100.0

Table 3.8: Chemical Business Organisations: Employment by Segment, 1980

SEGMENT	NO.	TOTAL EMPLOYMENT OF SEGMENT	PER CENT
I. Global Corporations	9	1,028,532	38.2
II. Global Restructuring Corporations	5	474,112	17.6
III. Multinational Corporations & Companies	52	967,902	36.0
IV. Large National Business Organisations	13	220,515	8.2
Total	79	2,691,106	100.0

account for 35.6 per cent and global restructuring corporations 14.1 per cent of the total sales represented by the set of 79 business organisations evaluated in the chemicals industry in 1980. In total, therefore, the two groups of global corporations account for almost one-half of the total sales. Contrasting these segments, the multinational corporations and companies accounted for 35.8 per cent of the sales and large national business organisations 14.5 per cent. This comparison of aggregate sales between the four segments emphasises the primary feature of organisational segmentation in the chemicals industry, which is an unequal distribution of market power.

The practical significance of each segment is demonstrated with reference to the employment generated by different types of business organisation (Table 3.8). In 1980, the two segments of global corporations controlled almost 56 per cent of the 2.7 million people employed worldwide in the business organisations examined. Conversely, the multinational corporations and companies employed 36 per cent, and the large national business organisations employed the remaining 8.2 per cent. If these figures are taken as being broadly indicative of the relative significance of different types of business organisation operating in the world economy, the two types of global corporations have the potential for the greatest impacts on employment.

The unequal size of segments, when evaluated in terms of aggregate sales or employment does, however, conceal the importance of individual business organisations and, therefore, the distribution of power within the chemicals industry. For instance, there are only nine global corporations, but these are roughly equivalent, measured in terms of sales volume and employment, to the 52 multinational corporations and companies. Of course, the concept of power as discussed here relates primarily to the characteristics of the size of the corporations concerned. This usage of the concept is intended simply as a means of understanding inequalities in inter-organisational relations as embodied in their structural characteristics and economic performance. Thus, although the results of the cluster analysis show that various measures of size are critical indicators of the power of a business organisation, it must be borne in mind that proven performance is also integral to this definition. In other words, the size and various other structural characteristics of a business organisation are the *outcome* of historical development and, therefore, surrogate indicators of established inter-organisational power relations. They are also the starting point of future developments, including corporate growth or decline. By specifying the number of business organisations of each type, a much clearer picture is, therefore, provided of the *concentration* of power within certain segments, and especially within global corporations.

Several questions are raised by this discussion of the distribution of power between and within segments of business organisations, not the least of which are the dynamics of segmentation. How do business organisations of different types relate to each other? Can business organisations move between segments and, if so, what are the main processes involved? Finally, how does the power of certain types of business organisations and segments help or hinder such transformations?

Power, Process and Organisational Transformation

A useful way of confronting these questions is to discuss events within the chemicals industry and also, where information is lacking, to supplement the discussion with examples of business organisations drawn from other industries. To this end, the pattern of segmentation described in the above study is illustrated schematically in Figure 3.2. The relative importance of the four types of business organisation which were identified is represented, as well as possible development paths involved in corporate transformation. It is a truism that very little, if anything, is known about the precise way in which business organisations are transformed, and especially the processes which are involved in this change, so the following discussion can only be tentative.

Theoretically, two sets of processes enable a degree of mobility in this segmented industry structure, and paradoxically, allow the established and more developed business organisations to maintain their own positions of power. The first set of processes are internal to the organisation and the second are external. Figure 3.2 shows the main area in which internal processes of growth and restructuring operate. These consist of growth by the establishment of facilities, product changes and product development, and geographical and organisational extension of the business organisation. However, it is clear that a number of obstacles stand to mitigate internal growth. The main obstacles are the transformation of a business organisation from a national to a multinational status, and also from a multinational to a global status. Taylor and Thrift (1982a) have identified these barriers as a series of gaps, which consist, in the main, of inadequate financial bases for development. These finance gaps, which include the celebrated 'Macmillan' and 'Radcliffe' (or venture) capital gaps (see Thomas, 1978), are present because of the inability, usually of smaller

Figure 3.2: Organisational Segmentation, Restructuring and Corporate Interaction

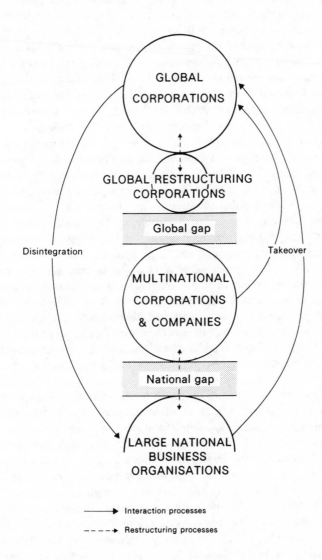

Note: Circle size is approximately equal to the market significance of each group.

firms, to gain access to capital for expansion by providing an established credit record. Basically, however, these problems are not overcome even at the level of the large corporation, which is faced with obtaining funds from a multiple-currency and increasingly international financial system (Aliber, 1970; 1971).

Growth by internal reorganisation does take place, allowing business organisations to evolve and transcend the barriers between these segments, but there are limitations. As Taylor and Thrift (1982a, p. 32) have stressed, 'it would seem reasonable to suggest that the greater the number of firms that cross a particular barrier, the more reinforced it becomes and the harder it is to cross'. However, the power of individual firms rather than just the number would seem to play a significant part in reinforcing barriers to corporate development. In this respect, the sheer size and features of the global corporations would appear to make the 'national' gap far more difficult to transcend. The organisational characteristics of global corporations, particularly their market spread, strong financial base and domination of the industry's production, make these business organisations a force to be reckoned with. For the smaller multinationals and large national business organisation, at least, growth by processes of internal restructuring seems an increasingly unlikely avenue of development. This type of growth can, at best, only be incremental, which would be insufficient given the starting point of such business organisations. Alternatively, it can be hypothesised that internal restructuring is an easier and more powerful means of growth for the larger established multinational and global corporations with access to resources, information and a capacity to cope with uncertainty.

Far more likely processes for the transformation of business organisations are externally located, often involving interaction with other organisations. These may include joint ventures, takeovers and mergers. A specific example of a merger from the chemicals industry is the recent trend for the larger corporations to buy up small producers of speciality chemicals, in order to carve out their own niche in the market. This process has taken on added importance because of the increasing decline in the market for heavy chemicals, which have traditionally been the 'cash-cow' of chemical corporations (*The Petroleum Economist*, 1982). The larger corporations have also realised that speciality chemicals alone can never pay their way (*The Economist*, 1982a), so that the success of the strategy ultimately depends on some of the major competitors shutting down parts of their own excess capacity in the heavy chemicals sector. The inevitable reluctance to make this move is underlined by the recent attempt by major chemical organisations to set up a swap-shop by which whole factories, managers, assets and workforces can be exchanged, leaving each individual firm to concentrate on its own specialities. The spatial repercussions of these types of processes are already becoming evident. For instance, ICI has announced a huge asset-swapping deal with BP which involved ICI closing part of its plastic facilities in the United Kingdom, transferring others to BP which would take similar steps with its own plants.

These examples drawn from the chemicals industry serve to highlight a further means of transformation operating in the model. Plants, companies and even subsidiary business organisations can be acquired by the larger organisations — especially the global and multinational corporations — in order to cross the development gap. An example of a global corporation expanding in this way is given by the American organisation Du Pont, which purchased the oil giant Conoco in 1980. The strategic reasons for this decision were part of Du Pont's policy towards backward integration and geographical diversification in Europe (*The Economist*, 1982b). Conoco's North Sea oil assets were the incentive behind the takeover by Du Pont, because of strong competition with other global chemical corporations in Europe (*The Economist*, 1980a).

Interaction with other business organisations, such as through mergers and takeovers, are a means of product, financial and geographical diversification open only to the largest of corporations, and they explain how it is possible for the structure of a business organisation to be radically transformed over a short period of time. Growth takes place in a series of 'quantum' leaps rather than incrementally. However, it would be wrong to assert these processes operate in only one direction. The recent collapse of the global electronics corporation AEG-Telefunken which is based in West Germany, raises the question of what might happen when large corporations are declared bankrupt.

Preliminary attempts to bail out AEG-Telefunken by the West German government foundered and recent plans involved a number of alternatives, including the selling off of some of the organisation's divisions and thinning down of the remaining elements (*The Economist*, 1982c). Presumably, the most profitable elements are the easiest to sell off and bids were received from a number of quarters, including Britain's GEC and the American electronics giant United Technologies and ITT, notably for AEG's profitable telecommunications and transport systems, and its power and engineering and industrial subsidiary (*The Economist*, 1983a). The remaining elements will, perhaps inevitably, be the hard core of unprofitable divisions which may be fashioned into national business organisations and smaller multinationals, or even closed altogether.

Conclusions

A tentative attempt has been made in this chapter to define the structure of business organisations empirically, concentrating on their geographical and organisational attributes of structure, as well as production and performance. The analysis supports the previous supposition that there are distinct forms of business organisation operating at an international level. However, the overall structure of business organisations in the chemicals industry is not uniform, and this seems to act to initiate, maintain and extend a basis of unequal power relations both between and within organisational segments.

In pointing out these elements of organisational structure, however, a number of caveats must be applied. To begin with, the study has been restricted to one sector and care must be taken not to apply features of organisational segmentation, which are specific to the chemicals industry, too broadly. The chemicals industry is unique in many respects, not the least of which is the expected above-average representation in terms of the number of global-scale corporations, compared to other industries.

A second limitation which must be applied relates to the sectoral analysis of business organisations. It can be concluded that a strict sectoral study would have fundamentally altered the pattern of segmentation which has been revealed by this analysis of business organisations. A study of the chemicals sector has been used only insofar as it acts as a starting point, and it includes many organisations whose activities stretch beyond the confines of industry definitions. Indeed, the study has emphasised how industries may overlap by using an organisational perspective.

A third caveat of the analysis is that it has involved a cross-sectional approach to operationalising the concept of business organisation segmentation, despite the inclusion of some dynamic measures of production and performance. What it has been unable to assess in any depth is how corporate organisation is transformed over time: in other words the dynamics and processes behind organisational segmentation. Although some of these processes were referred to in the final section of the chapter, no attempt was made to clarify their individual importance.

A final caveat to the study lies in the fact that organisational segmentation itself is only a conceptual framework in which studies of individual organisations can be evaluated. It does not undermine the importance of studies of individual enterprises but merely provides them with a contextual benchmark.

Notwithstanding these limitations, this chapter has demonstrated it is possible to define types of business organisation structures using data derived from published sources. Specifically, it has shown that an otherwise homogeneous group of multinational corporations can be broken down into groups of global, multinational and large national business organisations, each of which have their own distinct characteristics. To recap these findings, two groups of business organisations could be distinguished on the grounds of their: extensive, decentralised and highly multinational geographical attributes; large number of subsidiary companies held together in a highly differentiated structure; interests concentrated in the heart of the chemicals industry; large workforces; and substantial capital bases. Quite clearly, these business organisations deserved the epithet global corporation. However, despite these structural similarities, these two groups of corporations differed markedly by way of their performance. Whereas the global corporations displayed a record of success, with rapidly expanding profits and workforces, the group termed global restructuring corporations were performing only poorly and the significant shedding of jobs which has taken place inside these organisations can be seen as a reflection of this emphasis on restructuring.

Two other groups of enterprises were also highlighted. The first group was characterised by a relatively modest multinational structure, with considerably more orientation to the home country than the global corporations. Furthermore, these organisations had fewer but more independent subsidiaries, and were structurally less integrated, with a greater degree of downstream diversification in the industry. This set of enterprises displayed business and employment stability, and conformed to the traditional view of the multinational enterprise. The second group had by far the most restricted geographical structure, and were largely oriented to the economy in which the organisation was incorporated. Structurally, these organisations had fewer subsidiaries and a considerable degree of backward integration towards extractive/feedstock activities. These and other characteristics, such as their small workforces and capital-intensive production methods, led to this group being named large national business organisations.

In addition to these features, the discussion also raised several issues relating to the dynamic properties of the cross-sectional pattern of business organisation segmentation which had been described. An approximate correlation between the performance and structure of groups of business organisations was noted and evidently deserves further attention. Four themes — degree of decentralisation, host country characteristics, organisational structure and employment — were also extracted which serve to link these groups of organisations in a conceptual framework of segmentation. Several generalisations can be gleaned from these findings including:

1. a tendency toward geographical decentralisation with increases in the attributes of corporate size;
2. a change in host country characteristics associated with different types of structure, such as a greater relative and absolute presence in medium- and low-income countries in global and multinational corporations compared to large national business organisations;
3. added concentration of ownership, and greater structural differentiation and integration in global corporations, possibly to cope with activities which are functionally and geographically diverse; and
4. a relationship between performance and the magnitude and turnover rate of the workforces of business organisations.

The disparity between individual enterprises and groups of business organisations was revealed most clearly when the concept of power relations was introduced into the segmentation framework. Two measures — employment and sales — were used to illustrate these inequalities and they pointed to some important corollaries of the relative power of business organisations. Differences in the number as well as the size of the four types of organisation mean that there is an inevitable concentration of power within as well as between organisation segments, suggesting that the existence of different corporate structures poses problems for the expansion of smaller organisations, which are increasingly unable to meet the demands set by the corporations, or the financial and other hurdles set and determined by an economy now accustomed to serving these larger business organisations.

Rather than implying a *continuum* of organisational development, therefore, this analysis indicates an increasingly *segmented* sequence, where organisations are transformed by only a limited number of processes such as takeover, joint ventures, mergers, collusion and occasionally disintegration, most of which now lie external to the smaller organisation, and, seemingly, allow only growth by quantum leaps. In short, the existence of different types of business organisation strongly implies a highly *structured* industry, whereby growth and survival depend, to a large extent, on the methods and structure an organisation adopts. One example, which can be used to illustrate an outcome of the organisational structure present in the chemical industry, is the attention different forms of business organisation give to certain parts of the industry. For instance, the activities of global corporations were definitely concentrated in core chemicals, whereas multinationals were diversified downstream into other activities, and large national business organisations were integrated backwards into extractive and feedstock activities. There are two possible causes of this pattern: either it reflects the choices made by individual organisations or, more likely, it is a direct outcome of the power of global corporations, a few of which dominate the heart of the chemicals industry, acting to periperalise other firms into absorbing the remains.

It can be concluded that global corporations warrant further attention, especially with regard to their structural attributes about which very little is known. During this argument, the geographical and organisational elements of corporate structure were viewed separately, and yet the results have indicated a strong degree of concordance between the two. Thus, in order to expand an understanding of this relationship, and to provide a deeper insight into some of the dynamic processes underlying the pattern of segmentation in the chemicals industry, Chapter 4 examines the recent evolution of one global restructuring corporation, ICI.

4   The Geography of Corporate Restructuring: A Case Study of ICI

This chapter explores some of the inner workings of global corporations through a case study of ICI — a large chemical enterprise with its head-quarters located in Britain. However, such a study of ICI cannot be more than indicative of general processes operating within all global corporations. Thus, the discussion is empirical in content and descriptive in nature, drawing upon published information both internal and external to ICI.

As noted in Chapter 3, part of the importance of global corporations comes from their significance in terms of employment. Accompanying the huge workforces, which are a primary characteristic of the global corporation, is the impact that their restructuring can have on the international space economy. These spatial effects, however, have normally been only partially investigated with attention being confined to only one nation state. In common with the other global restructuring corporations from which it is abstracted, ICI has experienced difficulty in maintaining its performance especially since 1970, and has undergone a programme of restructuring, totally altering the form of the organisation. Thus, the thrust of this study is to examine the effects of restructuring on ICI's workforce, especially on the creation of a new spatial division of labour within the corporation. Following the brief outline of the main characteristics of ICI in the first part of the argument, the main causes of restructuring are then considered in the second part. A description of the main thrusts of restructuring in part three elaborates the changes in product emphases and the financing of adjustment which have taken place in ICI between 1970 and 1980. This review acts as an essential backcloth to a more detailed consideration of the geographical aspects of corporate restructuring in the fourth part of the chapter. In the final part, an attempt is made to draw together these various elements by illustrating the restructuring which took place within ICI in one year, 1980.

Imperial Chemical Industries

Imperial Chemical Industries (ICI) was formed by the merger of four companies in 1926, each well established in its own right: Nobel Industries Ltd, a powerful explosives company; Brunner, Mond and Company Ltd, a large alkali firm; British Dyestuffs Corporation and the United Alkali Company Ltd (Reader, 1970). Both Nobel and Brunner, Mond had been trading since the 1870s and the other two companies in the merger were, at that time, being threatened by imports and outmoded technology. The merger was partly a response to these threatening trading conditions. Further, the First World War had demonstrated to Britain that a united chemicals industry was essential to the country's defence as well as its industrial future (Reader, 1977).

In its formation year, ICI operated with assets of £69m and with interests only in Britain, Australasia and Canada. At the outset, the firm employed over 33,000 people and listed the following products in its portfolio: heavy chemicals; explosives and accessories; fertilisers; insecticides; dyestuffs; domestic chemicals; leathercloth; printing; sporting ammunitions; non-ferrous metals; paints; gas mantles; lamps and accessories; and welding plant and equipment (ICI, 1971).

By 1980, 55 years later, ICI had developed into a very different form of organisation, with a more extended international and product structure. A large number of products were still produced and marketed by the corporation, but under ten main business divisions — agriculture, fibres, general chemicals, organic chemicals, industrial explosives, oil, paints, petrochemicals, pharmaceuticals and plastics. ICI's geographical base by 1980 was equally broad. With factories in more than 40 countries and selling organisations in more than 60, ICI had been dubbed 'International Chemical Industries' (*The Economist*, 1980b) and was a global corporation in the true sense of the word. The distribution of ICI's factories and offices worldwide in 1980 are shown in Figure 4.1.

The corporate structure of ICI's activities in 1980-1 is shown in Figure 4.2. ICI (based in London) is the ultimate holding company for a larger group of companies. These companies are structured on the basis of area or regional divisions, the divisions being coordinated by executives who report annually to the parent organisation. The United Kingdom is the largest and most significant of these regional divisions and, unlike the other regions, is comprehensively sub-divided into several product divisions which perform relatively autonomously. The

Figure 4.1: The Worldwide Distribution of ICI's Factories and Offices

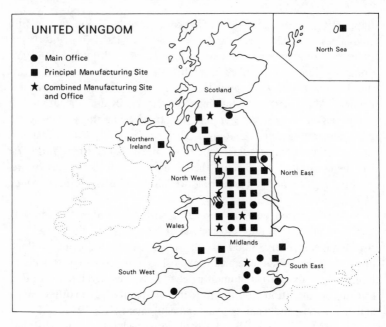

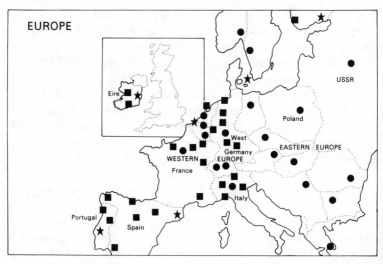

Source: Clarke (1982, pp. 95-8).

Figure 4.1 (continued)

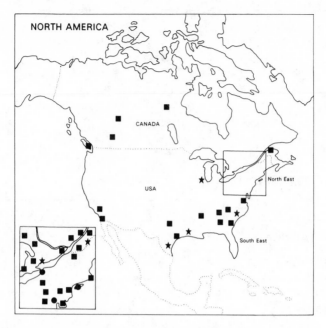

Figure 4.1 (continued)

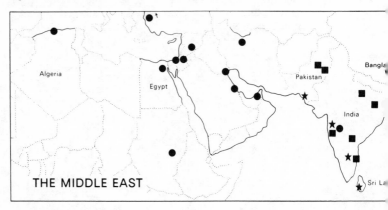

THE MIDDLE EAST

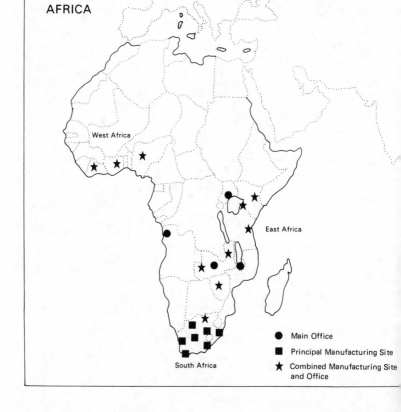

AFRICA

Figure 4.1 (continued)

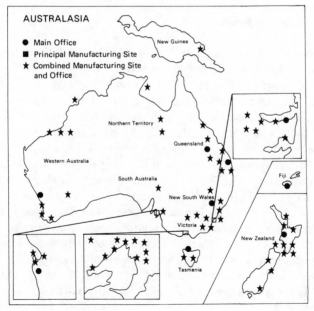

other regional divisions are Continental Western Europe, North America, South America, Africa and the Middle East, the Indian Sub-continent and Australasia and the Far East. Although companies within each of these divisions behave fairly independently, the parent company also consolidates the results of various businesses into worldwide product divisions for accounting purposes.

Figure 4.2: ICI: Corporate Structure, 1980

Source: Compiled from ICI (1981).

The Causes of Restructuring

In the first half of the decade 1970-80, ICI was still the stalwart of the British chemicals industry it had been set up to be in 1926. In 1974, the Chairman of ICI, Jack Callard, pointed out that the 'ICI Group is and will remain British-based, for two-thirds of our capital is invested here and 132,000 out of a total 201,000 of our people work here' (ICI, 1974, p. 1). Quite clearly, ICI's managers did not perceive the company was on the verge of a radical transformation.

Several factors coupled together in the mid-1970s to totally alter this situation. Initially, the oil crisis brought the chemicals industry to its knees. Then the British economy, on which so much of ICI's success had been based, began to falter. According to ICI, powerful unions and expensive labour in Britain only worsened the position. Furthermore, the gradual strengthening of sterling weakened ICI's export potential and made overseas production an imperative in many cases. Finally, the onset of world recession and soaring inflation set off fierce competition in a chemicals industry suffering from extensive overcapacity.

Before describing ICI's response to this situation the changes are briefly foreshadowed. ICI reacted to the quickening pace of change by substantial restructuring early in the 1970s, but apparently this was not enough. In 1978, Maurice Hodgson, the new ICI Chairman, exemplified the new spirit by emphasising that, in order 'to survive, ICI must match its competitors who have their bases in different political and economic environments. ICI has more than half its assets in the UK. These must be worked efficiently and continuously if we are to succeed' (ICI, 1978, p. 1). Over-reliance on the British economy, it seemed, was becoming too much of a risk. A new spirit was fostered. Potential overseas markets appeared to offer new outlets and a means to spread the risk incumbent on ICI.

The global potential was quickly embraced. From 1975 onwards, diversification was stepped up overseas and structural changes reflected this trend. In 1974, for example, ICI's operations outside the United Kingdom became of sufficient significance to warrant the division of the 'rest of the world' in annual reports into five separate regional categories: Continental Western Europe, the Americas, Australasia and the Far East, the Indian Sub-continent and Other Countries. By the end of the decade, ICI was a profoundly different organisation. Forced to adjust to economic stagflation and competition, Maurice Hodgson, still the Chairman of ICI in 1981, stressed 'the process of change in ICI will continue. Recession has eliminated any breathing space we might have had to adjust to a new world environment for chemicals in which growth rates will be lower than we have been accustomed to in the past. We are confident we can adjust the business to new requirements in product range, production capacity and territorial distribution' (ICI, 1981, p. 1). By 1981, the managers of ICI had greatly altered their attitudes. ICI had made fundamental changes in the three dimensions of products, capacities and geographical structure. Precisely how this was achieved, and the effects restructuring had, is now discussed.

The Restructuring of ICI

ICI responded to the rapidly worsening economic situation in the 1970s by a series of business changes, including emphasising new products and the running down of existing product lines in which market potential was declining, or which were not compatible with the organisation's interests taken as a whole. Occasionally during the decade, some structural changes *per se* also accompanied these new product initiatives. The nature and reasons for these changes are discussed below. The speed with which ICI responded to changes in the business environment can, it seems, be largely explained (at least superficially) by the ability to generate sufficient finance. This section, therefore, aims to summarise these restructuring initiatives before analysing the geographical component of corporate restructuring.

Product Segmentation

As outlined, ICI divides its activities into ten main product divisions, the sales and trading profits for which are shown in Tables 4.1 and 4.2.

Table 4.1: ICI Product Divisions: Sales, Selected Years (percentages)

PRODUCT DIVISION	1973	1976	1979
Agriculture	13	14	15
Fibres	12	9	7
General chemicals	15	15	16
Industrial explosives	4	4	3
Metals and engineering products	12	9	–
Oil	–	2	9
Organic chemicals	9	9	8
Paint and decorative products	8	8	7
Petrochemicals	11	14	17
Pharmaceuticals	4	4	5
Plastics	11	11	12
Miscellaneous	1	1	1
Total	100	100	100

Source: Various annual reports.

These tables illustrate the shifts in the product structure of ICI in two important respects. First, the proportion of ICI's total sales and trading profits accounted for by individual product divisions are emphasised. Second, restructuring between product divisions over time is also demonstrated. Rather than evaluating each product division separately, the discussion can be simplified and clarified by evaluating characteristics common to some of the divisions. Three criteria which can be used to this end are sales volume, net profits and the annual growth rate of profits for each division. Together they form the basis for a crude classification of divisions, a type of *product segmentation*.

Table 4.2: ICI Product Divisions: Trading Profits and Losses, Selected Years (percentages)

PRODUCT DIVISION	1973	1976	1979
Agriculture	14	20	24
Fibres	8	(2)	(5)
General chemicals	19	26	21
Industrial explosives	4	4	3
Metals and engineering products	10	6	–
Oil	–	(2)	12
Organic chemicals	8	12	1
Paint and decorative products	5	1	5
Petrochemicals	7	16	15
Pharmaceuticals	9	7	10
Plastics	10	8	9
Miscellaneous	2	(0)*	2
Royalty income	4	4	3
Total	100	100	100

Note: * Slight loss.
     Figures in brackets are trading losses.
Source: Various annual reports.

It must be emphasised that the criteria used in the classification of product divisions were tentative and specific to ICI, although their expression as percentages does mean that these results can be compared with those of other business organisations (Table 4.3). Thus, a division was classified as having a high sales volume if it accounted for over 15 per cent of the ICI total, and low if this figure was less than 15 per cent. Similarly, large profit earners were deemed to be those divisions contributing over 10 per cent to group profits. Finally, the annual growth rate of a division's profits was taken to be high when it accounted for above 10 per cent of the annual change in profits for ICI as a whole between 1970 and 1980. However, these criteria were used only as guidelines and where they conflicted, the profit growth characteristic was normally given precedence.

Table 4.3: Criteria Used to Define ICI Product Segments

CHARACTERISTIC	PRODUCT DIVISION AS PROPORTION OF TOTAL (per cent)	
	High	Low
Sales volume	> 15	< 15
Profit	> 10	< 10
Annual growth of profits	> 10	< 10

Product divisions were allocated to segments according to these characteristics. Compromise was occasionally required and in these cases, the growth rate characteristic was given precedence.

Source: Various annual reports.

Four product segments can be distinguished using these criteria. Product divisions allocated to Segment A display typically high sales volume figures, high profits and high annual growth rates for profits. For example, agricultural chemicals, ICI's top profit earner, expanded its sales from 13 per cent to 15 per cent, and its trading profits from 14 per cent to 24 per cent of the organisation's total between 1973 and 1979 (*Chemical Age*, 1980a). Another product division in this category is general chemicals which also grew rapidly, expanding its trading profits from 19 per cent of ICI's total in 1973 to 21 per cent in 1979. The addition of oil interests in ICI's portfolio in 1975 and the formation of a new product division, expanded quickly after initial losses, and by 1979 oil accounted for 12 per cent of total trading profits largely through the success of North Sea assets. These three product divisions are the most dynamic of ICI's acitivities.

Segment B consists of two product divisions, plastics and petro-chemicals (merged into one division in 1981), which have the characteristics of high sales volume, low profits and low profit growth rates. Figure 4.3 demonstrates how profits for these two product divisions have been attuned to cyclical variations in market demand (*The Economist*, 1981a) and overproduction of basic chemical feedstocks by the chemical and petrochemical industries. As an illustration of this fickleness, ICI mothballed 25 per cent of its capacity in certain plastics in 1979 (*Chemical Age*, 1979). Fortunes of these two divisions are, in fact, closely tied in production terms, changes in one balancing out changes in the other. Consequently, despite their important contribution to ICI's total sales (in 1979 these figures were 12 per cent and 17 per cent for plastics and petrochemicals respectively), they have experienced only a low rate of growth in trading profit earnings.

In contrast to product divisions in the first two segments, the fibres and organic chemicals divisions have been allocated to Segment C, which is characterised by products which have only low sales volumes, low profits and a neutral or negative growth rate in profits. As Tables 4.1 and 4.2 show, sales for the fibres division have declined consistently, from 12 per cent of ICI's total in 1973 to 7 per cent in 1979 and, more recently, the division has been returning loss after loss. Similarly, the organic chemicals division, which is essential to the production of intermediate chemicals for manufacturing dyestuffs, pigments and basic chemicals, followed a 'cash neutral' policy in the 1970s (*Chemical Age*, 1980b), with the aim of waiting for an upturn in trading conditions. The result has been a maintenance of a steady 8-9 per cent return of the total sales. Indeed, the flagging market for both fibres and organic chemicals has had a gross effect on ICI, which has been forced over the decade to reorganise these two product divisions more than any of the others. As Figure 4.3 illustrates, profits for the two divisions fell in 1973-4 and again in 1976-7, and in both cases an upswing in profits was concomitant with substantial restructuring of the divisions which included redundancies. After two rounds of such job cutbacks in 1979 and 1980, therefore, the two divisions again began to return profits.

The remaining product divisions of ICI — industrial explosives, metals and engineering products, paints and decorative products and pharmaceuticals (Figure 4.3) — have all displayed comparatively low sales volumes, low profits and low rates of growth in profits, the characteristics of Segment D. Proportionately, however, these divisions returned fairly constant sales and profits over the decade. The only exception was the pharmaceuticals division, the profit rates of which rose steadily. Within this segment, one of the major changes which

Figure 4.3: Divisional Trading Profits by Product Segments, 1970-80

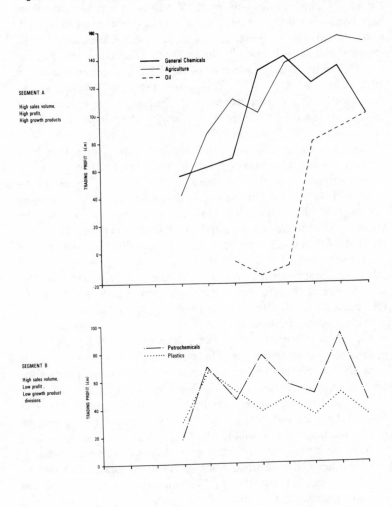

took place was in 1977 when ICI sold its interests in metals and engineering products, admitting that this area was at odds with the company's future (ICI, 1977).

New Emphases. To summarise this overview of the changes in the performance and product structure of ICI between 1970 and 1980, it is

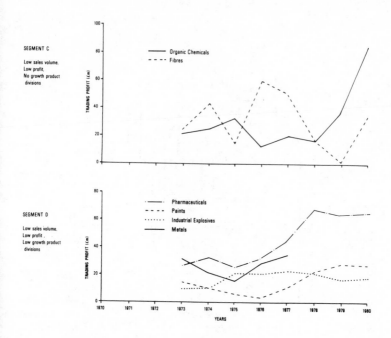

Source: Compiled from various ICI annual reports.

possible to identify three main emphases which are implicit within ICI policy:

1. During the period there has been an increasing pressure on the more dynamic product divisions, especially those in Segment A. These highly profitable and growth business areas have become, according to the relative proportions of sales and profits for which they account, the source for ICI's growth (see, for example, Figure 4.4).
2. A second emphasis which is discernible is the restructuring of certain product divisions to reduce the financial burden they impose. This is particularly so for the product divisions in Segment C, and it has had a twofold effect: increasing the viability of each division; and maintaining the profitability of ICI overall.
3. A final emphasis inherent in ICI's policy is the maintenance of established and stable product divisions as a collective mainstay of corporate profitability and a springboard for growth based on

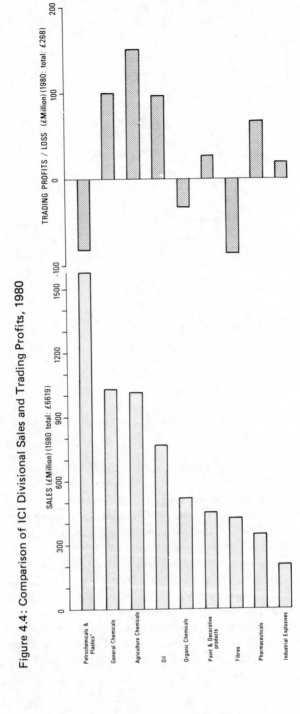

Figure 4.4: Comparison of ICI Divisional Sales and Trading Profits, 1980

Amalgamated. 1980

Source: Compiled from ICI (1980).

other product divisions. Thus, product divisions included in this category are those such as in Segment D, and it can be surmised that these divisions are either technically up to date, or they have been successful in forming their own market niche.

The Financing of Restructuring

To explain the dynamics of ICI's restructuring between 1970 and 1980 it is useful to explore the way in which these changes were financed. Finance capital is derived from three principal sources: retained earnings, share capital and loan capital. *Retained earnings* are the proportion of profits generated by trading which have been held back for future need as reserves of capital, or as capitalisation issues.

The second main capital source is *share capital*, which is derived from the selling of new shares issued on the stock market. Together, these retained earnings and share capital are the main internal sources of finance open to the organisation, but capital can also be raised by selling off of interests, companies and assets, and generated by deferring liabilities. The third source of finance is *loan capital* and this is essentially external to the organisation. Funds can be procured by issuing equity or through debt, with the second source being made over short- or long-term periods of repayment. A record of past performance and a potential for future earnings are the criteria required for funds raised through debt, whereas equity loans are capital raised through share issues based solely on the earnings potential of the organisation. The balance of capital inflows and outflows determines the cash-flow of the business organisation over time, and changes in cash-flow can act to temporarily restrict or enable corporate manoeuvreability, at least in the short term.

Financial changes which took place in ICI over the decade serve to demonstrate the effects on ICI's manoeuverability. ICI's profits reached a peak in 1973-4 and then again in 1976 and the changing structure of finance within ICI is made quite clear by Table 4.4 and Figure 4.5. Loan capital, in particular, gained in importance, rising from £2.7m (10 per cent of the total) in 1970 to £66m (29 per cent) in 1980. Retained earnings and share capital both displayed a downward trend despite their absolute significance. Several other trends are also evident from Figure 4.5. Expenditure peaked dramatically in 1974-5 and again in 1977-8, following growths in profits but coinciding with periods in which profits were depressed. Planning for this expenditure began at

Figure 4.5: Capital Expenditure and Finance in ICI, 1970-80

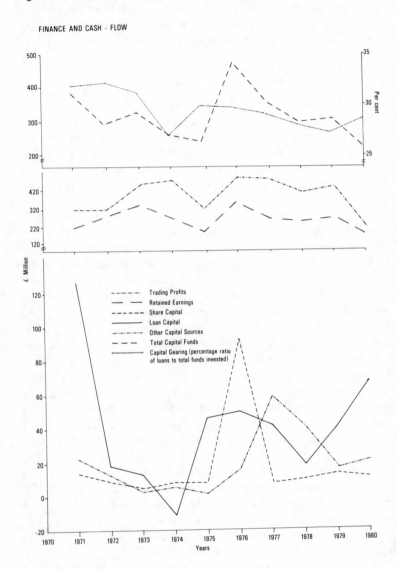

Source: ICI (1981).

Figure 4.5 (continued)

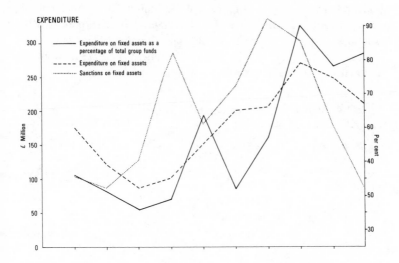

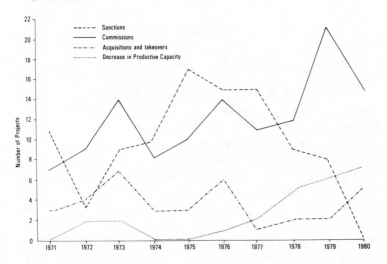

least one year before these dates, emphasising the time lag which is evident between the sanctioning and expenditure of capital; but the perception of the need for expenditure must have also pre-dated the sanctioning. The significance of the oil shock in 1973-4 and severe overcapacity in parts of the chemicals industry in 1977-8, were undoubtedly influential in providing a trigger to these changes.

Table 4.4: Sources of Finance Capital in ICI, 1970-80

SOURCES OF CAPITAL	1970 £ million	1970 Per cent	1975 £ million	1975 Per cent	1980 £ million	1980 Per cent
Retained earnings	197	71	188	77	132	57
Share capital	51	18	7	3	11	5
Loan capital	27	10	46	19	66	29
Other	1	1	1	1	20	9
Total	276	100	242	100	229	100

Figures are deflated to 1970 base level for comparison.
Source: Various annual reports.

By far the largest potential source of capital available to ICI was retained earnings. As Thomas (1978) points out, retained earnings are essentially 'liquid', and thus represent a source of finance which is comparatively readily accessible. ICI's use of retained earnings rose markedly in 1973 and 1976 and cash-flow was subsequently evened out by a gearing up of capital by increasing loans. Though the gearing ratio shown in Figure 4.5 actually varied very little from the 30 per cent mark, it must be stressed that even a small variation in this ratio can have a significant impact on corporate liquidity. In most cases, a rise in the gearing ratio for ICI foreshadowed an increase in the use of capital from other sources.

An additional feature of changes in the financing of ICI between 1970 and 1980 is the spreading effect which is created by complementary use of capital from different sources. Loan capital was at its lowest level in 1974 and 1978 when capital was being spent, and retained earnings and 'other' sources of capital remained high to balance out corporate finances. Bottoming out of retained earnings in 1975 led to an increase in loan capital to cover the interim period, 1974 to 1976.

Three characteristics emerge from the brief description of the pattern of financing in ICI:

1. *Capital availability* — sources of capital internal and external to ICI are characterised in terms of their quantities and the time over which they may be available.
2. *Cash-flow sequencing* — the cash-flow in ICI is occasionally maintained at a high level for a prolonged period of time by arranging capital from different sources sequential to one another.
3. *Leads and lags* — overall cash-flow governs the length of time between the perception, sanctioning and expenditure phases of development.

One way of conceptualing the interplay of these components of corporate finance is set out in Figure 4.6. This descriptive model shows that organisational cash-flow is comprised of capital from a number of sources, some of which (like loans) range over longer periods, and others (like retained earnings) which become available relatively quickly, only for shorter periods. Expenditure can be sanctioned only when capital resources as a whole are sufficient and, as a short-term contingency, expenditure can be deferred should conditions change. What is important to recognise is the relationship between capital drawn from different sources, and the effect environmental contingencies may have on the type of reaction an organisation might adopt at a particular point in time. As Thomas (1978, p. 16) has summarised in this respect:

> Where firms increased their assets slowly or at moderate rates then internal funds would generally be sufficient to cover capital expenditure. If firms expanded rapidly, then although profits would also be higher, the rise in savings would be insufficient to meet increased capital expenditure, thus leading to a demand for external finance.

From this viewpoint, it is possible to highlight the relationships between cash-flow and expenditure in ICI over the last decade, in order to explain the timing of capital projects. Thus, the pattern of expenditure tallies closely with the sanctioning and commissioning of individual capital projects (Figure 4.5).

A number of examples can be used to illustrate this point. The 1973-4 oil crisis brought a crash in the profits of several of ICI's product divisions, especially those which have close functional connections with the oil industry such as plastics and petrochemicals. In this case, the repercussion was an immediate sanctioning of expenditure in these product areas in ICI in 1974, followed closely by an increase in expen-

Figure 4.6: Corporate Finance, Cash-flow and Capital Expenditure

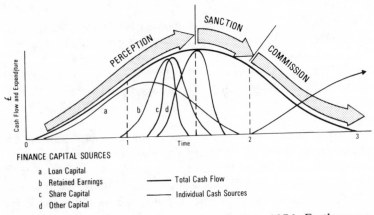

FINANCE CAPITAL SOURCES

a Loan Capital
b Retained Earnings
c Share Capital
d Other Capital

——— Total Cash Flow
——— Individual Cash Sources

diture in 1975 and a rush of capital projects in 1976. Furthermore, ICI's move into the oil industry in 1976-7, with the formation of a separate oil division, was enabled by a combination of increases made in loans, share issues, retained earnings consumption and from other capital investments which had been sold off.

In respect of these sources of capital, ICI was able to raise, for instance: £124m in international loans, including $50m (Canadian) of public debentures issued by CIL, the Canadian subsidiary of ICI; private issues of $15m (Australian) made by ICI Australia; and other sources which raised £75m in Swiss, Dutch and German currencies. In May of the same year, new stock issues were also made and this raised an additional £196m (ICI, 1976). Another source of capital used was raised in November 1977 by ICI selling its 63 per cent holding in Imperial Metal Industries Ltd, for £64m, which became available in two instalments, one in 1977 and another in 1978 (ICI, 1977). Many of these capital projects were, however, acquisitions and takeovers, especially those in 1973 and 1976. Part of the reason for this approach might be that these types of projects require less forward planning by ICI, compared to new green field projects.

The above discussion has broadly outlined the structure of ICI and the restructuring which took place between 1970 and 1980. It has aimed to provide a simplified view by emphasising, in particular, the growth business areas and contrasting these with business areas which are declining in importance. Product segmentation was introduced as a conceptual aid in this respect. The patterns and financing of re-structuring were also described and evaluated. The second section of this chapter uses this overview to address the geographical implications of restructuring within ICI in greater detail.

The Geography of Corporate Restructuring

This section describes the geographical dimension of restructuring in ICI by considering three related issues. First, ICI's spatial distribution is briefly assessed relative to world markets and growth regions in the chemicals industry. Second, the various processes or modes of restructuring used by ICI over the decade are described and their geographical importance is evaluated. Third, the geographical ramifications of the restructuring of ICI are described in the final section by reference to the effects on labour, and the creation of a changing spatial division of labour within the corporation.

Growth Regions

As Tables 4.5 and 4.6 illustrate, in 1970 53 per cent of ICI's sales were made outside the United Kingdom, which, as the headquarters of ICI, contributed 31 per cent of the group's £159m in trading profits. By 1975, the proportion of overseas sales had risen to 58 per cent while the contribution to profits made by overseas operations amounted to only 26 per cent. After 1975, the emphasis ICI placed on its overseas operations grew at an unprecedented rate. Although ICI's total sales increased to £5,715m in 1980, a growth of £2,616m on the 1975 figure, the proportion derived from overseas activities remained at a steady 58 per cent. In contrast, profits gained from overseas sales increased by a massive 25 per cent over the second five-year period from 1975 to 1980, despite ICI's total profits having fallen by £26m.

Table 4.5: Contribution of Sales outside the United Kingdom to Total ICI Group Sales, Selected Years

	1970	1975	1980
Group sales (£ million)	1462	3099	5715
Sales Outside United Kingdom (per cent)	53	58	58

Source: Various annual reports.

Table 4.6: Contribution of Profits outside the United Kingdom to
Total ICI Group Profits, Selected Years

	1970	1975	1980
Group profits (£million)	159	305	279
Profits Outside United Kingdom (per cent)	31	26	51

Source: Various annual reports.

This trend towards diversification outside the United Kingdom by
ICI emphasises not only the increases in the contribution of overseas
interests to the organisation's economic welfare, but also the increase
in overseas *production* which it represented. The reasons for the geographical shift of emphasis by ICI are to be found, in part, in the
significance of overseas markets (Table 4.7). Certain markets, especially
the United States, with 23 per cent of world chemical sales, and Western
Europe, representing 34 per cent of world chemical sales, offered the
greatest potential for expansion. Progressive overseas investment by
ICI during the 1970s mirrored the growth of sales overseas (see Table
4.8 and Figure 4.7), with expenditure in Continental Western Europe
and the Americas increasing by 4 per cent and 9 per cent respectively.

The results of the geographical shift in the centre of gravity of ICI
can be described at regional and local levels. At the regional scale,
ICI's overseas expansion has been extremely uneven since 1970. The
Americas, Australasia and the Far East and Continental Western Europe
divisions of ICI were the regions in which the greatest expansion was
concentrated. Ironically, this growth pattern has decreased the importance of the United Kingdom to the group's operations. At a local level,
it is possible to discern unequal spatial development by ICI within
regions. In Continental Western Europe, for example, development has
focused on the West German, French and British chemical markets,
which represented 9 per cent, 5 per cent and 6 per cent of the total
world market respectively in 1980 (Figure 4.7). In the Americas division, ICI has concentrated its growth in the United States, Brazil and
Argentina. ICI was one of the first European chemical organisations
to realise the significance of the United States as the largest single
chemical market in the world by opening operations there, and in the
1970s ICI invested more in that country than most of its American

Table 4.7: The Geographical Distribution of World Sales of Chemicals, 1980 (total = $US691 billion)

REGION	PER CENT OF TOTAL
United States	23
Total Western Europe	34
West Germany	(9)
United Kingdom	(6)
France	(5)
Other	(14)
Japan	11
Eastern Europe	19
Rest of World	13
Total	100

Source: *The Economist* (1981a, p. 57).

counterparts (*Chemical Business*, 1981). The Australasia and Far Eastern division also grew in importance, the proportion of total sales increasing by 4 per cent between 1970 and 1980. Developments here concentrated primarily on countries with assured supplies of materials and feedstocks such as Australia (*Chemical Age*, 1981a), and Indonesia, Singapore and Thailand (*Chemical Week*, 1980a), although the market potential each country offered was also a significant factor.

Modes of Restructuring

In a bid to focus upon the major processes of corporate restructuring used by ICI, and their geographical component, an attempt has been made to classify the frequency with which various modes of restructuring have been used between 1970 and 1980. The classification was made by a thorough detailing of the events listed in the annual reports issued by ICI. The spatial consequences of each mode can be gauged by their importance inside and outside the United Kingdom. Results of the survey are listed in Table 4.9.

Table 4.8: Geographical Analysis of Group Capital Expenditure, 1970-1 to 1979-80 (percentages)

DIVISION	1970-71	1971-72	1972-73	1973-74	1974-75	1975-76	1976-77	1977-78	1978-79	1979-80
United Kingdom	64	62	67	65	72	61	67	61	57	54
Continental Western Europe	14	18	7	7	8	9	9	13	16	20
The Americas	12	10	14	18	14	23	17	15	16	16
Other Countries	10	10	12	10	6	7	7	11	11	10
Total	100	100	100	100	100	100	100	100	100	100

Source: Adapted from ICI (1980, p. 11).

Figure 4.7: Divisional Breakdown of Sales and Investment Expenditure by ICI, 1970-80

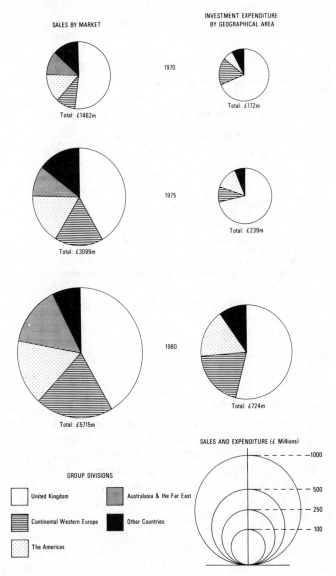

Source: Compiled from various ICI annual reports.

Table 4.9: Modes of Restructuring of Manufacturing Operations in ICI, 1970-80

MODE		NUMBER	PER CENT OUTSIDE UNITED KINGDOM
Subsidiaries sold or closed[1][2]		20	35
Subsidiaries:[1][3]	Sanctioned	97	46
	Commissioned	121	37
	Acquired	38	58
Companies formed		20	65
Joint ventures		25	76
Licensed production[4]		6	83
Transfers of production		6	50

Notes: 1. Plants, R & D facilities, oil platforms, companies.
2. Temporary shutdown, partial capacity cutback, closure and plants sold.
3. New plants.
4. Other companies licensed to produce or market ICI products or use ICI processes.
Source: Various annual reports.

The results indicate that the preferred modes of corporate growth are by the establishment and acquisition of companies and plants rather than on-site expansion. During the period under observation, ICI commissioned 121 new plant extensions. (The term 'plant' is used widely to include totally new sites and the extension of existing sites by significant expansion of capacity or the opening of a new 'unit'. This broad definition is required because the traditional definition of a single-plant manufacturing site does not apply to the chemicals industry, in which many locations are large multi-functional complexes.) Other preferred modes of expansion were by the formation of companies (20 cases) and joint ventures with other companies (25 cases). Some cases were classified to more than one category so as to gauge the significance of each mode. Thus, ICI's joint venture with Teijin of Japan, which resulted in the formation of a new company (Teijin Agrochemicals Ltd), was classified under 'companies formed' and 'joint ventures'. Another subsidiary, Fibremakers New Zealand Ltd, which closed two sites in 1980 and transferred capacity to an existing site, was similarly categorised under 'subsidiaries sold or closed' and 'transfers of production'.

The remaining modes of restructuring proved less important. Least popular was licensing of production to other companies (six cases) and production transfers (six cases). The major means of corporate rational-isation was by the selling off of subsidiaries and companies, of which 20 cases were reported over the decade.

The real significance of the various modes of restructuring lies in their geographical distribution within ICI. Table 4.9 lists the proportion of each mode accounted for by overseas operations. Quite clearly, certain modes are more commonly used than others. Though a large number of new subsidiaries were set up overseas as well as in the United Kingdom, other processes had added importance. In particular, whereas 35 per cent of subsidiaries closed or sold were outside Britain, 54 per cent of sanctions and 63 per cent of commissions for new plants were located in the United Kingdom. Of the subsidiaries which were acquired, 58 per cent were located outside Britain. In addition, 65 per cent of companies formed, 76 per cent of joint ven-tures and 83 per cent of licensed projects took place overseas. This pattern suggests that these modes of expansion either involve less risk than the establishment of subsidiaries on green field sites, or they may simply reflect the age of existing capital stocks in each region.

Various modes of restructuring, according to the evidence described here, are used selectively by ICI in different geographic areas, that is, inside and outside the United Kingdom. According to the number of subsidiaries sold or closed, disinvestment is taking place more rapidly inside than outside Britain by ICI, and capital investment overseas is quickly gaining importance and may roughly equal or exceed domes-tic investment. Overall, the restructuring initiatives used broadly mirror the apparent emphasis on new regions by ICI. On the surface at least, the combination of processes used overseas differs from those used in Britain, with special emphasis on acquisition, and the formation of companies, often in the form of joint ventures and licensed production. While these patterns may reflect differences in legal environments, they also indicate a structural basis for geographic expansion overseas which contrasts with domestic patterns, caused perhaps by environ-mental uncertainty inherent in spatial diversification.

The Changing International Division of Labour within ICI

The effects of restructuring within ICI and especially the emphasis on new regions between 1970 and 1980 had profound spatial effects. This section of the discussion aims to describe the implications of corporate restructuring by focusing on the changing spatial division of labour within ICI. As Table 4.10 demonstrates, the spatial division of labour within ICI was in a state of flux during the period under examination. In 1970, only 28 per cent of ICI's 190,000 workers were located outside Britain; in 1975 this figure was 31 per cent; and by 1980, 41 per cent of the much reduced labour force of 143,200 worked outside the United Kingdom.

Table 4.10: Contribution of Employment outside the United Kingdom to ICI Group Employment, Selected Years

	1970	1975	1980
Employment ('000)	190,000	192,000	143,200
Employment Outside United Kingdom (per cent)	28	31	41

Source: Various annual reports.

A detailed breakdown of employment by regional divisions within ICI between 1970 and 1980 is given in Table 4.11 and is graphically illustrated in Figure 4.8. The most apparent feature is the substantial decrease in the size of the total workforce. Employment in ICI rose from 190,000 in 1970-1 to 201,000 in 1973-4, and then fell off gradually to 192,000 in 1975-6. Only after this watershed year did employment begin to decrease rapidly to a level of 143,200 in 1979-80. Over the ten-year period, therefore, ICI shed 29 per cent of its 1970 workforce. This is the most profound feature of ICI's newly emerging international division of labour, a declining worldwide labour force.

The second feature is the dramatic drop in employment in the United Kingdom. This trend is accentuated after 1975-6 when, in the space of approximately one year, the labour force was cut by 37,000. Over the decade as a whole, ICI's employment in Britain fell by as much as 38.5 per cent and it is important to note that of the 52,700 jobs lost from ICI in the United Kingdom, only 5,900 were effectively 'transferred' to other ICI regional divisions. Clearly then, by far the greatest number of jobs (46,800) have been rationalised and lost altogether.

Examining employment by regional divisions reveals a third important trend. Although employment increased within the divisions taken together (excluding the United Kingdom) from 53,000 in 1970-1 to

Table 4.11: Employment in ICI Divisions Worldwide, 1970-1 to 1979-80 (thousands of employees)

DIVISION	1970-1	1971-2	1972-3	1973-4	1974-5	1975-6	1976-7	1977-8	1978-9	1979-80
United Kingdom	137,000	132,000	130,000	132,000	129,000	132,000	95,u00	92,500	89,400	84,300
Continental Western Europe					16,000	11,800	11,000	10,700	10,700	10,800
The Americas					23,000	19,700	19,900	19,500	20,200	19,900
Australia & the Far East	53,000	67,000	69,000	69,000	13,000	12,900	12,400	15,700	15,500	15,700
Indian Sub-continent					10,000	10,800	10,800	11,000	10,500	10,600
Other Countries					5,000	4,800	4,900	1,800	1,900	1,900
Total	190,000	199,000	199,000	201,000	196,000	192,000	154,000	151,200	148,200	143,200

Source: Clarke (1982, p. 99).

Figure 4.8: Divisional Breakdown of Employment in ICI, 1970-80

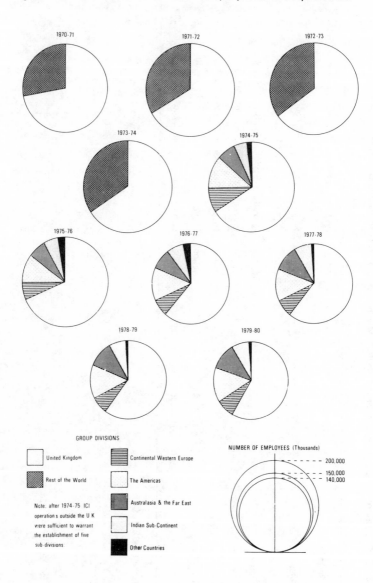

Source: Clarke (1982, p. 100).

69,000 in 1973-4, and then fell to 58,000 in 1979-80, all except two regional divisions recorded an absolute loss in employment. Only the Indian Sub-continent has retained an even balance, and Australasia and the Far East, actually experienced a growth in employment. Consequently, it is possible to establish that the trend towards decentralisation of employment from the United Kingdom within ICI, has been spatially selective and uneven.

Geographical diversification of production within ICI deserves more detailed attention, and has been illustrated graphically in Figure 4.9. The expansion of 3,700 jobs experienced in Australasia and the Far East between 1974 and 1980 demonstrates, to some degree, the 'centre-periphery' movement of production which has been described by a number of authors, with Australia itself acting as a linchpin (see Utrecht, 1978; Alford, 1979; Taylor and Thrift, 1981b). But the exact extent to which growth has concentrated either on Australasia or on the Far East is hard to ascertain because of their amalgamation into one operational division by ICI. By simultaneous use of employment figures from various sources, however, it is possible to compile a disaggregated view of these employment trends. Figure 4.10 makes a comparison of Australasia and the Far East with ICI worldwide, but also breaks down the first component into its two constituent elements, Australia and South East Asia. The importance of this illustration is that it demonstrates how, in terms of employment, ICI's growth has concentrated within the regional division on the South East Asian element and not on Australia, which exhibits employment trends similar to those for ICI as a whole. It is also important to recognise that regional growth need not necessarily lead to a growth in regional employment, as the cases for Continental Western Europe, the Americas and parts of Australasia and the Far East demonstrate.

What this description of changes in the international division of labour within ICI emphasises is that employment figures alone do not explain how production is still expanding in some regions. Evidently, there is some connection with the changing form of manufacturing production. So far, however, changes in the magnitude, form and geographical spread of production within ICI have been considered separately, and it is difficult to evaluate changes in the corporation's spatial division of labour without referring to how these factors interrelate. How, for example, can the decrease in employment in the petrochemicals division in the United Kingdom and its growth on the Continent be explained? A full explanation requires the consideration of individual acts of restructuring of production, such

Figure 4.9: The Geographical Diversification of Production within ICI

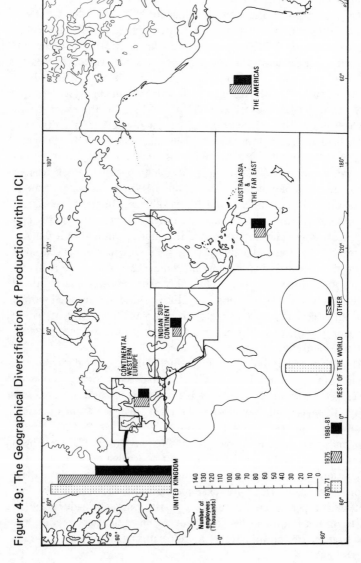

Source: Clarke (1982, p. 102).

Figure 4.10: Comparison of Employment Trends in ICI Australia and
the ICI Group, 1970-1 to 1980-1

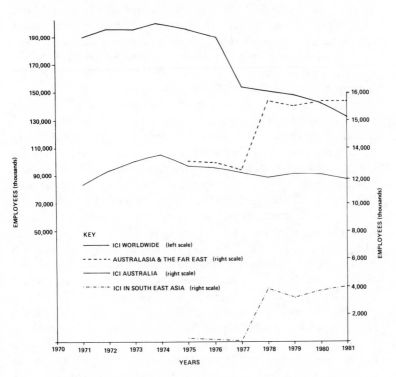

Source: Clarke (1984, p. 147).

as closures, redundancies and openings over a shorter period of time.
It is also necessary to relate these individual activities to the strategic
continuity of ICI's policy over the decade. This is now done for a
single year, 1980.

Structural Change and Strategic Continuity: A Year in the Life of ICI

The trend towards decentralisation of production within ICI away from
the United Kingdom — so evident within the decade under discussion —
was reinforced by each annual initiative. The development of ICI in

1980 illustrates this point well. In this year, a deepening of world recession made trading conditions difficult for a company whose product divisions sell as much as three-quarters of their output abroad (*Sunday Times*, 1980a). Profits fell dramatically during the year, especially from the United Kingdom, Continental Western Europe and American divisions (*Daily Telegraph*, 1980). In tandem with earlier trends, the company forecast a similar annual round of job losses comparable to 1979 (*The Times*, 1981a). The forecast was not wrong. ICI shed some 6,000 workers worldwide in 1980.

Product divisions that were hardest hit were those which formed over half of ICI's total business, especially those in product Segments B and C described earlier. These included dyestuffs, petrochemicals, plastics and fibres (*The Economist*, 1980c), so there was a continuing need to move towards more profitable commodities (*The Economist*, 1981b) and also to rationalise operations in the ailing product divisions (ICI, 1980). ICI's emphasis on these forms of restructuring during the decade had a direct bearing on it becoming the world's fifth most successful chemical company according to *The Economist* (1981c). The global spread of ICI's factories and a diverse product range allowed ICI to weather 1980 by taking a number of initiatives. The primary objective was to cut back on surplus capacity, a situation common to all Europe's nine largest man-made fibres producers (*The Economist*, 1981d). Ironically, it was Britain, as a 'geriatric home' of industry (*The Economist*, 1981e) within ICI, which came off worst in the 'chess game' of 1980. There, at least 6 per cent of the manufacturing labour force are employed in chemicals of one form or another, so that trouble for a large chemical corporation such as ICI meant trouble for British workers.

Geographical Rationalisation

In 1980, fibres, petrochemicals, plastics and the organic chemicals divisions were the hardest hit by ICI's rationalisation, in part because their production was closely interrelated. In each case the United Kingdom operations bore the brunt. The fibres industry continued to come off worst of all and a number of factors combined to worsen the situation for the division, the worst of which was a massive 30 per cent fall in consumption (*Financial Times*, 1980a). Continual losses by the division for six years led to ICI management adopting an aggressive attitude towards fibres in 1980, asserting that such losses 'could not be allowed to continue' (*Chemical Week*, 1980b). ICI's fibres rationalisation policy was spurred on by the fact that by October

1980, 60,000 jobs had been lost by closures and streamlining in the fibres, textiles and clothing industries in Britain in only ten months, with over 100 textile mills having closed alone (*Chemical Week*, 1980b). In 1979, for example, ICI had employed over 25,000 people in the fibres industry but, by the end of 1980, the division's workforce in Britain had been cut back to 7,500 but with an output equivalent to 1971 (*The Times*, 1980).

Geographically, fibres rationalisation by ICI was disparate. In 1980 two more fibre plants were closed, one at Kilroot in Northern Ireland where 1,100 jobs were lost, and another at Ardeer in Scotland where there were 700 redundancies. It is perhaps ironic that many of the plants closed, especially those in Northern Ireland, were at the forefront of the industry's technology. Companies such as ICI, Court-aulds, Hoechst, Du Pont, Monsanto and British Enkalon had invested over £17m on improvements to their Irish plants in the decade up to 1980, but many of them had been forced to shut or operate on short time because of overcapacities in synthetic fibres production (*The Economist*, 1981f). Carrington Viyella, in which ICI was a 49 per cent shareholder, also closed four plants and made 2,000 redundancies (*The Economist*, 1980d). Similarly, some of ICI's major textile com-petitors made cutbacks: Coats Patons having axed 4,000 since 1979, Tootals closing six plants and making 3,000 workers redundant in 1979 and Courtaulds cutting its labour force by 7,000 in the 18 months from June 1979 to December 1980.

Further job losses were spread across the synthetic fibres plants and the petrochemical plants which supplied them. At Pontypool (Wales), Doncaster (Yorkshire), Radcliffe (Lancashire), Wilton (Tee-side) and the divisional headquarters at Harrogate in Yorkshire, 20 per cent redundancies were felt. The major plant at Wilton on Teeside became fully loaded only because of these cutbacks and the parallel closure of the Ardeer unit in Scotland (*The Economist*, 1980a). But the cutbacks were not confined entirely to ICI's British plants. Even in the company's rapidly expanding West European market, jobs were lost at the Oestringen plant in West Germany. The ultimate effect was to reduce manpower in the company's West German facilities to 8,500, as against 25,000 in 1975 (*Financial Times*, 1980b), so that in total, 4,000 jobs were axed in the fibres division, representing a significant proportion of the 6,000 jobs lost within all product divisions of ICI worldwide. The majority of these were lost in Britain.

What is evident, therefore, is that rationalisation trends in the fibres industry were not uniform. Polyester and acrylic fibres felt the full effects and, by halving its capacity in the United Kingdom, ICI's policy followed the 'selective elimination of underutilised plants and unprofitable commodity products' (*Chemical Week*, 1980b, p. 19). ICI was not alone in this policy. Rhône-Poulenc of France similarly withdrew into speciality polyester products, leaving Hoechst of West Germany to dominate the market, Akzo of the Netherlands concentrated its polyester production onto two integrated sites in West Germany and Holland; and Hoechst of West Germany and Du Pont of the United States both pulled out of acrylic fibres altogether, leaving the field to Bayer, Courtaulds and Monsanto (*The Economist*, 1981d).

A decision was also made by ICI in 1980 to merge the plastics and petrochemicals divisions in order to cut overheads, and to scale down heavy chemical research (*The Economist*, 1981g). In the United Kingdom, 500 workers were, therefore, made redundant at the Hillhouse plant in Lancashire and 600 more at the soda-ash plant at Northwich in Cheshire (*Daily Telegraph*, 1980). In addition, one-quarter of the Mond plastics division's workforce, based on Merseyside, Cheshire, Teeside and Derbyshire, faced redundancy over the three years beginning in 1980, with an expected loss of 3,000 jobs. The polythene plant at Stevenage, Hertfordshire, was also ordered closed in 1980, with 840 redundancies (*The Times*, 1981b).

The closure of outdated British plants by ICI was frequently accompanied by a change in the method of production in those remaining plants. Several such cases were reported in 1980. Recession in the textiles industry had a profound impact on the organic chemicals division of ICI because of the reduction in the demand for dyes as a number of customers ceased production. Highly automated plants were opened at Huddersfield (Yorkshire) and Stevenston (Scotland), both of which were to produce industrial biocides (*The Economist*, 1980e). These moves can be explained in part as an attempt by ICI to remove competition in the industry, as the Stevenston hydrochloric acid plant was only owned partly by ICI — in 1980 it purchased the remaining 50 per cent by taking over Acna UK, the company which had previously been run jointly with Montedison of the United States (*Chemical Age*, 1980c). The purchase took place even though ICI had committed itself to reduced spending in the organics division which bought the company.

Further modernisation took place in other divisions, including the paints division plant at Stowmarket and agricultural division's Billingham plant, designed to produce high-protein animal feed from natural gas using highly developed biotechnology, representing the most advanced plant of its kind in Europe (*Financial Times*, 1980c). One important case which illustrates ICI's strategy of concentrating on areas in which it has a strong technological and manufacturing ability has been the move upmarket in the fibres division. The most obvious case in point is the production of the polyester fibre, Mitrelle, to imitate silk, at Pontypool (*The Economist*, 1981b; *Daily Telegraph*, 1981).

The Geographical Extension of Production

Plant modernisation and closures were, however, an essential precondition of geographical extension of production globally by ICI. Thus, the plastics division's strategy was primarily one of extending activities abroad. The goal was local, market-oriented production and is typified by a series of projects in Europe and North America (*The Economist*, 1980e). The emphasis on local production in these two markets represents an example of ICI's general policy in the 1970s which, as stated by Sir Maurice Hodgson, the ICI Chairman, noted that 'if we can supply markets. . .by exporting from the UK we will. . . but this is not always a feasible operation' (*Chemical Age*, 1980d).

In Europe, geographical diversification by ICI was centred on the construction of a plant at Wilhelmshaven in West Germany, commissioned in 1980. This complex parallels the Teeside plant in Britain, and it gave ICI manufacturing bases for polymers in both the United Kingdom and the Continent. Construction of the plant has enabled ICI to accelerate the closure of older, less economic units — those in the United Kingdom — as part of a programme to reduce operating costs. For instance, the modernisation of the Hillhouse plant mentioned above involved closing two old plants and opening two new ones, keeping in line with the company's aim to replace older units with modern plants (*Chemical Age*, 1980e). A similar case is described in the United States, where in 1980 a new plant in Hopewell in Virginia took over production of polyester film previously supplied from older ICI plants in the Netherlands and Scotland (*Chemical Week*, 1981). However, operating costs are not merely a function of labour. In the chemicals industry, energy considerations also form a significant cost factor.

A major force behind ICI's move into Western Europe was the pressure provided indirectly by the British government, which affects many of its costs, making them generally higher than on the Continent (*Chemical Week*, 1980b). For example, ICI had been worried about increasing energy costs in Britain for a number of years, and as the company itself noted:

because of the UK Government's high-cost energy policy, as applied through the tariff adopted by the electricity supply industry, UK consumers with a steady high-load electricity usage (including ICI as chlorine manufacturers) currently pay twice as much per unit as their Continental European competitors pay for a similar supply (ICI, 1980, p. 11).

Electricity amounted to 80 per cent of costs of chlorine production in ICI's Mond plastics division (northern England). Electricity costs, which are 50 per cent cheaper in West Germany, therefore, had a strong bearing on the opening of the plant in Wilhemshaven to produce chlorine (*The Economist*, 1981h). In this highly modernised plant, ICI employed no more than 40 process workers on any single shift (Richardson, 1981). In the same chlorine and derivatives business in Cheshire and on Teeside, ICI employed 11,500 workers. It takes little to imagine what might happen, should production in Britain become too costly.

One final point needs to be mentioned about the construction of the Wilhemshaven plant. That is, the plant was aimed at local production for the European market. The dying British car market, for instance, each car of which had traditionally contained around £54 worth of ICI products (including such things as fibres for seat covers, paint for the body, plastics for hoses and soda-ash for glass) (*Sunday Times*, 1980b), forced ICI to look to Europe for alternatives. The Wilhelmshaven plant, therefore, acted as a 'doorstep' producer to the West German motor company, Volkswagen.

This process of geographical extension of production in Western Europe typifies ICI's policy for expansion. Since 1960, ICI's sales in Continental Europe have increased by 300 per cent, its market share has trebled, and Europe now contributes 20 per cent towards the group's sales. In addition, plenty of potential still remains.

ICI's European expansion has been described in detail by Allan (1981). Market growth for Continental Western Europe has been forecast at a far higher rate than in the United Kingdom, and it has formed a strong basis for British exports as well as being a large producer of goods in its own right. Nevertheless, ICI's manufacturing base on the Continent has increased markedly for some of the reasons described above. In 1960 ICI had no factories in Europe; by 1980 it had 18. The result of this expansion has been a rapid increase in ICI's employees in Europe, which rose from 762 in 1960 to 10,889 in 1980. Indeed, the close relationship between sales and investment expansion has continued, as Figure 4.11 demonstrates. It is also important to point out that ICI's expansion in Europe was particularly marked after 1973-4 and it is likely that Britain's joining of the European Economic Community in 1973 had a profound impact on ICI's investment strategy: in terms of removing barriers to the expansion of production facilities on the Continent, but especially in promoting the EEC as a 'single' large market to approach the significance of that of the United States market.

Figure 4.11: Sales and Investment by ICI in Continental Western Europe, 1960-80

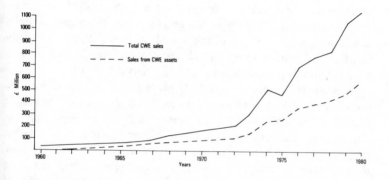

Source: Allan (1981, p. 78).

The close ties between the problem of geographical extension of production and energy, resource and sales considerations described above for Europe are given added weight by the fact that many European chemical companies are now building new capacity in North America and the Middle East. In these two regions, a plentiful supply of cheap natural gas provides an attractive alternative to naphtha-based chemicals produced in Europe. In fact, the output of these plants is replacing both products and employment that would otherwise have come to European plants (*The Economist*, 1981a). For example, in 1980, ICI's $US600m petrochemical plant came on stream at Corpus Christi in America. Owned jointly with Champion Petroleum and Solvay of Belgium through the Corpus Christi Petrochemical Company, the ethylene plant is designed to take ICI downstream to sources of ethylene feedstocks for fibres and plastics (*The Economist*, 1980b). In part, this plant again duplicates production of the Wilton plant in the United Kingdom, but it has the advantage of being able to use a wide variety of chemical feedstocks, so that it is extremely flexible (*European Chemical News*, 1980).

We have considered, on the one hand, the rationalisation taking place in the United Kingdom petrochemical industry and, on the other hand, the opening of new productive capacity in West Germany and North America. These initiatives taken in 1980 seem to suggest a continuity of ICI strategy in the 1970s and 1980s, a trend towards geographical diversification. Whether either of these two new plants will eventually replace productive capacity in Britain, especially in the north west and north east, is still a matter for conjecture. But what must be remembered is that large global corporations such as ICI, while they have a strategy, do not have a 'grand design'. The international structure of production must, by necessity, remain flexible. The importance of the Wilhelmshaven plant, for example, is not only to gain local market access and cheaper energy supplies, but also to integrate into the overall global production network of ICI.

In this sense, it matters very little whether a large, capital-intensive plant is opened in, for instance, Europe, North America or the Middle East. The internal flexibility of these multi-product sites and the elasticity of their external relations between plants makes global integration less of a problem today. Corporations, like ICI, are now able to take advantage of government incentives, cheap resources and various financial arrangements at both regional and international levels. For instance, various regional development policies operating in the United Kingdom have attracted major companies, but because infrastructural and financial incentives are usually offered, the tendency has been to attract capital-intensive industries. Labour-intensive industries have located in the south east (*The Economist*, 1980f).

Such incentives also apply on an international scale in competition between regions which might be far apart. For example, the United Kingdom development areas can compete with the emerging free production zones of the Asian countries. In this light, global companies have a strong hold over national governments. ICI Australia's plan to start a big $A500m petrochemical project at Point Wilson near Geelong in Victoria (*The Economist*, 1981i) is a good example of this. The plan has subsequently been shelved, with the blame being put squarely on the shoulders of the Australian Federal government's policies (*The Australian*, 1981). A similar plant has been commissioned in Canada, but its future remains in doubt.

To sum up, the particular initiatives taken in 1980 by ICI served

:o reinforce the overall corporate strategy in the period 1970 to 1980, and it is possible to distil five main features of ICI's policy from the discussion, all of which were aimed at responding to the recession which has hit ICI's main business areas:

1. rationalisation and closure of plants primarily in Britain;
2. opening of new, occasionally parallel plants in other divisions such as Continental Western Europe;
3. interaction between 1 and 2 to produce a shift in the geographical centre of gravity of ICI, and a change in the corporate division of labour;
4. changes in the products produced; and
5. changes in the process of production and, possibly, changes in the labour process, as geographical restructuring has taken place.

The individual initiatives taken in 1980, therefore, combined to reaffirm the continuity of ICI policy of the previous decade, which was a trend towards selective geographical rationalisation and diversification at a global scale. This trend continued in 1981. The British workforce was cut to 73,000 as a result of the fibres division being pruned to a few premium fibres, the plastics and petrochemicals divisions being merged to cut overheads, and investment being concentrated in a few key profit areas (*The Economist*, 1981j). The flexibility of ICI's network of plants is the key to the continued success of the company, especially in times of recession. The strategy retains profits for the company, but does little to increase the stability of jobs for individuals in the different countries in which ICI operates. Major job losses within individual national economies, such as the United Kingdom, must increasingly be explained at the international level. Redundancies within one part of the world and job creations within other regions are effectively two sides of the same coin. Within the new international division of labour of the corporation described here, individuals, in whatever part of the world they may work, must increasingly come to realise that, in the words of one ICI manager, 'they respond to the divisions, they work with me, but they work for ICI' (Richardson, 1981, p. 87).

Summary

This chapter has described some of the main components of change in organisational structure which accompany the internationalisation of production at an advanced stage of development within a so-called global corporation. The case study of a period of radical restructuring within ICI in the 1970s has also brought out the intimate relationship which exists between the changing spatial division of labour within large corporations and the changing structure of production. By drawing together information on particular plant openings, closures, expansions and contractions in the period from 1970 to 1980 it has been possible to suggest reasons for the changing location of employment which is taking place within ICI worldwide. However, it is to be expected that this pattern will go on changing through time, especially since large corporations can 'quickly abandon. . .locations. . .switching the destination of their next round of investment should the conditions for profitable production change' (Hudson, 1981, p. 26).

According to a recent survey of ICI's development, it is still regarded as employing too many people; operates too many unprofitable divisions; and has too many of its assets in Britain (*The Economist*, 1982d). In line with this belief, ICI has, since 1980, continued to cut its workforce especially in the United Kingdom, with 9,600 more jobs lost in 1981, 6,000 in 1982 and more in 1983. Most of these losses stem from unabated rationalisation in the fibres division and even in the United States, where ICI has been relatively successful, it has decided to pull out of fibres by selling its stake in Fiber Industries (*The Times*, 1983a). However, in the early 1980s, the plastics and petrochemicals division has replaced fibres as the biggest loss-maker, and rationalisation is now being extended to this division even in the traditionally safe area of research and technical services (*The Times*, 1982).

ICI has also extended its policy of moving out of bulk chemicals and commodities, except for top-of-the-range products, where it has no choice but to remain involved. Paralleling this policy has been a concentration on speciality products. These initiatives include, for example: the production of bacterial-based polymers through the formation of Marlborough Biopolymers Ltd (*The Economist*, 1983b); lacquers and coatings through the acquisition of the Midlands-based firm Arthur Holden (*The Times*, 1983b); and the development of 'heart drugs' by the pharmaceuticals division (*The Economist*, 1982e). Overall, ICI's pick-up in the first six months of 1983 owes much to the decision to switch to higher margin products, coupled with buoyant markets in North America, West Germany, Scandinavia and Holland (*The Times*, 1983c). Other changes of direction within ICI which have enabled this upturn include the formation of a speciality chemicals subsidiary (rather than an additional division as in the old mould of management) based in the United States, which operates with a team of European 'fishermen' directed to pluck out and develop the recession-proof, high-growth, value-added products from existing divisions, and on which ICI's growth depends (*Sunday Times*, 1983). Also, under the radical directorship of John Harvey-Jones, ICI has had its cumbersome main board cut back to five executives, moved out of its prestigious headquarters located in costly central London, and into a number of provincial centres, invoking greater independence for each of its divisions. Certainly, therefore, the 1980s are likely to see significant changes within ICI, in keeping with those of the 1970s.

The discussion has illustrated that corporate restructuring within ICI had a distinct geographical dimension. In retrospect, it appears that much of the spatial dynamics of restructuring can be explained in terms of the characteristics of individual locations and the position they occupy within the business structure of the organisation. The product segmentation framework outlined at the beginning of the chapter offers a starting point for such a perspective. Thus, Table 4.12 and Figure 4.12 illustrate the potential for growth and rationalisation in spatial terms in ICI, by calculating the relative representation of manufacturing plants and sales offices for each of the four product segments. The location quotient is designed to highlight whether each regional division has an above- or below-average representation of each product segment (<1.00 is below average, >1.00 is above average). Under current conditions, it is possible to hypothesise that rationalisation, which has predominantly affected segments B (plastics and petrochemicals) and C (fibres and organic chemicals), would have the greatest impact in the United Kingdom, Continental Western Europe and South America; whereas Africa, the Far East, Australasia and North America would be least affected. Alternatively, most of the development in the growth Segment A (general chemicals, agricultural chemicals and oil) and the stable product Segment D (pharmaceuticals, paints and industrial explosives) would be likely to be concentrated in the Far Eastern, Australasian and North American divisions.

Conclusions

This chapter has described changes in the structure of a single global corporation, ICI, over several years. The analysis was qualitative rather than quantitative, the aim being to bring out the geographical dimensions of the structure of large business organisations, in order to illustrate

Table 4.12: The Regional Distribution of Manufacturing Units and Sales Offices by Product Segments within the ICI Group, 1981

GROUP REGIONAL DIVISIONS	TOTAL NUMBER OF UNITS[1]	PERCENTAGE OF GROUP TOTAL	LOCATION QUOTIENTS[2] BY PRODUCT SEGMENT A	B	C	D	E
United Kingdom	59	16.3	1.38	1.31	1.85	0.47	–
Continental Western Europe	46	12.7	0.20	1.31	1.25	0.73	2.46
Middle East and India	41	11.3	0.77	0.63	1.12	0.75	2.21
Africa	30	8.3	0.90	0.57	0.96	1.03	1.51
The Far East	17	4.7	1.33	0.51	–	1.32	0.44
Australasia	86	23.7	1.05	0.90	0.27	1.47	0.70
North America	51	14.0	1.24	0.85	1.01	1.21	0.15
South America	32	9.0	1.13	1.62	1.44	0.61	0.71
Total	362	100.0					

Notes: 1. Including production units and sales offices.   2. Comparing the distribution of units by product segments: A. High sales volume, high profit, high growth product segment. B. High sales volume, low profit, low growth product segment. C. Low

Figure 4.12: The Global Division of Production within ICI, 1981 (number of manufacturing units and sales offices by product segment)

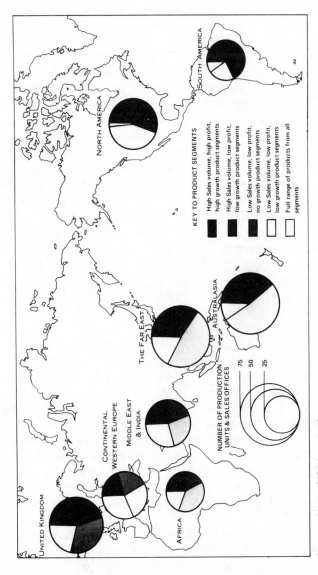

KEY TO PRODUCT SEGMENTS

High Sales volume, high profit, high growth product segments

High Sales volume, low profit, low growth product segments

Low Sales volume, low profit, no growth product segments

Low Sales volume, low profit, low growth product segments

Full range of products from all segments

NORTH AMERICA

SOUTH AMERICA

UNITED KINGDOM

CONTINENTAL WESTERN EUROPE

MIDDLE EAST & INDIA

AFRICA

THE FAR EAST

AUSTRALASIA

NUMBER OF PRODUCTION UNITS & SALES OFFICES

75
50
25

Source: Clarke (1984, p. 145).

some of the detailed mechanics of the global restructuring corporations previously identified. Quite clearly, ICI's attempt at diversification has two components: a shift out of the United Kingdom into potential growth areas at an international scale; and a deliberate move to concentrate production on new products. However, the discussion has also shown that it is not possible to refer to either of these aspects in isolation, as they work in tandem.

The case of ICI showed that the growth and expansion by global corporations has significant impacts for the international space economy, because of the extremely uneven nature of restructuring. Thus, ICI's growth in regions like Continental Europe, North America and South East Asia took place simultaneously with ICI's rationalisation of its existing operations in Britain, thereby highlighting three features: a higher turnover rate of establishments in the main centre of operations to replace older capital stocks and inefficient equipment; overseas expansion by methods which minimise risks, such as by joint ventures with other business organisations and licensing of products and processes; and a tendency to create a more extensive and decentralised spatial structure. Each of these factors combines the need to view the operations of business organisations as structural wholes, rather than just their component parts, in order to understand possible interrelationships between local changes in the structure of industry, in areas which may be far apart. As Dicken (1977, p. 139) has summarised in this respect:

In the most highly developed multinational enterprises an international division of labour is practised in which individual plants specialize in those activities for which their comparative advantage is greatest in relation to other plants within the enterprise. The objective is the attainment of overall corporate goals rather than necessarily maximising the profitability of individual units. Thus profits of one component unit may be used to cross-subsidize the losses of other component units. Further, new plants may be opened, old ones expanded, contracted or closed down, or activities shifted between one unit and another as and when corporate strategy deems such adjustments to be necessary.

This comment does not imply establishments themselves are becoming more mobile, but merely that it is their *association* as parts of the same corporation which creates a potential for restructuring on a global scale. What is also evident is that this process of restructuring is apparently bound up with the position individual plants occupy within the corporate structure. Indeed, the changing international division of labour which has been described is, to a large extent, a direct outcome of these types of processes operating within a single business organisation. However, by adopting such a descriptive framework, it has not been possible to identify individual employment changes because of the sheer scale of the problem of collecting and interpreting such data, even for one corporation. An important task, therefore, is to provide a more rigorous framework against which these changes in plant employment within the evolving spatial division of labour of the corporation can be described and specified. This is the objective of Chapter 5.

5 Plant Centrality in Organisational Structure

This study has amalgamated concepts derived from industrial geography on the spatial structure of business organisations with those from the structural contingency model on organisational structure. In doing so, it has bridged the gap which exists between theories of the overall structure of business organisations and theories of the place of component 'sub-units' or plants within this structure. The ICI case study has underlined the importance of plant position in organisational structure and highlighted the need to specify this relationship more fully. This chapter addresses the problem by attempting to measure and calibrate the centrality or peripherality of separate plants and sub-units within the structure of one business organisation, ICI. The study is a cross-sectional analysis that comprised the paints division of ICI in 1980.

Adopting a narrower empirical perspective than was attempted in Chapter 4 is necessary to facilitate the discussion and a detailed analysis and calibration of plant structures. However, looking at only one division of ICI imposes an important constraint on the analysis in that only one part of the multi-plant, multi-divisional structure of ICI is being evaluated without considering the relationship of that division to the other parts of the corporation. The study, therefore, cannot form conclusions on the structural aspects of interrelationships between product divisions. Also, the term 'division' is used loosely in this context to refer to the broad business area of which the plants are a part. As was shown in Chapter 4, ICI's product divisions do not function coherently on a global scale, but are used mainly for accounting purposes and are subsumed within the area divisions.

Coupled with this more focused analysis of the paints division is the problem of working with small populations. Although the survey had a 57 per cent response rate, making the sample of 18 plants large in relation to the total population, the small population raises the problem of suitable techniques of data analysis. A further constraint on the analysis is that the cross-sectional approach used does not allow the dynamic aspects of intra-organisational centrality and peripherality to be pursued. Thus, it has not been possible to evaluate the effects of, for instance, plants being bought or sold on the existing organisational structure.

Within these limitations, the main aspects of centrality and peripherality of plants within a single organisational structure are defined and more fully specified in empirical terms. The aim is to set up and operationalise a conceptual framework against which other processes operating at the plant level within one business organisation can be evaluated. Consequently, this analysis acts as a necessary backcloth to the assessments of labour dynamics and technology which are discussed in Chapters 6 and 7. There are three parts to the argument: the reviewing of concepts applicable to a definition of centrality; the description and measurement of the main dimensions of the operational domain and the intra-organisational relations of each plant; and the specification of attributes of the environmental and organisational relations of individual plants and the construction of centrality indices.

The Definition of Intra-organisational Centrality

The concept of centrality has already been introduced in Chapter 2 to help understand the structure of sub-units or plants within large business organisations. The term centrality was originally used by the Aston group to identify the locus of authority for decision-making in the organisation (Pugh *et al.*, 1968). This concept was later operationalised to explain *inequalities* in organisational structures, couched in terms of power relations (Hickson *et al.*, 1971; Hinings *et al.*, 1974). As a heuristic device for conceptualising intra-organisational structure, the centrality framework is a useful aid, but in practical terms and also along certain theoretical dimensions, the concept was found wanting (Child, 1972a; Donaldson, Child and Aldrich, 1975). It is the purpose of this section to highlight these deficiencies and thereby to establish the objectives of this chapter. The aim is to operationalise and more fully specify some of these criteria and subsequently to elaborate upon the basis of plant centrality in organisational structure.

To begin, the power of a sub-unit or plant has been deemed by the Aston group to be determined by the 'charter' granted to it by the parent organisation (Hickson *et al.*, 1971). Thus, the key to defining the importance or intra-organisational centrality of a plant lies in evaluating the distribution of authority within the business organisation (Pugh *et al.*, 1969). The Aston group has stressed that the allocation of authority is represented, in practical terms, by the *task* or activities which each plant performs. The centrality of the task of a single plant is composed of four elements: the ability of a plant to cope with environmental uncertainties; the ability of the organisation to substitute the function carried out by the plant; the level of importance the organisation attaches to the work carried out by the plant; and the ability of the plant to control contingencies which may arise in its plant structure (Hickson *et al.*, 1971).

Three interrelated problem areas are associated with this framework. First, because the Aston work focused on the task of the subunit (equivalent to the attention given to plant function in industrial geography), this has tended to divert attention away from other factors which are equally important, particularly the effects of organisational evolution. As the ICI case study illustrated, the expansion and contraction of business organisations has tangible spatial and temporal dimensions, with the result that individual plants will have contrasting histories, each having been established or acquired at very different 'points of onset' (Taylor and Thrift, 1982c; Massey and Meegan, 1982). Indeed, it is to be expected that the historical, spatial and ownership position of a plant are all closely intertwined in organisational structure. The consequence of an organisation's evolution will almost inevitably alter the basis for the distribution of power within a multi-plant organisation and, therefore, the centrality of each plant within that structure.

A second problem is related to the conceptualisation of organisational environment in space. Organisation theory in general and the structural contingency model in particular both stress the effects of variations in the characteristics of the environment on features of organisational structure, but they are not related directly, a weakness also commented on in the geographical literature (Marshall, 1982; McDermott and Taylor, 1982). Following Taylor and Thrift's (1979) lead, the introduction of a spatial component to the structural contingency model can resolve this initial dilemma, because environmental characteristics are shown to be affected not only by the position of the plant within the organisation, but also by its geographical location. From this perspective, spatial variation in the environmental characteristics within an organisation can be conceptualised as a series of environmental domains surrounding each plant, as Chapter 2 explained.

A third problem stems from the lack of appreciation of how historical factors and spatial structure interact within the centrality framework.

Interplay between these two factors is manifest in a number of ways, but the three most important have been summarised by McDermott and Taylor (1982) as: factors specific to individual locations and places; imperfect diffusion of information between [and within] organisations; and the cumulative impact of different management practices over time. These factors mean that the centrality of any plant is determined by its relationship with its local environment, as well as its position and function within the organisation. Thus, two sets of forces which affect the plant can be distinguished — *intra-organisational relations* and also *inter-organisational relations*.

From the above discussion, the *history* and *position* of a plant are critical components of its intra-organisational relations, in addition to the *task* it performs. Description of inter-organisational relations at the level of the domain must encapsulate both the composition or *internal characteristics* of the environment and the wider constraints or *external linkages* of the domain to the wider global environment. These criteria are used as starting points in the empirical analysis which follows.

Approaching the idea of centrality in this way does not deny inter-action between these two sets of factors (Figure 5.1). For example, plant managers are important mediators in this respect, simultaneously determining strategy and responding to environmental stimuli (Reeves and Turner, 1972; Ouchi, 1977; Ouchi and Maguire, 1975). Good management is a factor in maintaining and increasing the power of a plant in an organisation, significantly lengthening its 'life-cycle' (e.g. Schmenner, 1983; Stobaugh and Telesio, 1983). Thus, the aggregate plant composition of a region will impart an effect on the environment itself. Alternatively, the way in which plant managers perceive and respond to their environment can act to alter the importance of a plant to the business organisation (e.g. McDermott and Taylor, 1976; Neville and Taylor, 1980). Therefore, this study merely serves to clarify the organisational and environmental criteria which determine plant centrality in organisational structure, thereby providing a possible framework for these types of research in the future. In the following section, an attempt is made to define some empirical measures of plant centrality.

Specifying the Domain and Intra-organisational Relations

To explore the basis of plant centrality, this section serves to specify the configuration of the domain and intra-organisational relations

Figure 5.1: Conceptualising Plant Centrality in Organisational Structure

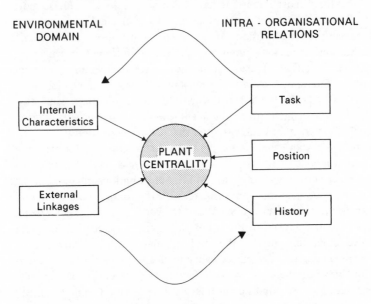

of each plant by identifying some workable dimensions which can be used to analyse the paints division of ICI.

The Domain

As Chapter 2 established, the domain is the potential environment of the plant and determines the group of organisations with which it might interact (Thompson, 1967). At this broad level of specification it is necessary to describe the context of the plant, rather than to establish direct and actual linkages with other organisations in the form of the task environment. In this analysis, which is concerned with plants located in a number of countries, a practical way of describing the operational domain of a plant is by equating it with the national environment. The primary reason for taking this level of specification is that data are readily available and easily constructed. This level of analysis has been discussed in detail by a number of authors, identifying three dimensions of a country's environment which are relevant to an assessment of risk: political, economic and legal (Robinson, 1981; Burton and Inoue, 1983). However, for the specific purposes of this analysis, six dimensions of the domain can be identified and used. These are outlined in Table 5.1.

Political Attributes. A number of practical examples show that political attributes are an important aspect of the business environment despite the apparent intangibility of assessing the political attributes of a plant's operational domain. Many organisations employ specialists to evaluate the risk associated with investment in particular types of economies, and political considerations are prominent in these assessments (see the *National Times*, 1983). Similar techniques can be employed to evaluate ongoing risk where plants are already located. These issues are especially important because, though not readily quantifiable, simple rank assessments of countries can be used. Even such simple indicators help to establish the extent to which the political system regulates or interferes in business in the plant's domain. From available information, three simple indices can be devised: *centralisation of the political system*, which is evaluated by ranking the countries in which the plants are located, relative to one another on a scale from a highly centralised to a highly decentralised system; attitude towards *currency control*, which is classified as free, liberal or strict; and the record or *extent of intervention* in the economy (i.e. a surrogate for which is the number of formal currency devaluations over a ten-year period).

Economic Attributes. In contrast with political factors, the economic attributes of a national environment or domain are easily quantifiable. *Gross national product* (GNP) forms a succinct measure of aggregate wealth, and *GNP per capita* indicates how the wealth is distributed within a country. Measures of economic stability or instability are also important and three complementary indicators can be used: *rate of inflation, growth in the money supply* and the level of the government's *budget deficit*.

International Trade Structure. To describe the trade structure of a national domain simple indicators such as *import trends* and *export trends* were compiled, using 1975 as a base year. Also the *orientation of trade* internally and with developed, developing and centrally planned economies has been determined, though in order to evaluate the type and magnitude of trade, two more elaborate indices were constructed. An index which measures the degree of specialisation in the trade of an economy is, for example, the proportion of primary products among total exports. As trade in primary products is more

Table 5.1: Variables Used to Describe the Domain

DIMENSION	OPERATIONAL VARIABLES	SOURCE NOTES
POLITICAL ATTRIBUTES	Centralisation of the political system	Rank rating of countries from 1 (highly decentralised) to 10 (highly centralised)
	Currency control	Rated as 'free'(1), 'liberal'(2) or 'strict'(3). (Picks' Currency Yearbook, 1980)
	Extent of intervention	Number of currency devaluations 1978-1979 (Picks' Currency Yearbook, 1980)
ECONOMIC ATTRIBUTES	GNP, $US m, 1980	IMF (1982)
	GNP per capita, $US m, 1980	World Bank (1982)
	Rate of inflation, %	Annual average 1970-1980 (World Bank, 1982)
	Growth in the money supply, %	Annual average 1973-1980 (UN, 1983)
	Budget deficit, % 1980	IMF (1982)
INTERNATIONAL TRADE STRUCTURE	Import trends	1975 = 100 (IMF, 1982)
	Export trends	1975 = 100 (IMF, 1982)
	Orientation of trade by types of economy, %:	UN (1981)
	(i) developed markets	
	(ii) developing markets	
	(iii) centrally planned economies	
	(iv) internal trade	
	Stability, %	$\dfrac{\text{Exports of primary products} \times 100}{\text{Total exports}}$ Derived from World Bank (1982) data
	Vulnerability, %	$\dfrac{\text{Exports + imports} \times 100}{\text{GNP}}$ Derived from World Bank (1982) data

Category	Variable	Source
INTERNATIONAL CAPITAL STRUCTURE	Current account balance of payments, $USm, 1980	World Bank (1982)
	Debt Service Ratio, %	$\dfrac{\text{Government bonds} + \text{medium and long-term borrowings}}{\text{Exports}} \times \dfrac{100}{1}$ Derived from World Bank (1982) and OECD (1982a) data
	Foreign investment, $USm, 1980	Net investment (World Bank, 1982)
	Official Development Aid, $USm, 1980	Net receipts from all sources (OECD, 1982b)
INDUSTRY FACTORS	Production trends	1975 = 100 (IMF, 1982)
	Demand, %	$\dfrac{\text{Public} + \text{private consumption}}{\text{GNP}} \times \dfrac{100}{1}$ Derived from World Bank (1982) data
	Energy consumption trends, %	Annual average 1974–1979 (World Bank, 1982)
	Total industrial labour force, %	As percentage of total labour force (World Bank, 1982)
	Growth of industrial labour force, %	Annual average, 1970–1980 (World Bank, 1982)
SECTOR FACTORS	Volume of chemical exports, $USm, 1980	UN (1981)
	Chemical exports as a proportion of total exports, % 1980	UN (1981)
	Δ " " " " " "	UN (1981)
	Balance of trade in chemicals, % 1980	UN (1981)
	Scale	Number of establishments, 1979 (UN, 1980)
	Competitiveness	Δ " "
	Size of chemicals sector workforce, 1979	UN (1980)
	Δ " " " " " "	UN (1980)
	Number of employees per establishment, 1979	$\dfrac{\text{Size of chemical sector workforce}}{\text{Scale}}$ (UN, 1980)

International Standard Industrial Classification (ISIC) at 2 digit level (35), 'Chemicals, Petroleum and Plastics'.
Note: Δ Annual rate of change.

volatile than other aspects of international trade, this index forms an indicator of the degree of *stability* in an economy's trade structure. Finally, the magnitude of trade was assessed as the total volume of trade (imports plus exports) relative to GNP, that is, the wealth of the domain. This index evaluates the *vulnerability* of the domain to fluctuations in international trade.

International Capital Structure. An additional gauge of the degree to which a national domain is tied into the international economy is provided by its capital structure and, in particular, the level of surplus or deficit owed overseas and the volume of overseas capital circulating in the economy. Two measures can be used to evaluate the level of surplus or deficit: the *current account balance of payments* position, which takes into account differences in imports and exports, including unrequited official and private transfers of capital; and the *debt service ratio*, defined as the level of debt outstanding on government bonds and medium- and long-term loans, relative to exports. This ratio is one of the several rules of thumb commonly used to assess the ability of a country to service its national debt (World Bank, 1982). Two further variables, the level of *foreign investment* and *official development aid*, can be used to describe two contrasting elements of circulating overseas capital in the domain. In both cases, negative figures point towards countries which are net investors and donors respectively.

Industry Factors. At a more specific level, characteristics of manufacturing industry in a national domain are likely to impinge on the operations of a particular plant. *Production trends* can be summarised as an index relative to 1975. Production levels and *demand* or consumption can be evaluated as an index measuring public and private consumption as a percentage of gross national product. Other variables indicating the broad nature of production are *energy consumption trends*, the size of the *total industrial labour force* and the average annual *growth of the industrial labour force*.

Sector Factors. Paints production falls into the chemicals industry category which, at an international level, is the most specific level at which comprehensive data can be collected to describe the national domains. To evaluate the structure of trade in chemicals, several criteria are available. These include the *volume of chemical exports*; *chemical exports as a proportion of total exports*; the *rate* at which this proportion of total exports is growing; and the *balance of trade in chemicals*.

The nature of the production environment can be assessed according to the *scale* of production (number of establishments) and the *competitiveness* of the sector (rate of change in the number of establishments). Other important sectoral characteristics of the domain are the *size of the chemicals workforce*, the *rate of change of the workforce size* and the *number of employees per establishment*.

Intra-organisational Relations

In order to describe the characteristics of a plant within the larger organisation to which it belongs, two broad dimensions can be identified (Taylor and Thrift, 1982c). The first set of variables relate the plant to the business organisation in question, and the second set indicate its production characteristics (Table 5.2).

Organisational Factors. The initial discussion in the introduction of this chapter emphasised the history of the plant and its intra-organisational position as two important components of the relationship of a plant to its parent business organisation. Three complementary variables are important in describing the history of each plant. First, the *age* of the plant measures the number of years the plant has been in operation and, if it was acquired, a second variable is the *length of time* since the plant was taken over. This second variable measures the proportion of the plant's total lifespan for which it has been part of the organisation to which it presently belongs. The third variable is the *status* of the plant and indicates explicitly whether the plant has been established as a branch plant or alternatively whether it was acquired by the organisation.

A further four variables can be compiled to indicate complementary aspects of plants within a business organisation. Whereas the *hierarchical position* of the plant within the ownership structure of the corporation was stressed by the literature, it would also be useful to investigate the effect of the *geographical position* or location of the plant within the business organisation. In addition, the Aston studies also emphasised the importance of the task of the sub-unit. When operationalising this concept, it must be borne in mind that the task of a plant is relative to the organisation itself, hence the concepts of 'pervasiveness' and 'substitutability' developed by the Aston group (Hinings *et al.*, 1974). Precisely how the plant extends its influence through the organisation (literally, pervades), can be summarised in the *scale of task* which it performs. A simple measure of *substitutability* is the number of other paints plants owned by the

Table 5.2: Variables Used to Describe Intra-organisational Relations

DIMENSION	OPERATIONAL VARIABLES	SOURCE NOTES*
ORGANISATIONAL FACTORS		
History	Age	Number of years since opened
	Length of time acquired	By present organisation
	Status	Using binary data to illustrate whether plant is a branch plant or an acquired plant
Position	Hierarchical position	Number of companies in the ownership chain back to the parent business organisation (derived from Dun and Bradstreet, 1982)
	Geographical position, kilometres	Shortest distance (Great Circle route) from corporate headquarters
	Scale of task, %	$\dfrac{\text{Plant output}}{\text{Total input of plants owned by immediate parent}} \times \dfrac{100}{1}$
	Substitutability	Number of other plants owned by the immediate parent
PRODUCTION FACTORS		

		Product ranks
	Technological scale	4 automotive and industrial paints 3 domestic paints 2 paint preparations 1 other paint products Plant output × technological diversity
Method	Small-batch production, %	Proportion of total equipment dated pre-1975
	Repetition flow-line production, %	Proportion of total equipment dated post-1980
Scale	Output, 1980	Millions of litres of paint and equivalent products produced
	Δ Output	
	Total energy costs, 1980	$USm
	Energy intensity	$\dfrac{\text{Output}}{\text{Energy costs}} \times \dfrac{100}{1}$
Product Structure	Product range	Number of product types produced
	Product specialisation	Orientation of production towards industrial paints (+1.0) or domestic paints (−1.0)

Notes: * Unless otherwise stated all data is for 1980. Δ Annual rate of change.

immediate parent in the same national domain, and this indicates the potential which exists for the business organisation to replace the task a plant performs, within the existing structure.

Production Factors. Measures have also been developed to describe in detail the form of production, task or function of each plant. Four categories of characteristics are important in this respect: the form of technology, methods of production, scale of production and product structure. Of these categories, technology is the most difficult to represent in statistical terms and it is necessary to develop surrogate indices for this purpose, such as the *technological complexity* and *technological scale* of each plant. Complexity is important because it represents an historical record of technological development. In the paints industry, in particular, individual types of paint are produced by technologies which differ in complexity from the production of most other basic products, ranging to paint preparations (powders, resins, additives and so on), domestic and industrial paints. Thus, it is possible to rank and add together these scores for the technologies used in each plant which, when divided by the number of technologies, can be used to represent complexity. An added dimension of technology is its scale or capacity (Gold, 1981). A representative measure of the scale of technology, therefore, is the number of technologies used, weighted by the establishment's total output.

To describe the methods of production employed (the distinction from technology being based on the configuration of technology and manpower in production), it is possible to make a distinction between unit, batch and process production (Woodward, 1965). There is a fundamental and practical distinction in the paints industry between *small-batch production* and *repetition flow-line production*. These two methods do intermesh, as in mixed batch production, but the relative importance of these methods is significant and can be represented by the proportion of total production for which each method accounts. Scale of production can be measured by a number of variables, of which the total *output* of the plant is the most significant, and the dynamics of scale can be represented by the annual rate of *change in output*. Other measures include the *total energy costs* to run the plant and its *energy intensity* (energy costs relative to output).

Finally, to describe the product structure of a plant, two factors are important. These are *product range*, represented by the number of product areas in which the plant operates — automotive and industrial paints, domestic or decorative paints, paint preparations, and 'other' paint products — and *product specialisation* or the degree to which production in the plant is concentrated on the domestic or industrial end of the product range.

Data Reduction

The sets of variables representing different aspects of intra-organisational centrality were used to produce a data set which describes the domain and intra-organisational relations of the plants of ICI's paints division operating worldwide. A postal questionnaire survey was circulated to all plants and a 57 per cent response rate was achieved, representing a relatively large sample of eighteen plants drawn from ten countries. Thus, the objective of maintaining the structural integrity of a corporate approach was achieved within practical limits. The locations and ownership structures of the respondent plants are shown in Table 5.3. Other data were gathered from the secondary sources shown to describe the domains of each of the plants (Table 5.1).

However, as these criteria are only a priori measures of plant centrality, it was considered necessary to test the various data sets in order to remove redundant and overlapping variables. Bearing in mind the small size of the population (not the sample), the objective of parsimony led to a confrontation with the inadequacy of many analytical techniques. Blalock (1972) pinpointed this dilemma that results from the very fact that social science research is often concerned with focusing on small populations, where assumptions of normality cannot be made. Cohen (1977, p. 6) summarises the problem neatly:

> The reliability (or precision) of a sample value is the closeness with which it can be expected to approximate the relevant population value. It is necessarily an estimated value in practice, since the population value is generally unknown. Depending upon the statistic in question, and the specific statistical model on which the test is based, reliability may or may not be directly dependent upon the unit of measurement, the population value, and the shape of the population distribution. However, it is *always* dependent upon the size of the sample.

The problem lies in finding statistical techniques appropriate to the analysis of these data sets, as most depend on the availability of large samples drawn from large populations. Non-parametric statistics (see Siegel, 1956) are especially applicable in these cases, but because of their looser assumptions they are inherently less powerful. There-

Table 5.3: Plant Ownership Structure and Location

COUNTRY	OWNERSHIP STRUCTURE	PLANT LOCATIONS
United Kingdom	Paints Division	Slough, Stowmarket
West Germany	Deutsche ICI GmbH	
	: Hermann Wiederhold KG	
	:. Hermann Wiederhold GmbH	Hilden
Canada	CIL Incorporated	York Works (Toronto), Vaughan Centre
	. CIL Paints Incorporated	(Toronto), Montreal Works
Australia	ICI Australia Ltd	Clayton, Footscray (Victoria), Cabarita
	: ICI Australia Investments Pty Ltd	(New South Wales), Rocklea (Queensland),
	.. Dulux Australia Ltd	Port Adelaide (South Australia)

India	Alkali and Chemical Corporation of India Ltd	Rishra, Hyderabad
Pakistan	ICI (Pakistan) Ltd	
	.. Paintex Ltd	Lahore
Zambia	ICI Zambia Ltd	
	.. Dukon Paints Ltd	Kitwe
Malaysia	ICI Malaysia Sdn Bhd	
	.: ICI Paints (Mal) Sdn Bhd	Selangor (Malaysia)
	.:. ICI Paints (Singapore) Pte Ltd	Jurong (Singapore)
	ICI Paints (Thailand)	Laksi (Thailand)

Source: Compiled from Dun and Bradstreet (1982).

fore, the application of multivariate techniques to a small population such as that constructed here has a number of problems, the most notable of which relate to assumptions on normality and homoscedasticity. These effects decrease as the sample and population size increase (Bennett and Bowers, 1976).

Despite these problems, the application of factor analysis can be justified as an exploratory exercise (Mather, 1976; Tukey, 1969), given that it might be possible to apply other multivariate techniques in the future. Factor analysis, however, is an accessible and easily worked technique. Indeed, it is 'merely a measurement tool to define a concept or concepts within a clearly defined social model. . .This is a job factor analysis does well and we can ask little more of any tool that it does its job well' (Taylor, 1981, p. 265).

Factor analysis was used to evaluate individual variables and compress the most meaningful combinations of variables (in terms of the proportion of data variance for which they accounted) into a series of factor solutions to achieve an economy of description in the data set (Davies, 1971). As Cattrell (1966, p. 191) noted, factor analysis is 'a generalised method for making invisible influences visible, at least to a first approximation to their form'. The data were standardised to remove the effects of large variables and then a matrix of variable correlation coefficients was constructed to establish the association between variables. The small number of cases in relation to the number of variables meant that each case could only be related back to the factor solutions when the number of variables was at least one less than the number of cases. Consequently, it was necessary to run several tests on each of the sub-sets or variable dimensions. Those variables in which the response was recorded in a binary form had a Harman proportional coefficient substituted (see Tinkler, 1971) for the existing Pearson product moment correlation coefficient, because these are not suitable for dichotomous data. The correlation matrix formed the input to an R-mode (case-by-case) factor analysis which produced a number of factor dimensions of the data, or composite variables. Each composite variable describes a portion of the variance in the data and the convention of withdrawing factors with eigenvalues of less than one was followed (Daultrey, 1976).

Factor analysis was employed in preference to a principal components solution because the method extracts the effects of co-variance between variables produced by underlying factors (Goddard and Kirby, 1976). Although factor analysis can only make a best estimate of communality because of this approach (communality is the squared multiple correlation between a given variable and others in the matrix), these estimates can be improved significantly through a process of iteration. The factor solutions can also be rotated to produce theoretically meaningful dimensions of the data, without altering its structure. A varimax-orthogonal technique of rotation was used not only because it simplifies the column structure of the matrix in preference to the rows, but also because it destroys generality in favour of simplifying differences in the data (Davies, 1971). Both these characteristics help provide a clearer and more easily interpretable picture.

In order to relate the extracted factors back to the plant cases, the process of factoring requires the calculation of the inverse of the correlation matrix. As noted, this procedure was not possible when both domain and intra-organisational variables were taken together because the determinant measure of the condition of the matrix was close to zero. Calculations based on such fine limits can result in significant computational errors and an ill-conditioned matrix. Mather (1976) draws an analogy of the ill-conditioned matrix with the problem of determining the exact point of intersection of a pair of straight lines which is easy when the lines are perpendicular, but is difficult to evaluate precisely as the angle of intersection is reduced. Lines which cross but are close to parallel correspond with the ill-conditioned matrix. To circumvent this problem, which is caused entirely by the large number of variables relative to cases, the factoring procedure was split into several analyses, each of which corresponded with a particular dimension of domain and organisational structure defined previously: political attributes, economic attributes, international trade and capital structure, industry and sector factors, organisation factors and production factors.

Constructs of Centrality

Seventeen factors were produced by factor analysis and these represent, in effect, constructs of domain and intra-organisational centrality. The results are set out in Tables 5.4 and 5.5, with eleven attributes describing the domain and six attributes describing the intra-organisational context of each plant. According to which of the original variables contributed strongly to the production of a factor (loadings were considered significant when they were above −0.5 or 0.5), it is possible to interpret these constructs through the association between the variables.

Table 5.4: Domain Factors

FACTOR	FACTOR NAME	PER CENT OF VARIANCE EXPLAINED	VARIABLE	LOADING	VARIABLE	LOADING
I	Index of wealth and political democracy	74.8	Centralisation	-0.86317	GNP per capita	0.98901
			Currency control	-0.61381	Budget deficit	0.73283
			Extent of intervention	-0.56928	GNP	0.65325
II	Currency stability	25.2	Growth in the money supply	-0.61060	Rate of inflation	0.76345
					Extent of intervention	0.73571
					Currency control	0.72554
III	Trade vulnerability	62.2	Trade orientation to developed markets	-0.75333	Trade orientation to developing markets	0.91780
					Export trends	0.83101
					Import trends	0.76250
					Vulnerability	0.68871
IV	International market structure	37.8	Trade orientation to developed markets	-0.65118	Trade orientation to centrally planned markets	0.86401
					Internal trade	0.71879
V	Foreign investment	62.5			Foreign investment	0.98777
VI	Aid dependency	37.5			Official development aid	0.73081
					Debt service ratio	0.56114

VII	Manufacturing productivity growth	66.3		Production trends	0.93421
				Energy consumption trends	0.76841
				Growth of industrial labour force	0.53970
VIII	Newly industrialising	33.7	Total industrial labour force	−0.94347	Growth of industrial labour force	0.77410
IX	Scale of chemicals production	47.2		Volume of chemical exports	0.94809
				No. of employees per establishment	0.88192
				Size of chemicals sector workforce	0.80719
				Balance of trade in chemicals	0.75065
				Scale of chemicals industry	0.52136
X	Chemicals sector growth	36.6		Competitiveness	0.97303
				Δ Chemicals sector workforce	0.93622
				Scale of chemicals industry	0.81060
				Size of chemicals sector workforce	0.51967
XI	Chemical export dynamics	16.2	Chemical exports as a proportion of total exports	−0.74271	Chemical as a proportion of total exports	0.82371

Note: Δ Annual rate of change, compounded 1970-80.

Table 5.5: Intra-organisational Factors

FACTOR	FACTOR NAME	PER CENT OF VARIANCE EXPLAINED	VARIABLE	LOADING	VARIABLE	LOADING
I	Plant position	62.0	Scale of task	-0.75145	Substitutability	0.97874
					Geographical position	0.85473
					Hierarchical position	0.70454
II	Length of membership	25.7	Hierarchical position	-0.57985	Length of time acquired	0.68891
					Age	0.57522
III	Plant status	12.3	Status	-0.70387	Age	0.61635
IV	Scale of production	65.8			Total energy costs	0.97276
					Output	0.93799
					Technological scale	0.91704
					Energy intensity	0.89089
V	Specialisation	22.2	Small-batch production	-0.47501	Product specialisation	0.93221
					Product range	0.49116
					Technological diversity	0.42361
VI	Production technology	11.9	Technological complexity	-0.65307	Product range	0.82491

Interpretation of Factors

Of the domain variables, six load heavily on Factor I, split evenly on a bipolar relationship. All three attributes of the political structure of the environmental domain — centralisation, currency control and the extent of intervention — display a strong negative association with budget deficit, GNP and GNP per capita. As the negative variables describe aspects of democracy in the political system and the positive variables indicate the level of wealth in the domain, the results can be evaluated as representing an *index of wealth and political democracy*. What this means is that the wealthiest environmental domains are also those with decentralised political systems.

Factor II picked out several variables which described currency trends in plants' national domains. Thus, rate of inflation, extent of intervention and currency control all had high positive loadings. Only one variable, growth in the money supply, was related negatively to this factor. Tentatively, therefore, this factor can be interpreted as measuring *currency stability*.

Two factors are significant in terms of isolating dimensions of the international trade structure of each domain. Four variables relate positively to Factor III, namely trade orientation with developing markets, export trends, import trends and vulnerability. In such domains, therefore, the economy is not directed to relationships with developed country markets (in fact this variable loads negatively), so business organisations in these locations are trading largely with developing country markets and are doing so to an increasing extent. The combination of the openness of the economy, together with instability of developing country economies, means that this factor highlights a dimension of *trade vulnerability*. Three variables are associated with Factor IV. These were trade orientation to centrally planned markets and internal trade, which are positive, and trade orientation to developed markets, which is negative. Together, these variables clearly summarise the *international market structure* of the domain. Consequently, such environments are characterised by a limited trade structure which is aimed primarily at markets other than those of the developed nations, mainly centrally planned economies.

Factors V and VI form straightforward measures of *foreign investment* and *aid dependency* respectively in the international capital structure of individual national domains. The foreign investment factor gives an indication of the level of external control in the economy. The relationship between countries with a high debt service ratio and large amounts of official development aid on the aid dependency factor needs little explanation.

Factor analysis of the form of industry in each domain produced two distinct dimensions. High positive growth in production trends, energy consumption trends and growth of the industrial labour force are characteristic of Factor VII, and form an apparent measure of *manufacturing productivity growth* in individual national economies. Complementing this measure, Factor VIII highlights the growth of the industrial labour force variable, which is negatively associated with the total industrial labour force, that is, the measure of industry employment as a proportion of total employment. The growth in industry employment relative to the rest of the economy is a classic feature of countries which are *newly industrialising*.

The three final factors produced in this set of analyses relate to the chemicals sector. Several variables load heavily on Factor IX, including volume of chemical exports, number of employees per establishment, size of chemicals sector workforce, balance of trade in chemicals and the scale of chemicals industry. Taken together, these variables are indicative of aspects of the *scale of chemicals production*. Some of these variables such as scale of chemicals industry and size of chemicals sector workforce also related to Factor X, but more importantly this factor emphasised the growth aspect of the industry, especially the rate of growth in the number of chemical establishments (competitiveness) and annual rate of change of the chemicals sector workforce. As a result, this factor can be used to represent the *chemicals sector growth*. Two variables load heavily on Factor XI, chemicals as a proportion of total exports, which loads positively, and the annual rate of change of chemicals exports as a proportion of total exports, which was negative. Quite clearly then, Factor XI is a measure of *chemical export dynamics*.

Six factors emerge from the analyses of data describing the intra-organisational characteristics of each plant (Table 5.5). The most important variable loading on Factor I is substitutability, which is indicative of the number of other, similar plants owned by the parent business organisation, and hence of the potential for a plant to be replaced. Two other variables are also important, the geographical position and hierarchical position of a plant. The scale of task, which loaded negatively against these three variables, implies that the functional importance of the plant declines as each of the other variables increase. In other words, Factor I is a measure of *plant position* within an organisation.

Two variables which load positively on Factor II are the length of time acquired and the age of the plant, which relates in a negative fashion to hierarchical position. What this pattern implies is that the older plants are located higher up the ownership hierarchy. As the suggestion is that the hierarchical structure of plants embodies the historical record of plant development, younger plants being found away from the ownership core, Factor II is appropriately labelled *length of membership*. The negative relationship between plant status and age which is the characteristic of Factor III stresses the fact that older plants tend to be those which have been acquired rather than established as branch plants and the factor is, therefore, an indicator of *plant status*.

In contrast to the first three factors, Factor IV emphasises features of the *scale of production*, including total energy costs, output, technical scale and energy intensity. However, small-batch production relates negatively to product specialisation, product range and technological diversity on Factor V. This combination of variables suggests that repetition flow-line production is, by implication, associated with either specialised production, or plants which have a large product range and are more technologically diverse. The index is a representative measure of the level of *specialisation* of a plant. Finally, Factor VI highlights *production technology* because it emphasises that where production extends across most of the product categories, technology is less diverse, and this is probably to be attributed to the scale economies associated with these forms of technology.

Indices of Centrality

The preceding analyses have served to operationalise a number of attributes of the centrality of plants within organisational structure, as well as the features of those plants' environmental domains. It is now quite feasible to categorise each of these factors as definable dimensions of the broad concepts which were extracted from the literature (Figure 5.2). Intra-organisational relations have several features, especially the position, history and task of a plant. According to these results, the history of a plant is more or less analogous to its position within the organisation. The three remaining variables describe aspects of the task of the plant, including its specialisation, scale and technological structure. Of the eleven factors which described the environmental domain of the plant, six emphasise the domain's internal characteristics and five the external linkages of the domain.

So far, however, each of these attributes has been described only

Figure 5.2: Domain and Organisational Attributes of Plant Centrality

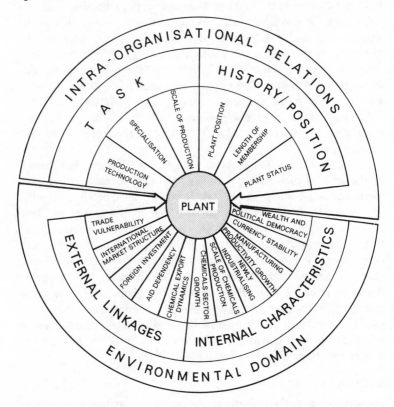

in isolation. To conceptualise how these factors interrelate, it is useful to combine these variables. There are three principal reasons for attempting this integration. First, there is the need to understand the relative direction and strength of influence of individual variables. Second, it is important to be able to place actual cases in some order, according to the total effect of these dimensions of domain and intra-organisational centrality. Third, it is important to understand the relationship between a plant's domain characteristics which stem from its location and its particular intra-organisational position.

Two indices were constructed to summarise the concepts of intra-organisational and domain centrality separately. The indices were produced by a simple process of adding the final factor scores for each case onto the factor variables, after these scores had been weighted according to the amount of variance in the data which each composite variable explained (see Tables 5.4 and 5.5). Each case was then assigned to the two scales calibrated to range from 0 to 100 (Figure 5.3).

The index describing the environmental domains of each plant (Figure 5.3) summarises the relationships between the eleven factors shown in Table 5.6. Central domains such as Canada, Australia, West Germany, Singapore and, to a certain extent, the United Kingdom, are typically affluent and democratic, with stable currencies. They are, however, also more vulnerable to fluctuations in trade patterns because of their orientation of trade towards the world's developed country markets. Other factors combine to show that the central domains are to be found in the established industrialised counties of the world, the major sources of foreign investment and the centres of large-scale chemicals production. At the other extreme, countries offering peripheral domains are usually poor and undemocratic, with unstable currencies. In terms of trade, these countries are less vulnerable, but growing exports are oriented towards developing country markets. These locations are also typified by large amounts of foreign investment and aid and they display high rates of productivity growth typical of newly industrialising nations. The chemical sector is of growing significance in these peripheral economies, examples of which include Pakistan, India, Thailand and Zambia.

The intra-organisational relations of plants located in this range of national domains displayed a somewhat different arrangement (Figure 5.3). Plants such as Stowmarket and Slough (United Kingdom), and Cabarita and Clayton (Australia), occupy central positions. As such they are less substitutable, usually acquired plants, with a longstanding membership in the organisation. Production in these plants takes place on a large scale, and is specialised and technologically diverse, employing repetition flow-line methods. In contrast, peripheral plants have a low position in the corporate hierarchy, as recently established branch plants. These plants are small and less specialised, catering for the domestic paints market, and production technology is concentrated on small-batch production methods. Such plants include, for example, Jurong (Singapore), Rishra (India) and Kitwe (Zambia).

The low level of association between the domain and organisational centrality of individual plants was confirmed by a Spearman's rank correlation test (r_s = 0.3849). The value of this coefficient shows clearly that plants which are central in organisational terms are not necessarily located in central domains. Likewise, peripheral plants are not always located in peripheral domains. There is an extremely important corollary to this argument, which is that the intra-organ-

Figure 5.3: The Centrality of ICI Plants on Domain and Organisational Indices

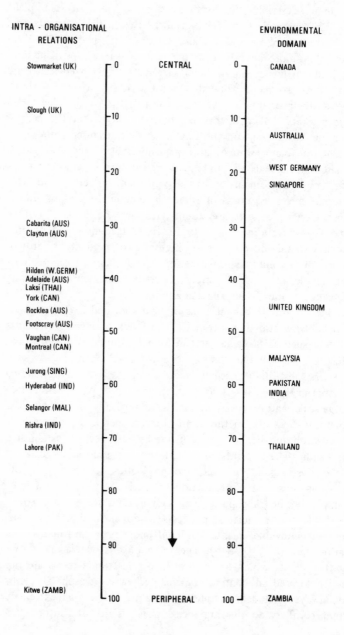

Table 5.6: Characteristics of Central and Peripheral Plant Domains and Intra-organisational Relations

PLANT DOMAIN	CENTRAL	PERIPHERAL
Index of wealth and political democracy	rich/ democratic	poor/ undemocratic
Currency stability	stable	unstable
Trade vulnerability	high	low
International market structure	developed markets	developing markets
Foreign investment	low	high
Aid dependency	low	high
Manufacturing productivity growth	low	high
Newly industrialising	low	high
Scale of chemicals production	large	small
Chemical sector growth	high	low
Chemical export dynamics	low growth	high growth

PLANT INTRA-ORGANISATIONAL RELATIONS	CENTRAL	PERIPHERAL
Plant position	high	low
Length of membership	long	short
Plant status	high (old, acquired)	low (new, branch plant)
Scale of production	large	small
Specialisation	domestic	industrial
Production technology	diverse, repetition flow-line methods	concentrated, small-batch methods

isational centrality of a plant is likely to take precedence, because it can override the centrality of a domain. In many cases, however, the relationship between the organisational centrality of a plant and the centrality of its domain are likely to reinforce one another, with large plants locating in large markets, large markets perpetuating the plants' growth, and so on. The degree of circularity in this argument is undeniable, but it is important to realise that this is precisely the reason for a plant's central existence, because the longer it is able to survive, the more power it accumulates relative to other plants in the same organisation. Pfeffer (1981, p. 290) summarises this issue:

> Once in power, in other words, power can be used to take action and acquire resources which will provide at least as much if not more power in the future. Power has within it the source of its own perpetuation. The combination of these. . .effects makes change in the distribution of control in organizations incredibly difficult and unlikely.

Conclusions

This chapter has made an initial attempt to describe the position of individual plants within a large business organisation. In doing so, the analysis has attempted to operationalise the concept of centrality as a conceptual device for understanding the inequalities that exist between plants and sub-units within organisational structure. To achieve this end, facets of the intra-organisational relations of individual plants, including their task, position and historical evolution were developed. Some broad measures of the environmental domains of the plants studied were also devised. The two sets of characteristics were then encapsulated in indices describing the overall organisational and domain centrality of the plants. The composition of the two centrality indices illustrates the relative strength, directions of influence and interrelationships between the various features of a plant's intra-organisational relations and environmental domain. From the case study of the plants belonging to the paints division of ICI, two alternative propositions can be established relating to plant centrality.

First, results from the study show that scarcity and an embedded position within a business organisation are features integral to the creation of a central plant. In essence, these establishments are the survivors, those with a longstanding membership, in part because the organisation has been willing to continue developing these plants, enlarging them, carving out a specialist role for them to serve and investing in technologically intensive methods of production. In contrast, peripheral plants, because of their more recent history — usually established as branch plants — occupy a superficial position within the organisation, with a definite but only small role to play. The position of these establishments is more precarious simply because there are more of them, and they do not attract as much individual emphasis. What this generalisation suggests as a first proposition, therefore, is that the position and history of a plant are critical influences on its centrality, and thereby on the network of power relations within a business organisation. In other words, there is a dynamic aspect to plant centrality in organisational structure which is represented as an accumulation of power by virtue of an establishment's survival, as well as the task it performs.

Second, with regard to the environment of a plant, the results suggested that central domains of plants are to be found, in general, in the established industrialised countries, and it seems likely that such locations will be conducive to the creation of plants central to business organisations, with the two influences reinforcing one another. Similarly, peripheral domains which are located in the world's developing countries are more likely to promote plants which are peripheral, rather than central, to the business organisation. As the analysis demonstrated a lack of a direct relationship between domain and organisational centrality of plants in ICI's paints division, a second proposition must be that either organisational or domain centrality is the stronger influence on individual plants. However, to evaluate the relative importance of these propositions, it is necessary to examine their influence on other dependent plant characteristics.

The task remains, therefore, to integrate these characteristics of organisational structure and locational environment with more detailed information on the internal operation and performance of the same plants. By doing this, it should be possible to test the significance of plant centrality in organisational structure and explain some of the dynamic properties of location, both in organisational and geographic terms. A useful focus to examine and evaluate the organisation-environment nexus and, hence, to establish the effects of each, is in the area of labour dynamics at the plant level. This is the purpose of Chapter 6.

6 The Effects of Plant Centrality on Labour Dynamics

A framework has been developed for describing the structural position of plants within business organisations, summarising the characteristics of their environmental domains and intra-organisational relations as two centrality indices. These indices established the relative importance of each plant and location to the organisation. The configuration of the measures of centrality suggested that the overall context of production varies significantly between plants, not only in terms of, for instance, the size and attributes of the market and industrial environment, but also in relation to the historical evolution, function and technologies used in each plant. This chapter relates these empirical measures to a separate set of data highlighting aspects of employment in the same 18 plants of the paints division of ICI. The chapter's objectives are threefold: to consider the importance of individual attributes of centrality; to gauge the relative impact of the revealed attributes of intra-organisational relations compared with the attributes of each plant's environmental domain on labour dynamics; and to illustrate the combined effect of these centrality criteria in contrasting plants. Through this analysis, a more elaborate specification of the significant structural forces impinging on production at the plant level inside the business organisation will be provided, which may help explain their patterns of labour use. It is also intended to reflect on directions of causality within this framework.

The resultant analysis draws on additional information on employment gathered in surveys of ICI paint producing plants. While most of the variables used in the centrality framework were inherently cross-sectional in nature, some variables incorporated into the analysis also provide an approximation of changes in the environmental domain and organisational contexts of these plants. However, the model developed in Chapter 5 operates without detailed reference to time, and is unable to incorporate the processes operating in the industrial environment at the plant level. It is hardly likely that the picture described in 1980 represents an equilibrium situation. Rather, it is the outcome of historical and evolutionary processes that are still operating. Thus, in an attempt to incorporate elements of change in the analysis, some employment variables have been constructed to measure rates of change. Similar, but more detailed time-series data gathered from case studies of individual plants of contrasting centrality are included in an attempt to demonstrate the concrete outcomes of these forces at the establishment level. Complementary use of these general and specific perspectives of plants should help to provide a more detailed understanding of processes operating inside the establishment.

In the analysis which follows, the argument is developed in three stages. In the first section, approaches used to investigate aspects of employment and labour dynamics in industrial geography and related disciplines are compared with those which have been adopted in a broadly termed 'business organisation' perspective. This part of the discussion serves to highlight the conceptual gap which exists between the business organisation and the plant. It also emphasises the need to examine labour dynamics in relation to factors inside the plant, as well as within the structural context of the business organisation and its environment. Key attributes of labour dynamics are then described, and are used as dependent variables in a stepwise multiple regression procedure in the second section. This set of analyses is designed to pick out the main factors of the environment and organisation which can be used as a basis for understanding patterns of labour use in different locations within the business organisation. Finally, case studies of several plants of varying degrees of centrality are used to elaborate and highlight some of the main effects of plant centrality on labour dynamics.

Approaches to the Analysis of Labour Dynamics

The dynamic attributes of employment and labour use are a central focus in industrial geography, since they represent a particularly important aspect of the tangible repercussions of industrial change. There are a number of ways of approaching these issues and the business organisation approach is perhaps the most recent to be developed in industrial geography, if the early work of the 'enterprise school' from McNee (1960) onwards is not included. It is the purpose of this section to highlight the potential of this business organisation approach for evaluating labour dynamics and to point out some of the more fundamental features of employment which need to be addressed. In order

Figure 6.1: Approaches to the Analysis of Labour Dynamics

LEVEL OF
DISSAGGREGATION

to facilitate discussion, a distinction is made between the levels at which labour has been examined by geographical and related disciplines, comparing these with the business organisation perspective adopted here (Figure 6.1).

Geographical and Related Approaches

As Figure 6.1 illustrates, it is possible to distinguish three broad levels at which research on labour has been tackled within industrial geography and related disciplines: labour has normally been examined with regions and/or industrial sectors as the main analytical units at an aggregate level; plant survey data has been a popular approach at a regional level because of the relative ease of accessibility to this type of information; and some studies have adopted an anthropological approach to evaluating the social processes operating at the establishment level.

Regional and sectoral approaches to labour dynamics have normally used data which is disaggregated from individual business organisations, either in the form of data bases derived from industrial sectors, or as plant level survey data made on a regional or sectoral basis. Regional and sectoral data have frequently been used in combination, both at a national scale and in the analysis of individual regions and sub-regions. Fothergill and Gudgin's (1982) work in the United Kingdom, for example, concentrates on the construction of 'regional employment accounts' and relies heavily on a series of shift-share analyses of four structural variables — mix of industries, urban structure, size structure of factories and regional policy — to explain how regional employment change differs from the national average. Fothergill and Gudgin's work can be criticised on the grounds of interpretation as well as technique: not only does it have a narrow explanatory base arising through the limited number of variables which are incorporated, but it also ascribes any regional variation in employment change simply to a different mix of these four factors.

Other work, such as that by Keeble (1976), demonstrates the usefulness of approaching employment from a national level. Keeble uses shift-share methods to disaggregate the structural elements which help explain regional variations in employment, but he points out that the technique is less suitable in the treatment of sub-regional variations. To help understand specific locational changes, Keeble is a proponent of the 'components of change' approach, which evaluates employment change as a product of six components of firm dynamics — births, deaths, expansions, contractions, emigrations and immigrations — at an establishment level. These data are available only in an aggregate form. Thus, the main application for studies using this type of data is in providing an explanatory backdrop to more detailed disaggregated approaches (e.g. Gillespie and Owen, 1981), concentrating as it does largely on changes in the magnitude of employment in regions and sectors.

To develop analysis at this level, Massey (1979) and Townsend (1982a) contend that it is useful and possible to assess other aspects of labour using sectoral data on a regional basis. Specifically, they assert occupational criteria can be determined. Also, Massey and Meegan (1979a) emphasised the necessity of distinguishing between net employment shifts caused by the combination of changes in output and labour productivity.

Some of these leads have been pursued in other structural work (Massey and Meegan, 1979b; 1982), and they differ from the approaches outlined above in the emphasis they give to the causes rather than simply employment effects of industrial reorganisation. Thus, Massey and Meegan's (1979b) work in Britain began by classifying elements of the electrical engineering sector according to whether they were restructuring due to overcapacity and high costs, to achieve scale advantages, or to maintain or increase market standing. The second stage of the approach required a move from these sub-sectors to case studies of company reorganisation. In the third stage, employment changes were divided into four types: absolute loss, locational loss, absolute gain and locational gain. The magnitude of these employment changes was then related back to sub-sectors on a regional basis in a fourth stage. Next, Massey and Meegan divided the employment effects on an occupational basis (e.g. ratio of administrative to other employees, skilled to semi-skilled ratio, male-female proportions) and, in the final stage, employment changes at an occupational level were tied down by location in development areas or non-development areas. What Massey and Meegan were able to do by attempting to divide aggregate data and then re-aggregate them in spatial terms, after accounting for the influence of individual firms, was to establish some of the fundamental causes of labour dynamics by focusing on the forms of production reorganisation (intensification, rationalisation and technical change) as they relate to the reasons for restructuring. This approach is based on the premise that 'production change and location change are integrally related. Analytically there is no simple movement from production change to its resulting spatial change' (Massey and Meegan, 1982, p. 144).

There is a problem, however, associated with Massey and Meegan's approach which arises in the transition from sectoral to organisational data. Indeed, as the authors note, '"sectoral restructuring" is. . .often difficult to pin down precisely in terms of related product-ranges' (Massey and Meegan, 1979b, p. 165). The problem is in defining sectors which are reasonably 'closed', that is, those which do not suffer from overlap by individual organisations into other sectors. As the electrical engineering sector in Birtain was defined as being relatively closed by Massey and Meegan, the overlap problem is not so evident as it might be in other sectors. But the problem still arises whether or not such a transition is practically and theoretically sound, especially in sectors other than electrical engineering. Is it, for instance, possible to separate the employment effects initiated by *sector*, from those begun by the *organisation*? This problem is particularly evident in the case of organisationally overlapping sectors, and it implies there is some limitation as to the conclusions which can be made on labour dynamics in organisations when the data are derived from sectors.

A similar criticism can be levied at the work of Walker and Storper (1980) and Storper (1982) in their analyses of job content characteristics in different industrial sectors in the United States. This work begins from the same starting point as Massey and Meegan, in that the production or labour process is viewed as a vital component of the spatial division of labour, so the two concepts must be integrated in a single theoretical context (for an elaboration, see Storper and Walker, 1983). The question arises, however, whether job content (such as skills required in the work process) can be analysed from sectoral data, divorced as this is from an organisational context. Certainly, there are some limitations to the job content model Storper and Walker propose, because changes in labour arising through alterations to production can only be inferred from aggregate data sources; and even then, the data are filtered through sectoral definitions. In short, the problem of organisations overlapping official definitions of sectors may mean that such models are applicable only in explaining sectoral and not organisational labour characteristics.

The second level of approach to labour dynamics in industrial geography involves the use of disaggregated plant data. In this approach, the plants investigated are normally drawn from sectoral data bases and they are, therefore, disembodied from the business organisation, even though ownership connections and other structural variables may be included, as is the case with McDermott's (1976) work on the electronics industry in Scotland. Even so, external linkages and not employment are the focus in many of these studies. A step further is taken by McDermott and Keeble (1978) who examined employment using sector breakdowns and inserted an organisational component. Analysis at this level requires survey work, and criteria such as employment size, the proportion of non-operatives, wage and salary levels and output per employee were compared between establishments by McDermott and Keeble. While analysis at a plant level and the insertion of an organisational context resolves, to a considerable degree, the reservations on employment criteria expressed for more aggregate approaches, two problems still remain. First, as Massey and Meegan (1982) point out, most plant studies of this type compare establishments from widely different functions, histories and organisational contexts, and the effects of these variations on labour dynamics have not yet been fully explored. Second, they do not examine the processes operating inside each plant.

Concern for this lack of appreciation of historical and situational detail has prompted the construction of individual plant 'anthropologies', using a variety of techniques, including external observation, participant observation and interviews. This is the third and most disaggregated level at which labour dynamics have been investigated. Overall, attention is given to identifying the processes operating inside the plant – which can only be inferred from other levels of analysis – but the studies differ widely in content and focus. For example, Coriot's (1980) study of assembly line organisation in Renault factories concentrates on the characteristics and organisation of production technology in use, establishing the implications of automation for labour organisation, whereas Ireland's (1982) satirical novel of work in an Australian petrochemical complex is designed to highlight social aspects. In between these two extremes are several case studies aimed at eliciting the socio-technical basis of production and industrial conflict, including insights into work in car plants (e.g. Beynon, 1975; Friedman and Meredeen, 1980) and chemical complexes (e.g. Nichols and Beynon, 1977; Gallie, 1978).

Abstractions from these case studies and the theoretical literature (e.g. Aglietta, 1979; Banaji, 1977; BLPG, 1977; Braverman, 1974; Burawoy, 1979; CSE, 1976; Edwards, 1979; Friedman, 1977a, 1977b; Gorz, 1976; Merkle, 1980; Palloix, 1976; Rose, 1975; Sohn-Rethel, 1976; and Zimbalist, 1979) place the labour process at the heart of plant employment dynamics, because of its role as a crucial mediator in industrial transformation and because it acts as the pivot of a constant struggle over production in which management obtains the 'consent' of workers to co-operate in the pursuit of profit (Burawoy, 1979). When management fails to re-exert control, there is a tendency to alter the form of the labour process in an attempt by managers to maintain the upper hand. Consequently, a continuity of change can be expected. The logic behind these transformations in the labour process is illustrated in Table 6.1.

Notwithstanding the valuable insights which these in-depth plant studies provide, a number of conceptual and practical weaknesses are inherent in the anthropological approach to labour dynamics. The transnational location of many major elements of production (Clegg, 1980), for instance, means that the corporation now has the upper hand and can segment production facilities both functionally and spatially, thereby dividing labour groups and isolating contractual negotiations (Clarke, 1981; Clark and Massey, 1982). Although it is possible for a labour process to develop with apparent continuity in individual plant locations, the structure of the multinational corporation

Table 6.1: Form and Transformation in the Labour Process

PHASE OF LABOUR PROCESS	CHARACTERISTICS	CONTRADICTION OF TRANSFORMATION
Manufacture	Simple co-operation of crafts. Division of labour.	Emergence of factory allowed centralised capital investment in machine form (fixed labour).
Machinofacture	Machines introduced. Gradual commodification of labour.	Factory-produced collectivised labour, highlighted need to manage.
Scientific Management	Empirical gathering of knowledge of production process. Dissociation of conception from execution in labour process. Labour appended to machine.	'Efficiency drives' to eliminate labour.
Fordism	Control over the pace of assembly by a semi-automatic assembly line. Institutionalisation of class struggle in collective bargaining.	Inability to divide work tasks evenly in time to co-ordinate with uniform machine pace; problems of human strain and motivation.
Neo-Fordism	Automatic production control. Recomposition of tasks in production.	Superficial worker autonomy produces rising demands for worker participation and democracy in the labour process.

Source: Clarke (1982, p. 111).

theoretically cuts across this sequence, so that different labour processes such as Fordism, scientific management and neo-Fordism, each performing a similar task, may possibly be found in different locations. Exactly how the organisational forces interact with other local factors to affect these processes is, as yet, uncertain. For example, labour process theory implies that the more advanced forms of work organisation are more labour efficient, because, in part, they have invested in capital-intensive methods of production. However, efficiency is affected by a number of criteria, not the least of which are the underlying social and cultural differences of individual workforces, and local wage and salary levels. These factors will undoubtedly affect the relative productivity of plants in internationally separated locations. It can be concluded that before it is possible to make generalisations on locationally separate labour processes within large business organisations, it is first necessary to investigate variations in these labour criteria between plants in order to establish causal relations, and as a prelude to more detailed studies.

The Business Organisation Approach

In contrast to these geographical studies, a business organisation approach to labour dynamics differs in the explicit attention given to the *corporation* as the primary unit of analysis and in the concern for organisational structure. Within this framework, it is possible to distinguish between studies of employment depending on their level of analysis of corporate operations, that is, whether they examine the total international structure, national or regional sub-structure, or establishment of the business organisation. Only a handful of studies have examined the international operations of business organisations as a totality, such as Teulings's (1981) work on the Dutch group, Philips, and Clarke's (1982) study of the changing spatial division of labour in ICI (see Chapter 4). These studies have three distinctive characteristics in the way they approach labour. First, their 'top-down' approach means they are able to refer to employment in aggregate terms, but they differ from other geographical approaches in that they are an aggregation of a single organisation. Second, the distribution of employment is examined either structurally, within product divisions, or spatially, within regional divisions. Third, despite a few anecdotal references to changes in plant employment, it is difficult to relate broad patterns of labour dynamics experienced at the corporate level to individual locations.

The majority of business organisation studies, however, have tended to approach employment issues at the level of the organisation's national or regional operations. The reasons for the relative abundance of these studies are numerous, but some include problems of data accessibility and comparability at an extra-national level, parochiality and, of course, pragmatism. Many examples adopt a synthetic approach, using sectoral data as background, and then progress to tease out the component accounted for by large business organisations. Massey and Meegan's (1979b) work (mentioned above) is applicable here to a certain extent, but the work of Dicken, Lloyd and others is perhaps more typical. Lloyd and Reeve's (1982) study of industrial restructuring in north west England is a good example of this level of business organisation approach. Lloyd and Reeve initially sketch the employment background of the region by sector and compare this with the United Kingdom as a whole, but then begin to flesh out the key corporate employers in a 'bottom-up' approach. The issues regarding labour this type of regional study raises stems from the parts of the business organisation the region possesses. They concentrate especially on the proportions of skilled and unskilled employment and wage rates (Dicken and Lloyd, 1979). This approach is significant in its ability to paint an overall picture of corporate employment, but the problem is that employment changes are more often than not only seen in aggregate terms and cannot be tied down to the plant level, except on occasions.

Townsend (1981, 1982a, 1982b) illustrates how it is possible to remedy this deficiency by collecting material on the employment effects of establishment closures, redundancies and wastage by business organisations, reported for the United Kingdom in sources such as the *Financial Times* and which can be tied down to individual locations. Undoubtedly, this is a useful method for monitoring employment at a national level, specifically because it acts to 'strip away the present anonymity of. . .corporations' impact on the employment geography of Britain' (Townsend, 1981, p. 37). What it does not enable is the formation of a clear overall picture of corporate labour dynamics other than redundancies, nor does it allow the magnitude of corporate employment to be assessed – only of specific changes.

A recent study of West German multinationals operating in the United Kingdom by Watts (1982) and a case study of the largest business organisation, Hoechst, begin to address the problem of determining the magnitude and locational distribution of corporate employment at an establishment level. In addition, Watts's study of Hoechst shows how it has been possible for the national workforce of the organisation to grow rapidly after 1969 with the acquisition of the Berger group of companies and their constituent plants. Also, in a study of the major global corporations involved in the Australian chemicals industry, Clarke (1984) has demonstrated how it is possible to piece together the pattern of business organisation employment in a national context, from knowledge about their ownership structures.

Very few studies have dug beneath these patterns to expose the processes operating on labour at an establishment level, from the business organisation perspective. A study at this scale has been conducted by Adrian and Evans (1984) on Borg-Warner's Albury Wodonga plant in New South Wales, in which a preliminary attempt was made to calculate the potential direct and multiplier effects on employment of the possible closure of the site. In contrast, Bassett (1984) has drawn out some of the varied employment fortunes of plants owned by large business organisations in the Bristol area, noting, for example, that the local Bristol ICI plant has escaped the worst effects of global restructuring because of its place in the more profitable chemicals and agricultural divisions of ICI.

A detailed study of three plants owned by Fiat in southern Italy helps to understand some of the broader implications for labour of processes operating inside the plant (Amin, 1984). Amin explains Fiat's decentralisation into southern Italy against a background of broader changes, including a response by the company to growing labour militancy and urban congestion around its Turin headquarters. The move has involved the relocation of a restructured and technically more flexible labour process, divided between three plants, to areas where labour is cheaper, less skilled and more tractable. The plants occupy a subordinate position within Fiat. Amin's work emphasises the importance of understanding the structure of production as an integral element of corporate organisation and labour dynamics.

Broader implications of the business organisation approach to labour dynamics at the establishment level are the effects of the position, task and status of the site in the organisation. In a review of the plant literature by Watts (1981), the tentative conclusion is formed that both job mix and job stability are related to the status and function of the establishment, but that three issues are central to testing this hypothesis: job mix, quality of employment and skill mix.

Job mix is likely to depend on the status of the plant – whether it is a branch plant or independently owned – because of the tendency for administrative, marketing and other boundary-spanning functions such as research and development, to be located in the more central and independent plants. Thus, status will affect the balance of administrative to shopfloor workers – the 'administrative ratio' (Hower and Lorsch, 1967; Thompson, 1967) or 'control' functions (Törnqvist, 1970). This is an important issue because, as Child (1973) has pointed out, the administrative ratio is a confused term in the organisations literature, more often than not being applied at the level of the business organisation, rather than at the level of the plant. The other issues identified by Watts – quality of employment and skill mix – may vary between plants of different status. In terms of job stability, Watts also established that there is circumstantial evidence to suggest externally owned plants may be more likely to close, hence making their workforces redundant or, alternatively, that employment change rates may differ between types of plants. These conclusions are reinforced by the organisational literature which asserts that the mixture and stability of jobs may relate to the routineness and certainty of work the establishment undertakes (Hage and Aiken, 1969; Tushman, 1979), as well as the technology employed and the characteristics of the environment (Freeman, 1973).

Overall, therefore, a business organisation approach to labour dynamics does allow structural characteristics to be related to internal labour markets (Friedman, 1977a; Doehringer and Piore, 1971) and also to a principal agent involved in labour market segmentation (Edwards, Reich and Gordon, 1975; Danson, 1982). Also, through simultaneous use of business organisation and plant data, it has proven possible to identify corporate dominated labour markets in spatial terms (e.g. Taylor and Thrift, 1983; Blackburn and Mann, 1979).

Labour Dynamics and Plant Centrality

The above comparison of the main levels of analysis of labour dynamics which have been used in industrial geography and the business organisation perspective has served two functions: to isolate the approach that this chapter might adopt; and to identify the issues which are central to understanding labour dynamics.

At the highest level of aggregation of regional and sectoral data, the various approaches which have been used highlight a principal weakness, which is the assumption that sectoral data somehow can be translated directly into conclusions on the labour dynamics of organisations, even though business organisations overlap these divisions to a considerable extent. As sectoral definitions effectively apply a filter to reality, these approaches are, therefore, more gainfully employed to construct the explanatory background for labour dynamics at national, regional and even sub-regional levels. At the second level of disaggregated plant data this same problem applies. Plant data are usually only assigned to sectors and they are, therefore, often devoid of organisational contexts. Unless the relationships between the plant and the organisation are detailed more fully, it can be suggested that conclusions on labour dynamics will be erroneous.

Some of these weaknesses are remedied by the business organisation approach, which attempts to maintain the structural integrity of corporate operations. Examination of the international operations of organisations as a whole helps to place national employment changes, where appropriate, in a corporate context, and also aids in overcoming national research myopia by using a top-down perspective. However, the sheer scale of organisations' operations often creates its own problems, so that labour dynamics have been treated in an aggregate way in order to handle the information. At the level of analysis of organisations' national operations, there has been a tendency either to approach employment by tracing the ownership of plants in a traditional bottom-up way, or to maintain the top-down perspective and fail to translate corporate aggregations to the establishment level. Even the analyses of corporate redundancy data only examine the negative aspect of labour dynamics, and where the magnitude of an organisation's employment has been able to be gauged, there are often difficulties in converting these figures to a plant level.

Divorced from these aggregate levels of analysis are the plant studies, which have a reciprocal set of problems. In the plant anthropologies, for example, the problem arises as to whether or not labour dynamics are determined by locational factors or the position of the plant within the business organisation. Establishment level studies adopting a business organisation approach have failed to come to grips with this same problem, apart from occasional generalisations regarding job mix and job stability, which are only tentatively related to the plant's organisational context and environmental characteristics.

In short, a conceptual gap exists between aspects of labour dynamics viewed at an establishment level and more aggregate levels of analysis. This is the case whether traditional geographical approaches or the business organisation approach is adopted. At this stage, then, the key issue lies in relating the changing patterns of employment inside the plant to wider organisational and environmental constraints, and, in this sense, the plant centrality framework developed in Chapter 5 offers a suitable means to approach this objective.

In addition to demonstrating the existence of this conceptual gap, the discussion in this section has also emphasised three main dimensions of labour dynamics that can be used as guidelines within the empirical analysis which follows. The first dimension is *job stability*, and critical features in this respect are the size of the establishment workforce and the rate at which employment is growing or declining in the plant. A second dimension is *job mix*, including the occupational make-up of the plant. It would be useful, for example, to address variation in the plant administrative ratio in the context of different domains and intra-organisational relations. *Production efficiency* is the third dimension which affects labour dynamics at the plant level. Criteria which are needed to compare production between plants are, for instance, the levels of total labour costs, and the capital intensity of production. Furthermore, each of these factors is likely to affect productivity levels and the rate at which the productivity of a plant is changing, so these are necessary summary measures of plant performance.

The Measurement of Labour Dynamics and Relationships with Plant Centrality

As a means of testing the possible effects of plant centrality in the structure of business organisations on labour dynamics, data were collected on an establishment basis for each of the 18 plants surveyed in the paints division of ICI in Chapter 5. These data were designed to elicit information on the aspects of job stability, job mix and production efficiency.

Two variables were used together to describe job stability. *Workforce size* was the first (simply the total number of people employed in the plant) — a figure including both shopfloor and administrative staff. The second variable, *rate of employment change*, represented the number of jobs lost or gained annually by the plant. Taking these two variables together indicates the magnitude as well as the rate of employment change. A single variable, the plant *administrative ratio*, was also constructed as a preliminary indication of the job mix in the establishment, measuring the administrative staff as a percentage of the total employment of the plant.

Additional variables were used to indicate attributes important to the efficiency of production. The first variable, *productivity*, was simply the average output per person, and this was also calculated annually as a variable measuring the *rate of change in productivity*. These first two indices are directly comparable between plants, but they say nothing about the levels of productivity. The efficiency of a plant is relative to the *capital intensity of production*, because it is perhaps to be expected that plants with the largest amounts of investment in equipment will have higher productivity levels, or output per person. A surrogate measure which was used to assess capital intensity was the ratio of the total energy costs needed to run the plant compared to that plant's total wage bill. The *total labour costs* are also important, as this variable indicates the overall significance of labour in monetary terms to production, rather than the cost per person, so these last two variables are complementary.

These seven labour variables measure the state of production in individual plants in 1980, as well as their change over time. To provide comparable results, energy and labour costs have been converted to United States dollars for the analyses.

The seven variables describing aspects of labour dynamics for each of the eighteen plants were used as dependent variables in a stepwise multiple regression procedure, and were regressed against the scores for each plant recorded on the seventeen independent variables or factors developed in Chapter 5 to describe the attributes of their environmental domains and intra-organisational relations. Stepwise multiple regression is an improved version of forward-selection regression in which independent variables can be added to, and removed from, the regression equation in order to improve the fit of the regression line, at each 'step' or stage in the analysis. A variable which is included in the equation at an early stage may become superfluous at a later stage because of overlap, or the inter-relationship with other variables in the equation. The resultant model for each dependent variable, therefore, includes a number of independent variables which account for a proportion of the variance in the data. The partial-F statistic stresses the significance of the individual variable at the final stage of the analysis and describes its strength and direction of influence. The R^2 value, or percentage of unique variance in the data which is explained by each variable, is a second criterion on which the equation is judged. Finally, the cumulative R^2 is the total variance which is explained at the final stage of the procedure by all variables. This figure is the sum of all the individual R^2 values.

The procedure used follows that described in detail by Draper and Smith (1966, pp. 171-2), King (1969, pp. 145-8) and Ferguson (1977, p. 36). The process of adding and removing variables to and from the individual equations followed a pre-set criterion closely, and continued until they had been met. Thus, any variable included in the equations must have exceeded the F statistic for inclusion which determined the confidence level based on the number of cases. At subsequent stages, each independent variable was re-examined and removed if it fell below the F value for withdrawal, which was pre-set in the same way. Although the final regression equation represents the 'best fit' using the available independent variables, it must be noted that those variables with a lower individual R^2 coefficient were not necessarily less significant, but merely accounted for variance which was as yet unexplained.

Stepwise multiple regression tests were conducted separately on the domain and intra-organisational factors developed in Chapter 5, to test for the effects of these attributes on the seven labour variables. The two sets of independent variables were also tested together to establish their relative importance. In the results of the analyses which are set out below, the variables which proved significant in the equations are listed and interpreted.

Workforce Size. Several attributes of the environmental domain of the plant proved to be significant determinants of the size of its workforce (Table 6.2). The first variable, scale of chemicals production (Factor IX, F=0.73885), was the strongest indicator and shows that the size of a plant's workforce correlates with the overall size of other competing establishments and the scale and international importance of the local chemicals sector. Bound up with this explanation is a second variable, international market structure (Factor IV, F=0.50254) which describes the orientation of trade to centrally planned markets and the proportion of internal trade in the domain. What is significant is that the positive association between a plant's workforce size and this variable indicates larger workforces are located in domains which are not related to trade with developed market economies. This feature might be interpreted as an effect of a large local market and trade with the more dynamic economies where the chemicals sector is growing, rather than with saturated developed markets. With regard to the paints industry, this interpretation is sensible as most plants tend to serve national rather than international markets, so that the size of a plant workforce is proportional to the market size of the domain. Workforce size is also related to currency stability (Factor II, F=0.45024) in a negative fashion. This relationship suggests that plants in domains characterised by fiscal instability have smaller workforces.

The intra-organisational relations of a plant also affected the size of the workforce. The scale of production (Factor IV, F=0.37745) of the plant was the most influential attribute and this probably reflects the location of the plant in a domain with a large market. Also important in terms of workforce size was plant status (Factor III, F=0.54929), suggesting that the large-scale plants with big workforces are also the older acquired establishments, rather than the newer branch plants. This conclusion is reinforced by the negative association of workforce size with plant position (Factor I, F=−0.41490), indicating that more people are employed in the older acquired plants which occupy a high position in the business organisation, probably because of the scale of their task, their inability to be substituted within the organisation and their central location in large markets.

Table 6.2: Stepwise Multiple Regression: Workforce Size

RANGE OF VARIABLES	SIGNIFICANT INDEPENDENT VARIABLES	FACTOR NUMBER	PARTIAL F COEFFICIENT	INDIVIDUAL R^2	CUMULATIVE R^2
(A) Domain	Scale of chemicals production	IX	0.73885	0.484	0.484
	International market structure	IV	0.50252	0.095	0.579
	Currency stability	II	-0.45024	0.085	0.664
(B) Intra-organisational Relations	Scale of production	IV	0.37745	0.304	0.304
	Plant status	III	0.54929	0.175	0.479
	Plant position	I	-0.41490	0.089	0.568
(A + B)	Scale of chemicals production	IX	0.69479	0.483	0.483
	Plant position	I	-0.49967	0.129	0.612

The inverse relationship which existed between the scale of chemicals production of the domain and plant position when domain and intra-organisational factors were tested together underlines these conclusions and shows the way in which the larger plants are located in the larger markets, thereby mutually reinforcing one another. These are the ideal conditions for large plant workforces.

Rate of Employment Change. The rate of employment change inside individual plants displayed a strong negative correlation with the scale of chemicals production (Factor IX, F=−0.88278) of the domain of location, and was positively associated with local currency stability (Factor II, F=0.42990) (Table 6.3). These findings suggest that the plants with higher employment growth rates are those which operate in domains where the sector is small but growing, with the implication that negative rates of employment change take place in domains in which the industry is already well established and possibly saturated, particularly in the developed country economies.

In terms of the effects of intra-organisational relations, the rate of employment change experienced in a plant was found to decrease with both plant status (Factor III, F=−0.61429) and scale of production (Factor IV, F=−0.47830). Practically, this means that the high status plants − those which have been acquired, are older and produce paints on a larger scale − are precisely those establishments which are shedding jobs. However, there is also the possibility that this feature simply represents the restricted scope for employment growth in large plants relative to small plants. Reasons for this tendency might be the capital intensity and economies of scale which are typical of large plants, but this theme is discussed further below. Scale of chemicals production (Factor IX, F=−0.89279) in the domain and length of membership (Factor II, F=0.51695) proved to be the most influential factors when the two sets of attributes were tested together. The negative relationship between these two factors appears to show that employment grows more rapidly in plants which have been a part of the business organisation longer, and which occupy a central position in the ownership hierarchy. Where the chemical sector of the domain is large, this tends to increase the rate of employment decline, possibly because of stiff competition between firms and an attempt to keep labour costs down in production.

Administrative Ratio. The proportion of a plant's total workforce involved in functions other than production − the support, boundary-

Table 6.3: Stepwise Multiple Regression: Rate of Employment Change

RANGE OF VARIABLES	SIGNIFICANT INDEPENDENT VARIABLES	FACTOR NUMBER	PARTIAL F COEFFICIENT	INDIVIDUAL R^2	CUMULATIVE R^2
(A) Domain	Scale of chemicals production	IX	-0.88278	0.730	0.730
	Currency stability	II	0.42990	0.050	0.780
(B) Intra-organisational Relations	Plant status	III	0.61429	0.390	0.390
	Scale of production	IV	-0.47830	0.139	0.529
(A + B)	Scale of chemicals production	IX	-0.89279	0.730	0.730
	Length of membership	II	0.51695	0.072	0.802

spanning or broadly termed administrative personnel — displayed little relationship with domain characteristics (Table 6.4). Chemicals sector growth (Factor X, F=0.37913) was the only attribute of any significance, explaining 14.3 per cent of the variance in the data. One possible explanation for an increase in the administrative ratio in these circumstances might be the need for the plant to monitor the complex and changing business environment in order to remain competitive. The intra-organisational attributes provided a broader explanation of the reasons for changes in the administrative ratio. Plant status (Factor III, F=0.66505) was an important determinant, with the older acquired plants like Slough and Stowmarket in the United Kingdom, Clayton, Cabarita and Port Adelaide in Australia, and Hilden in West Germany having the largest proportions of administrative jobs. These are the plants most central to the organisation overall, located in the largest markets, so the reason for this pattern can be explained in historical terms. Before they were acquired by ICI, these plants were already established centres of administration and production for their previous parent organisations, and the long period since they were acquired has merely served to entrench this administrative role. For example, both Slough and Clayton are headquarters for their own regional paints divisions, a vital reason for their large component of administrative employment compared to other plants.

The negative correlation of the administrative ratio with length of membership (Factor II, F=−0.37978) serves to underline this conclusion, with the newer, generally branch plants having a smaller proportion of administrative personnel. In addition, plants which have a complex production technology (Factor VI, F=−0.61019) have more administrative staff, perhaps either because of their labour saving propensity, which causes the proportion of administrative jobs to grow, or because of the need to control and buffer a much more complex production process. When the domain and intra-organisational attributes were used in a combined analysis, the two most significant factors were plant status (Factor III, F=0.70616) and production technology (Factor VI, F=−0.55687), and coupled with the trade vulnerability (Factor III, F=0.45825) of the domain, helped to reinforce the need for a high administrative ratio when the operational environment is uncertain.

Productivity. The productivity levels (output per person) varied considerably among the 18 plants, and, in terms of attributes of their domains, correlated negatively with foreign investment (Factor V,

Table 6.4: Stepwise Multiple Regression: Administrative Ratio

RANGE OF VARIABLES	SIGNIFICANT INDEPENDENT VARIABLES	FACTOR NUMBER	PARTIAL F COEFFICIENT	INDIVIDUAL R^2	CUMULATIVE R^2
(A) Domain	Chemicals sector growth	X	0.37913	0.143	0.143
(B) Intra-organisational Relations	Plant status	III	0.66505	0.192	0.192
	Production technology	VI	-0.61019	0.310	0.502
	Length of membership	II	-0.37978	0.072	0.574
(A + B)	Plant status	III	0.70616	0.192	0.192
	Production technology	VI	-0.55687	0.310	0.502
	Trade vulnerability	III	0.45825	0.104	0.606

F=–0.58604) and positively with the index of wealth and political democracy (Factor I, F=0.54344) (Table 6.5). The negative relationship with foreign investment may simply reflect the patterns of net investment in peripheral country domains, where there is less competitiveness to bolster productivity levels. The positive relationship with the second variable, the index of wealth and political democracy, indicates the capacity of the domain (or market) for paints. Hence, increases in wealth apparently correlate with increases in productivity.

Three attributes of a plant's intra-organisational relations accounted for over 50 per cent of the variance in productivity among the surveyed plants. First, length of membership (Factor II, F=0.57325) was a reasonable indicator of productivity levels, suggesting that the older plants may have higher levels of productivity either, for example, because they have had time to smooth out production problems or, more likely, because their past record of performance, *ipso facto*, has enabled them to remain as part of the business organisation longer. The plants with consistently low productivity levels are precisely those which are likely to be closed or sold off. Second, production technology (Factor VI, F=–0.50727) and third, specialisation (Factor V, F=0.45154) were correlated negatively with productivity. The reason for this relationship is that some plants have a number of production methods on the one site, in order to cope with a more diverse product range and also to allow for fluctuations in demand. Thus, they have low productivity levels, as do plants which produce a range of products with a weighting to the specialised industrial end of the paints range. Alternatively, the bigger plants specialise largely in producing paints for the domestic end of the market where there is a relatively high demand. Consequently, these plants are by definition mass producers, so their productivity levels are much higher.

When the domain and intra-organisational attributes were used in a combined analysis of productivity levels, factors such as foreign investment, specialisation and length of membership were again prominent. There was, however, a negative relationship between productivity and chemicals sector growth (Factor X, F=–0.66179) and chemical export dynamics (Factor XI, F=–0.46748). The structure of these two factors would seem to suggest that the plants with lower productivity levels are located in domains where the domestic chemicals sector is growing only slowly, if at all, and they have a limited share of the international market.

Two additional intra-organisational attributes shown to be important in the combined analysis were plant position (Factor I, F=0.74916)

Table 6.5: Stepwise Multiple Regression: Productivity

RANGE OF VARIABLES	SIGNIFICANT INDEPENDENT VARIABLES	FACTOR NUMBER	PARTIAL F COEFFICIENT	INDIVIDUAL R^2	CUMULATIVE R^2
(A) Domain	Foreign investment	V	-0.58604	0.214	0.214
	Index of wealth and political democracy	I	0.54344	0.232	0.446
(B) Intra-organisational Relations	Length of membership	II	0.57325	0.199	0.199
	Production technology	VI	-0.50727	0.177	0.376
	Specialisation	V	-0.45154	0.127	0.503
(A + B)	Foreign investment	V	-0.75320	0.215	0.215
	Plant position	I	0.74916	0.308	0.523
	Scale of production	IV	0.78585	0.105	0.628
	Specialisation	V	-0.59028	0.079	0.707
	Length of membership	II	0.77168	0.073	0.780
	Chemicals sector growth	X	0.66179	0.075	0.855
	Chemical export dynamics	XI	-0.46748	0.031	0.886

and scale of production (Factor IV, F=0.78585). This suggests two interesting variants. First, plants with more peripheral positions within the organisation have high productivity levels, probably because of their situation as part of a small network of branch plants, with the threat of substitution by other plants from within the subsidiary of the business organisation which owns them. Second, the largest of the central plants also have high productivity levels because of their scale of production which is energy and technology intensive. This similarity of productivity levels at the extremes of plant centrality and peripherality is, for quite different reasons, the mainstay of the high productivity of central plants relying on mass production advantages, and peripheral plants performing either by virtue of their tentative peripheral position within the organisation or, perhaps, because of the recent age of their capital stock, compared to central plants. It is interesting to note that the combination of domain and organisational variables accounted for over 88 per cent of the variance in the data, making this a powerful model of productivity.

Rate of Change in Productivity. Compared to productivity levels, the rate at which productivity is changing could only be explained by one variable, length of membership (Factor II, F=−0.49303) of the plant in the business organisation (Table 6.6). Nevertheless, over 24 per cent of the variance in the data was explained by this variable. The limited evidence available, therefore, suggests that the *growth rate* of productivity is lower in the older, more central plants. This situation may be due either to aging equipment or the difficulty of maintaining high growth in productivity simply through capital investment. Overall, an asymptotic relationship (S-shaped curve) might be suggested, with the rate of productivity increasing as the plant becomes more established in the organisation and then tailing off as production reaches a peak, although this sequence must remain as conjecture.

Capital Intensity of Production. As with the previous dependent variable, only one factor emerged to explain variations in the capital intensity of production, foreign investment (Factor V, F=−0.42743) in the domain of the plant (Table 6.7). On the one hand, this negative relationship indicates there may be some association between the capital intensity of production and the level of external control of the economy, which may explain why productivity growth rates can be higher in these locations. In peripheral country domains, production tends to be more labour, rather than capital, intensive. On the

Table 6.6: Stepwise Multiple Regression: Rate of Change in Productivity

RANGE OF VARIABLES	SIGNIFICANT INDEPENDENT VARIABLES	FACTOR NUMBER	PARTIAL F COEFFICIENT	INDIVIDUAL R^2	CUMULATIVE R^2
(A) Domain	-	-	-	-	-
(B) Intra-organisational Relations	Length of membership	II	-0.49303	0.243	0.243
(A + B)	Length of membership	II	-0.49303	0.243	0.243

Table 6.7: Stepwise Multiple Regression: Capital Intensity of Production

RANGE OF VARIABLES	SIGNIFICANT INDEPENDENT VARIABLES	FACTOR NUMBER	PARTIAL F COEFFICIENT	INDIVIDUAL R^2	CUMULATIVE R^2
(A) Domain	Foreign investment	V	-0.42743	0.183	0.183
(B) Intra-organisational Relations	-	-	-	-	-
(A + B)	Foreign investment	V	-0.42743	0.183	0.183

other hand, the level of foreign investment may simply reflect the gross level of overseas involvement in an economy, thereby correlating with the degree of wealth in the domain (total national GNP). Despite these speculations, it is difficult to extrapolate conclusions from this limited finding, especially without referring to the labour costs involved in each location, which is the last attribute of labour to be examined.

Total Labour Costs. The total labour costs of a plant are undoubtedly influential in terms of productivity and the capital intensity of production. There was a positive association between total labour costs and three domain attributes — scale of chemicals production (Factor IX, F=0.92302), chemical export dynamics (Factor XI, F=0.59658) and international market structure (Factor IV, F=0.58688) — and this combination of variables explained 90 per cent of the variance in the data (Table 6.8). The results emphasise the importance of the size of the domestic chemicals market and the significance of the overall scale of the chemicals sector in determining a plant's total labour costs. Also, the export dynamics of the chemicals sector are influential, as these domains are where the large plants with the large workforces are located. It can be contended, therefore, that total labour costs in these plants are high because they are located in markets with an established chemicals sector, geared up to the international economy.

Three attributes of intra-organisational relations were also useful in explaining total labour costs. Apart from the obvious relationship with scale of production (Factor IV, F=0.91835), total labour costs were affected by plant status (Factor III, F=0.58982) and production technology (Factor VI, F=0.38516), indicating the older acquired (high status) plants with larger product ranges were also those with the least technological complexity. These combined factors emphasise such plants are those with the most up-to-date equipment producing a defined range of products on a large scale, so that new technology seems to have been used to offset high total labour costs in these locations. However, because labour costs per person were not measured and compared directly between the plants, it cannot be stated that high cost labour was the principal cause of the observed tendency for central establishments to shed greater amounts of their workforce over time. Instead, it is only possible to infer that the more advanced rate of decline of the workforce in central plants is due to higher labour costs and the fact that the apparent investment in new technology — increasing capital intensity of production — in these locations has been made necessary for a plant to retain its central status in a

Table 6.8: Stepwise Multiple Regression: Total Labour Costs

RANGE OF VARIABLES	SIGNIFICANT INDEPENDENT VARIABLES	FACTOR NUMBER	PARTIAL F COEFFICIENT	INDIVIDUAL R^2	CUMULATIVE R^2
(A) Domain	Scale of chemicals production	IX	0.92302	0.761	0.761
	Chemical export dynamics	XI	0.59658	0.086	0.847
	International market structure	IV	0.58688	0.053	0.900
(B) Intra-organisational Relations	Scale of production	IV	0.91835	0.768	0.768
	Plant status	III	0.58982	0.093	0.861
	Production technology	VI	0.38516	0.021	0.882
(A + B)	Scale of production	IV	0.79426	0.768	0.768
	Scale of chemicals production	IX	0.78746	0.144	0.912

competitive environment. Such a conclusion could explain why there was an observed interaction between domain and organisation forces, particularly with regard to a plant's total labour costs. In the combined analysis, only two variables accounted for 91 per cent of the variance, scale of production (Factor IV, F=0.79426) of the plant and the scale of chemicals production (Factor IX, F=0.78746) of the domain. This is a prime example of the circular relationship between the plant and the domain which was underlined in Chapter 5.

Notwithstanding the complexity of the relationships between labour dynamics and attributes of a plant's domain and intra-organisational relations which have been demonstrated in this analysis, it is possible to form some general conclusions as to the effects of plant centrality on labour dynamics. As has been emphasised, it is rarely possible to reach the conclusion that an individual aspect of labour is determined by the position of the plant in the structure of the business organisation or, alternatively, by its environment. In fact, based on these results, it is more common for most aspects of labour dynamics to be affected by a combination of these forces. For instance, the size of the workforce, the rate of employment change, productivity and total labour costs incurred by a plant seem to be related to a mixture of environmental and organisational relations.

In some cases, however, it is possible to discern the dominant effect of either the domain or intra-organisational forces, which impinge on a plant and determine some of its labour characteristics. Thus, although the evidence was limited, the capital intensity of production seemed to be influenced more by the environmental domain than by factors operating within the business organisation. This feature is probably contingent on how the corporation evaluates the plant's operational environment, technologies being introduced which 'match' the surrounding competition, rather than being the most developed techniques which are available to the organisation. If this is the case, then it represents one concrete example of the effect of business organisations cutting across national boundaries and questions the notion of the international transfer of technology, a point also made by Newfarmer and Topik (1982).

Attributes of labour which were determined by organisational rather than domain forces were the administrative ratio and the rate of change of productivity of individual plants. In the case of both these variables, the status and length of membership of the plant as part of the business organisation were influential, suggesting that the administrative function of selected plants has been acquired and reinforced over time. A possible explanation for the falling rate of productivity in these plants was their advanced stage of development and their level of technological sophistication, which makes it difficult to make further improvements in the efficiency of production. In the newer, more peripheral plants, the rate of increase of productivity is likely to be greater because large gains can be made by simple changes in manpower organisation and the types of technology used in production.

An appreciation of the historical development of the business organisation and the position the individual plant occupies within this framework are necessary to make sense of a complex picture. The oldest and most established plants in ICI's paints division are generally located in central domains and, in point of fact, they reflect the broad pattern of temporal and geographical development by ICI, especially in Britain, West Germany and Australia. The British plants, at Slough and Stowmarket, and their Australian counterparts at Cabarita and Clayton, have, therefore, maintained their organisational centrality by virtue of their location in markets valuable to ICI. They have increased their importance simply by surviving and acquiring more power, be it in terms of their contribution to production or their administrative role, for example. Built into the structure of business organisations, therefore, is an *historical inertia* which is manifest as a network of power relations and which, it appears, has a direct bearing on the performance and operational characteristics of individual plants. Consequently, the newer branch plants are admitted or taken into the business organisation on an unequal footing from the start, and it is unlikely that they will be able to overcome the power wielded by the plants already well entrenched in the organisation. This conclusion is borne out by examining some of these generalisations on the effects of plant centrality on labour dynamics in detailed studies of individual plants.

Case Studies of Plant Labour Dynamics

The domain and organisational characteristics which affect various aspects of labour dynamics in the plants operating in the paints division of ICI have been described in detail. However, there are two constraints inherent in that exercise — the specification and elaboration of the current pattern of labour use, and the mode of variable-by-variable analysis which was adopted. Some insights into the way in which various components of plant centrality affect labour dynamics have been gleaned, suggesting the composition, direction and approximate strength of these causal relations. This assessment of labour dynamics can be extended through a series of case studies of plants which vary in their degree of centrality, operating in contrasting positions within the business organisation and in different operational environments.

Four plants were selected from those included in the survey, by means of the centrality indices developed in Chapter 5 and supplemented by additional information. The British plant at Slough was chosen as an example of one of the most central plants. This plant was established in the early 1900s by Naylor Brothers before being taken over by ICI. Slough's level of production, 46.7 million litres in 1980, is exceeded only by the plant at Stowmarket. Slough is also the headquarters and centre for the research and development operations of ICI's British paints division, employing 766 workers in 1980. Jurong in Singapore was selected as an extreme contrast and as an example of a peripheral plant. A branch plant opened in 1968, Jurong was intended to supplement ICI's main paint operation in Malaysia and is, in fact, one of three plants producing paints owned by ICI Paints of Malaysia (the third is in Thailand). In scale of output and in terms of employment, Jurong is many times smaller than Slough and in 1980 it produced only 3.1 million litres of paint and had a total of 220 workers. Between these two extreme cases, two Australian plants were chosen for examination as examples of 'semi-peripheral' establishments, to use Wallerstein's (1979) terminology. The older of these plants, Cabarita, is located in Sydney and was opened originally in 1920 by British Australian Lead Manufacturers before being acquired by ICI Australia-New Zealand in 1947. In 1980 the plant produced 14.5 million litres of paint with a workforce of 669 employees. A second plant at Clayton in Victoria was also selected, not only because of its more recent history — Clayton was established as a branch plant in 1957 by ICI — but also because it is now the headquarters for ICI Australia's subsidiary, Dulux Australia, and a centre for research and development initiatives. In 1980, Clayton had a workforce of 524 and a comparable output to Cabarita of 15.1 million litres.

As a means of comparing labour dynamics in the four plants, time-series data comparable with the criteria examined in the previous section were compiled for the period 1973 to 1980 (1973 was the earliest date for which data were available for all four plants). The data included changes over time in the output and employment levels, administrative ratios and several indices constructed to describe the structure of production such as capital intensity, productivity, labour costs per litre and the total energy and labour costs to run the plants. These data are set out in Figures 6.2 to 6.4. (Where appropriate, regression lines have been fitted to the data to illustrate the rate of change in each of these attributes and the slope coefficient from the regression equations (termed b) are used in the argument for evaluation purposes. A large negative coefficient represents a rapid decline in the attribute under examination, a high positive coefficient indicates a substantial growth.)

Figure 6.2 illustrates the magnitude of output and employment differences, which is a primary characteristic separating central and peripheral plants. The Jurong plant in Singapore, for example, produced only approximately 8 per cent of the output of ICI's Slough plant in the United Kingdom in 1980, and the two Australian plants both produced about 33 per cent of Slough's output. The rate at which output has changed in each location is less significant, and bears little relationship with plant centrality. Output increased less markedly and was cyclical in Slough over the period (b=0.21), whereas in the Australian (Cabarita b=0.26; Clayton b=0.27) and Singaporean (b=0.14) plants the trends were less discernible. These differences are likely to be the result of stiff market competition or recession in central domains, a conclusion which is borne out in the effect on plant employment levels. The rate of employment decline seems to have been marked in the central plants such as Slough where about 170 jobs were shed in the seven-year period (b=−24.44), representing 18 per cent of the 1973 workforce. The smallest changes seem to occur in the peripheral plants like Jurong where there has been a slight increase in the workforce size (b=2.67). Changes of this kind may indicate ongoing pressures to eliminate direct labour power from production in more central plants and domains because of the competitive nature of the operating environment.

What is particularly significant about these changes in employment levels is the apparent decline in the administrative staff as reflected in the administrative ratio (Figure 6.2). Unfortunately, data of this kind were not available over time for Clayton and Cabarita. Nevertheless, two features do stand out quite clearly when Slough and Jurong are compared. First, the number of administrative jobs grew rapidly in Jurong and declined markedly at Slough. Second, the administrative jobs represented 30 per cent of the *total* jobs lost at

Figure 6.2:
Plant Case Studies:
Output and
Employment
Structure

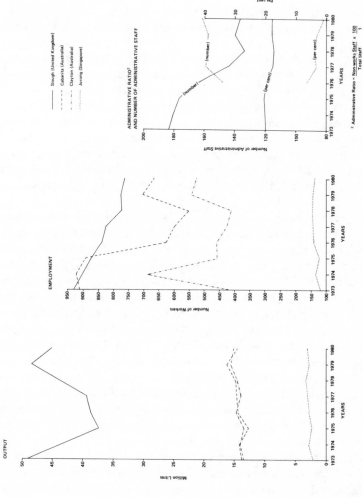

Source: Plant survey.

Slough and almost all the jobs generated at Jurong. The administrative ratio has, therefore, decreased in both locations, but from the data available, it is not possible to establish why these changes have taken place. It can be suggested, however, that the increase in administrative jobs at Jurong is associated with the plant's stage of development and its attempt to penetrate the regional market, in which case sales and marketing personnel are of primary importance. The fall in the administrative ratio at Slough is only relatively slight, indicating that the administrative jobs are also being affected by rationalisation as well as those involved in production. By comparison, at Jurong the proportion of administrative jobs is undergoing a decline relative to the production workforce — even though total administrative staff are increasing — because of an increase in the latter compared to the former. The wide discrepancy in the administrative ratio between central plants such as Slough (18 per cent) and peripheral plants like Jurong (1-2 per cent) may be due to a combination of differences in the administrative staff in central locations to monitor the more dynamic business environment.

In order to understand the dynamic aspects of employment in more detail it is necessary to address the nature of production. Figure 6.3 illustrates changes in the capital intensity of production and productivity levels over the period for the four plants. The feature which stands out from these illustrations is the wide differences in both the levels and growth rates in productivity between the plants. Productivity levels were, for example, over 60 per cent higher in Slough in 1980 than those of Jurong, and approximately 58 per cent higher than in the Australian plants. Furthermore, productivity was growing at a faster rate in Slough (b=1.84) compared to Cabarita (b=1.44) and Clayton (b=0.48) in Australia, and Jurong (b=0.67) in Singapore. One major reason for these patterns is undoubtedly the dramatic differences in the capital intensity of production. The capital intensity ratio has been calculated to take into account the real ratio of energy costs relative to labour costs. Thus, it is interesting to note that the ratio was approximately 27 per cent at Slough in 1980, 13 per cent in the Australian plants and only 4 per cent in Jurong. Superimposed on these scale differences are wide variations in the rate of increase of the capital intensity of production, which is much higher in central plants (e.g. Slough, b=1.27) compared to peripheral plants (e.g. Jurong, b=0.05).

Underlying the differences in the performance of central and peripheral plants which these figures demonstrate, there is also a fundamental

Figure 6.3: Plant Case Studies: Capital Intensity and Productivity

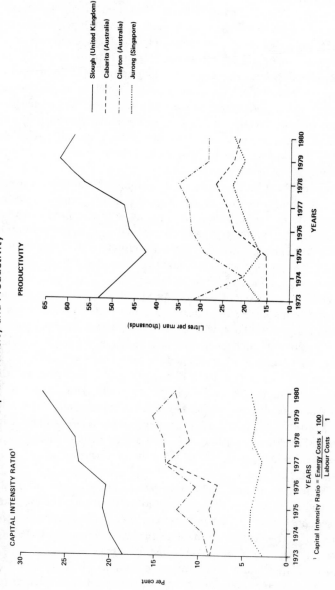

¹ Capital Intensity Ratio = Energy Costs × 100
                            ───────── ───
                            Labour Costs   1

Source: Plant survey.

disparity in the cost structure of production (Figure 6.4). The total labour costs again show up the variation between plants and the dramatic growth rate of labour costs in the United Kingdom as indicated by Slough (b=0.96) compared to Clayton (b=0.12) and Jurong (b=0.09), for example. A similar picture emerges when the total energy costs of the plants are examined, total energy costs growing rapidly in Slough (b=0.31) compared to Jurong (b=0.01). But these discrepancies in costs are not merely the result of the differences in output of central and peripheral plants. Rather, it is important to take into account the rate at which these costs are growing, which is a function of rising energy and labour costs to the plant, and inflationary tendencies in the domain in general, as well as those enabling the growth of output. Once again, this feature is a clear example of the interaction between the domain and organisational factors which are hard to separate.

The labour cost component of a single unit of output is a useful measure for comparing production in these plants (Figure 6.4). At the beginning of the period, labour costs per litre of paint produced were 17 cents (US) in Jurong, compared to 10 cents in Cabarita and 8 cents in Slough. These measures reflect the labour-intensive nature of production in peripheral plants compared to central plants, but the figures also show how the rate of labour costs per unit of output are rising in the two extreme cases of Jurong and Slough but for possibly quite different reasons. In the two Australian plants these costs are growing at a modest rate (b=0.61), whereas in Jurong labour costs per litre of paint (b=1.96) are approaching the levels they are in Slough (b=2.02). On the other hand, it is reasonable to suggest that the growth rate in Jurong is due to a combination of the rising cost of labour and the growth in the number of workers employed in the plant. On the other hand, the rapid decline in the workforce at Slough means that the marked growth in labour costs per litre can only be accounted for by a combination of rising labour costs per se and perhaps inefficiencies in the use of manpower, which belie the performance of the plant based on output alone.

These four plant case studies illustrate in more detail some of the trends and amplify some of the conclusions gained from the preceding cross-sectional survey of labour characteristics in the first part of this chapter. In particular, the results show the effects of a plant's historical inertia on the inter-plant power network in several ways. To begin with, the centrality of a plant gives an indication of its standing within the business organisation, but it may mask other factors such as the

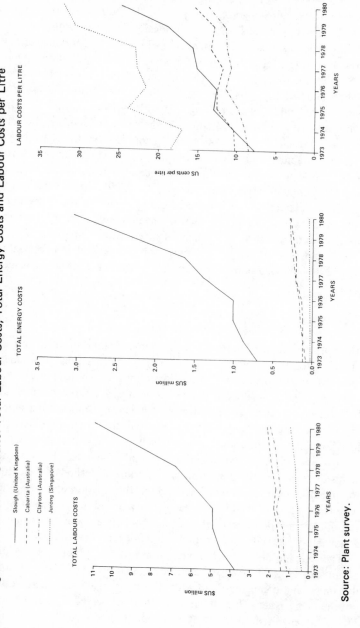

Figure 6.4: Plant Case Studies: Total Labour Costs, Total Energy Costs and Labour Costs per Litre

Slough (United Kingdom)

Cabarita (Australia)

Clayton (Australia)

Jurong (Singapore)

Source: Plant survey.

relative efficiency of production. As an example, the significant growth in labour costs at Slough may, in part, be due to the lack of competition inside the business organisation locally. In wider terms, this conclusion suggests that central plants might suffer from complacency, or at least a lack of competition from within the organisation, despite the apparent willingness of the organisation to invest in these locations. Some of the causal factors for this characteristic are likely to relate to organisational structure, particularly the existence of other plants owned by the organisation in the local domain. To illustrate this point, a characteristic of central plants like Slough is their lack of substitutability and the scale of their tasks. Thus, the two British plants (Slough and Stowmarket) had a combined output in 1980 of over 100 million litres, compared to 48 million litres for the five Australian plants, and 15 million litres in the case of the three South East Asian plants. Certainly, this is an attribute of plant centrality in organisational structure which deserves closer attention in the future, but it must suffice to know for the present that centrality does have significant implications for labour dynamics inside the plant.

Conclusions

The purpose of this chapter has been to investigate some of the effects of plant centrality within the nexus of organisation-environment relations at the plant level. The illustrations which have been used exemplify the complexity of these relationships and show that it would be erroneous to force an explanation of labour dynamics into a simple model. In fact, the argument has stressed the interaction between locational and organisational factors which must be taken into account, where appropriate, in explaining patterns of labour use. Put in wider terms of reference, the discussion has described a method of evaluating the organisational forces which are behind the creation of a new international division of labour, and has thereby served to describe some of the micro-scale processes sketched in a preliminary way in Chapter 4 at a macro-scale, and pinned within a definite analytical framework.

The chapter began by outlining some of the advantages and disadvantages of traditional geographical approaches to evaluating labour dynamics, and compared them with a business organisation perspective on the same issue. This theoretical argument served four functions. First, it recognised the lack of attention to specifying plant labour dynamics within organisational structure. Second, it highlighted the extent to which variations in plant function, history and organisational characteristics have been either underplayed or ignored. Third, it was hypothesised that the structure of multinational corporations would cut across the development sequence of individual plants, thereby raising questions regarding the comparative economies of production in contrasting locations. Finally, three main dimensions and operational variables of labour dynamics were isolated: job stability (workforce size; rate of employment change); job mix (administrative ratio); and production efficiency (productivity; rate of change in productivity; capital intensity of production; and total labour costs).

These criteria were used as dependent variables in a series of step-wise multiple regression analyses, so as to highlight relationships with the domain and intra-organisational characteristics of the plants belonging to the paints division of ICI. The size of a plant's workforce displayed a strong relationship with the size of the market and competing establishments of the domain in which it was located, but it was also shown to increase with the age of the establishment. However, the rate of a plant's employment change was negative or growing only slowly in central country domains, whereas the rate of employment growth was higher in developing country domains. This feature corresponded with a greater rate of job losses and shows that jobs are much more unstable in central than peripheral establishments. Coupled with these trends was a tendency for the mix of jobs to change with the dynamics of the chemical industry of a domain. Thus, the increase in the administrative ratio of a plant with domain centrality was attributed to the need to monitor increasingly complex business environments, as well as the size of the plant itself, so that peripheral branch plants had comparatively few support staff.

Productivity was influenced by the size of the domain's market, as indicated by the level of wealth, but the negative relationship with foreign investment was tentatively explained as indicative of a lack of competitiveness in peripheral domains which is unlikely to bolster productivity levels. Productivity was also higher in older establishments, either because production was more efficient, or because the less efficient (more peripheral) plants had been sold off or closed. The degree of specialisation was also important in this respect, with the central plants being, in the main, the mass producers and the more productive. Despite this feature, the rate of change of productivity was found to be much lower in central establishments, and it was suggested that these rates may tail off in the older plants because of the aging of equipment. However, the capital intensity of production was much higher, which was explained as an attempt to offset high costs of labour and falling productivity in these locations.

Results from the analyses show that in some cases it is possible to discern the dominant influence of characteristics of the environmental domain on aspects of plant labour dynamics, as was the case with the capital intensity of production. One possible reason for this was given as the domain providing the base-level for production, so that the type of technology which is introduced is contingent on the weight the corporation gives to the location, and on its perception of the technological environment. In other cases, the dominant influence of a plant's intra-organisational relations could be seen. The administrative ratio, for example, was related strongly to the status of the plant — being higher in acquired than branch plants, and in the plants with a longer standing in the organisation. Productivity changes were also influenced more by intra-organisational relations, with falling productivity growth rates in central plants and growing productivity growth rates in peripheral plants being explained by differences in the technical nature of production: productivity improvements being gained relatively easily in the later compared to the former, because of the wider scope for improvement through manpower organisation and technical means.

The mutual reinforcement of domain and intra-organisational characteristics was, however, clearly evident for the majority of the labour variables. It was obvious, for instance, that there was a direct interaction between establishments and market size in the case of the size of a plant's workforce, with large plants being located in large markets, small plants in small markets, and so on. Paradoxically, however, this same relationship has also affected the rate of employment change in a plant, which results in lower and negative growth rates in central establishments because of the need to keep labour costs down in order to remain competitive. Productivity was found to be similarly affected, being greater in the extreme central and peripheral plants for two different reasons: capital investment offsetting rising labour costs in central establishments; and the threat of substitution from within the organisation in the periphery acting to keep productivity growth rates up.

Overall, therefore, the results demonstrated the implications of plant centrality for labour dynamics, and emphasised the growing entrenchment of these inequalities, a type of *historical inertia* in the sub-unit structure of business organisations. A significant upshot of this conclusion is that plants which join the organisation at different points in time enter the structure on an unequal footing from established plants. Indeed, this important feature was illustrated by case studies of individual plants of contrasting centrality and histories in the United Kingdom, Australia and Singapore. These examples underlined the more fundamental changes in production in central compared to peripheral plants, especially their higher levels of output, larger workforces, greater proportion of administrative staff, higher levels of productivity and a more rapid growth in the capital intensity of production. There is also a growing inequality in production costs between these two extremes, with energy and labour prices growing more rapidly at the centre of the organisation than at the periphery. The apparent lack of internal competition in the organisation for central plants is reflected in their gross inefficiencies in manpower utilisation.

The analysis has shown, therefore, that patterns of labour use can be profitably explained within a business organisation's framework, but several caveats must of course apply to these conclusions, because of the narrow empirical focus. These results cannot be taken as indicative of those processes operating within other product divisions, but simply represent a structural explanation of patterns of labour dynamics which have been experienced within the one business area of ICI. Also, it is possible that the power of explanation could be improved by experimenting with a range of different variables. Notwithstanding these limitations, the centrality framework offers a supplementary perspective by which to view labour dynamics at a plant level within the business organisation and, when applied, it is possible to understand changes in labour use whilst making allowances for variations in attributes of a plant's operational environment and intra-organisational relations. The chapter has also indicated significant differences in the technological basis of production in plants of varying degrees of centrality, and it is the intention of Chapter 7 to describe the structure of production and to suggest possible causes for these variations in plant technology.

7   The Technological Basis of Plant Peripherality

Chapters 5 and 6 show that there is a significant relationship between the attributes of a plant's centrality in the structure of a business organisation and the patterns of labour dynamics which these establishments display. Thus, the form of production technology is an integral and important component of structural differentiation and plant peripherality, a point which has already been established in the organisations literature (Dewar and Hage, 1978; Hickson, Pugh and Pheysey, 1969; Harvey, 1968). By contrast, much of the geographical literature explains technology largely in terms of the attributes of location, organisational influences being reduced to a secondary position (e.g. Steed, 1971; Howells, 1983). Both of these perspectives suffer from a degree of determinism, in that they presuppose a direct relationship between technology and *structure*, or technology and *place*. Two problems underlie these partial conceptualisations of the determinants of technology: a failure to appreciate the existence of complex rather than simple relationships with organisational structure and social or cultural conditions (Blau *et al.*, 1976; Sutton, 1974); and an inability to deal with technology at the level of the sub-unit or plant, compared to the generalised view of technology within the business organisation (Comstock and Scott, 1977). These problems combine to underline the difficulties which are experienced when attempting to balance the role of an organisation's strategic choice in determining technology with those constraints placed on choice, imposed from inside and outside the business organisation. As Child (1972b, p. 6) has pointed out, 'any association between. . .[technology and structure]. . .may be more accurately viewed as derivative of decisions made by those in control of the organization regarding the tasks to be carried out in relation to the resources available to perform them'. As will be shown in this chapter, therefore, the form of plant technology exemplifies the influence of *organisational constraints* (e.g. resources available, the distribution of tasks, number of plants) on the one hand, and *locational constraints* (e.g. size of

214

market, domain technology, labour market conditions) on the other hand. How these two forces interact to affect production and the technological basis of plant peripherality is the subject of the discussion.

There are, however, practical problems in addressing plant technology which impose specific limitations on the analysis. The examination is restricted to case studies of only four plants which have been selected from the paints division of ICI. As noted previously, these plants were specifically chosen because of their contrasting degrees of centrality, and it is held in this discussion that these positions will broadly reflect changes in intra-organisational relations and the environment between central and peripheral plants. A further limitation is that these micro-scale studies are not intended to be quantitatively rigorous, but rather they are qualitative illustrations, designed to impart a feel for the processes operating inside the plant. Another limiting factor is that these impressions have been gained over a relatively short period of time, so they can only provide limited insights into the dynamic aspects of plant technology. At best, therefore, the discussion is an attempt to outline major differences in technology between plants through a cross-sectional examination of local plant managers' views on, and strategies for, dealing with technological change in different organisational and locational circumstances.

In examining the question of technology in plant peripherality, the argument is developed in three parts. In the first part, technology is defined and related to the limited evidence of the effects of organisational structure on technology — the theoretical implications being discussed within a business organisation framework in order to isolate those aspects of technology which require closer examination. The second part of the discussion makes four detailed case studies of technology in plants of contrasting degrees of centrality. Finally, insights into the context and dynamics of technological change within the plant are gained in part three through an evaluation of the perspectives of individual plant managers.

Technology and the Structure of Business Organisations

Before discussing the implications of the structure of business organisations for plant-level technology, two related problems have to be considered: the need to provide a specification or definition of technology which can be examined empirically; and the need to highlight the major points at which the structure of business organisations affect the development and form of technology. The intention is to assess some of the more problematic aspects of technology inside the large business organisation, which can be used as a springboard for the argument which follows.

Defining the Scope and Context of Technology

A key characteristic of attempts to define technology within the social sciences is the degree of ambiguity in most statements regarding the scope and context of the issue. Within the literature on organisations, for example, technology has been treated at certain times as a key variable, a major independent determinant of structure (e.g. Perrow, 1967; Woodward, 1965) and at other times simply as one of a set of impinging forces or as a dependent variable (e.g. Hickson, Pugh and Pheysey, 1969; Blau *et al.*, 1976; Child and Mansfield, 1972). A primary reason for this state of ambiguity is the way in which definitions vary in their relationship between technology and organisational structure. In some cases, technology is defined as an internal attribute of structure and, in others, as an exogenous environmental force (McDermott and Taylor, 1982). As Stanfield (1976) has emphasised, there is a need for studies to specify more fully which aspects of technology they are discussing and to limit conclusions to the bounds of their definition.

Technology has in fact been defined in a number of ways, but two stand out. At one extreme is the proposition that technology must be seen as the 'stock of all human knowledge' (Simon, 1957) or as 'the material form of the labour process through which the *underlying* [emphasis added] forces and relations of production are expressed' (Harvey, 1982, p. 100). This is the widest perspective on technology and it argues essentially that technical innovations are merely extensions or concrete forms of knowledge, so they cannot be divorced from one another. At the other extreme, technology is argued to be present in more tangible forms, as 'the sequence of physical techniques used upon the workflow of the organisation' (Pugh *et al.*, 1969, p. 102), 'operations technology' (Hickson, Pugh and Pheysey, 1969), or simply as 'nuts and bolts' technology (Pennings, 1975; McDermott and Taylor, 1982).

Despite the existence of these contrasting definitions, it must be emphasised that the narrower proposition is the more readily 'operationalised' as various studies have testified. Some research has propounded a more or less direct relationship between technology and the structure of organisations, with different production systems being viewed as points along a technological continuum. Woodward's (1965) classic study of 203 firms in south Essex is, perhaps, the archetypal example. In her view, production systems develop chronologically and, in so doing, their technical complexity increases, from unit and small batch technologies, through large batch and mass production, to process technologies. Other authors have questioned the idea that successive developments necessarily involve increasing technical complexity, but may actually result in an increase in technical simplicity (e.g. Harvey, 1968). Furthermore, the Aston studies (Hickson, Pugh and Pheysey, 1969; Pugh et al., 1969) classified technology at three levels — operations technology, materials technology and knowledge technology — but were only able to operationalise operations technology, using the variable workflow integration. Focusing on this practical and accessible form of technology demonstrates the difficulties associated with studies of this type.

Two elements are, therefore, central to the majority of the definitions of technology. These are the material and mechanical *equipping* of the work process as the first feature (a restricted definition of technology as machines), and the *sequencing* activities as an indication of the control exerted or constraints applied to labour in production as the second feature (an extended definition of technology as machines plus labour). Although the extreme categories of batch and mass or process production do have theoretical problems associated with them, they are useful heuristic devices because they emphasise both the organisation of technology and technical aspects. Indeed, batch (Reeves and Turner, 1972) and mass-output (Khandwalla, 1974) methods of production may reflect important differences in the environment and organisational forces affecting production, which are of direct interest to this study. Consequently, these tenets are used here as parts of a workable definition of technology with particular stress being laid on the organisation, sequence and equipment used in production. This definition of technology is preferred to the proposition of technology as information for practical reasons.

An additional problem relating to technology is the context within which it is being discussed. As was the case with the Aston studies, for example, it is often unclear which level of the business organisation is being addressed, with the result that organisations and their sub-units are frequently confused (Child, 1972a). There is a dichotomy between those authors who advocate concentrating on studying technology at the level of the business organisation (Hickson, Pugh and

Pheysey, 1969), and those who hold that it is more logical to investigate technology within organisational sub-units (Comstock and Scott, 1977). However, in keeping with the above definition of technology, it seems more appropriate to adopt the sub-unit or establishment of the organisation as the context for a discussion on technology.

Evaluating the dynamics of technology is a further problem area relevant to this study. Oakey, Thwaites and Nash (1982, p. 1075) have stressed that 'far too frequently in the past, writers on technological change have used the terms innovation, diffusion, and adoption without making the critical distinction between product and process innovations'. This distinction is important for at least two reasons: products and processes are vital ingredients of technology, and both can be bought, sold and transferred; and it is held that process innovations are more readily available and diffused over space because of the relative confidentiality of product innovations. Consequently, product innovations are said to be a better indicator of the indigenous innovative potential of a region (Oakey, Thwaites and Nash, 1982). As the objective of this analysis is to evaluate the implications of organisational structure for technology only *process innovations*, which are deemed to be more mobile, are examined.

A final problem vital to the definition and scope of technology is the ability to measure the significance of any individual technological innovation. Gold (1981), in a review of the industrial economics literature on technology over the past 25 years confronted this problem and concluded that simple techniques, such as counting the number of firms or plants using an innovation, fail to indicate its real significance. Nevertheless, this is the major method which has been used in industrial geography to assess the degree of spread of technological innovations (see Oakey, Thwaites and Nash, 1980 for example). Gold (1981, pp. 249), therefore, suggested that the 'output associated with an innovation provides a more effective reflection of the extent of its utilization', though it is by no means an ideal measure.

The thrust of this discussion, therefore, is to focus on the issue of technology as the equipment, sequence and organisation of elements of production operating inside the plant, rather than the somewhat more fluid view of technology as information or knowledge generated by, and entering, the business organisation. Furthermore, the distinction between definitions of technology simply as machines or as machines plus labour is retained, in order to throw some light on the effects of different technologies on labour. This definition addresses the process and not product innovations aspect of technology. A useful guideline to gauge the significance of individual innovations of this type is to evaluate the output associated with the technology.

Theoretical Implications of Business Organisation Structure for Technology

In examining the possible ways in which the structure of business organisations might affect technology inside the plant, the scope of this analysis is narrower than most of the studies in the organisations literature. As these studies have concentrated mainly on isolating dimensions of causal relations of technology on organisational structure, this issue is recognised but not addressed. Instead, the aim is to conceptualise certain areas where business organisation structure is likely to impinge on plant technology.

A characteristic of approaches to technology in industrial geography is the tendency to use plant data entirely divorced from the parent business organisation. This feature is evident in the work by Thwaites (1978) and Oakey, Thwaites and Nash (1980), in which the effects of industrial sector, enterprise and plant size, and organisational attributes on technological innovation are assessed. As these types of studies focus upon the implications of technological change at the establishment level for regional development, the business organisation component behind these changes has remained underdeveloped. Indeed, the issue of technological change at a plant level within the individual business organisation was significant only by its absence in a recent survey of British and American research themes on technological change (Malecki, 1980a).

The business organisation perspective's potential contribution to understanding technological change can be illustrated by reference to Howells's (1983) case study of the diffusion of technology in an application of filter-down theory in the British pharmaceuticals industry. He established that there was sufficient circumstantial evidence to suggest that the degree of technological sophistication of an enterprise might be influenced by locational factors such as settlement size, degree of urbanisation and distance from corporate headquarters. In testing these assumptions empirically, Howells (1983, p. 154) concluded that 'there appeared to be no particular relationship between the technological sophistication of a firm or manufacturing plant and its location'. Although he did refer to other work which had shown that the position of the plant in the hierarchy of the parent corporation may be a significant influence on plant technology, Howells failed to follow up this assertion.

Howells's study illustrates two weaknesses underlying the plant level approach to technology: the tendency to treat the establishment, firm and industry sector as rough equivalents, with results from each being used interchangeably; and the usual sectoral approach to identifying plants to be studied is not necessarily representative of the mix of establishments in individual business organisations (Taylor, 1983). As Taylor (1983, p. 107) has noted succinctly in this respect:

> large business organisations will have distinctive combinations of. . .leader, intermediate, laggard and support companies. . . However, for a variety of internal and external reasons, not all managerial teams may be willing to meet this competitive challenge, making large business organisations, as well as their constituent companies, very variable both in character and performance.

In other words, conclusions on technological structure from disaggregated plant studies can only be limited because they are likely to be unrepresentative of the full spectrum of plants belonging to business organisations, especially if such studies adopt a regional approach. These conclusions can, therefore, only be couched in local terms, because they say nothing about the range and variations in the structure of technologies *within* the business organisation. Thus, even Taylor and Thrift's (1982b; 1982c) study of iron foundry establishments in the West Midlands, which adopts a bottom-up approach, can only make inferences relating to possible variations in technology within a business organisation. As a means of resolving this dilemma, a single plant needs to be examined in relation to its position in the corporate structure, and relative to other plants in the business organisation which may be situated elsewhere in the region, nation, or even in another country.

What is more, the significance of the business organisation's perspective on plant technology becomes increasingly evident when it is realised that technological innovations (especially product technologies) are not usually widely available and that one of the few channels available for diffusion is either the business organisation or licensing arrangements (Oakey, Thwaites and Nash, 1982). It is hardly surprising, therefore, to find some conflicting conclusions emerging from the geographical literature. Although Oakey, Thwaites and Nash (1980) were able, for example, to establish that innovations in large corporations were introduced initially in the branch plants, this is perhaps true only for the plants in the sample. When Taylor (1983) reworked the same data set used by Oakey, Thwaites and Nash, he showed precisely the opposite trend, with innovations being introduced first into the higher status plants and then gradually diffusing out to the branch plants. Part of the reason for this confusion may lie in the detail with which plants were defined. The first study, for instance, only classified plants as either 'headquarters plants' or 'branch plants'. Alternatively, Taylor's analysis also identified two groups, 'innovative group plants' and 'laggard branch plants', but there was an important sub-group of 'divisional headquarters plants' within the first group. There is the distinct possibility that innovative group plants may have been classified under the branch plant status by Oakey, Thwaites and Nash, in which case this would considerably raise the latter's innovative potential in relation to the former. What emerges from both the studies, however, is that the diffusion of innovations within the large business organisation usually involves the low technology product and process innovations which are nearing the end of their life-cycles.

The situation in which process technology may diffuse through the organisation is analogous to the theory that large multinational corporations progress through an exporting phase to the production of established products overseas, in order to elongate the standard-isation phase of a product and to give time for new products to be researched and developed (Vernon, 1966; Taylor and Thrift, 1983). In comparison, insights into the effects of the position of a plant within the business organisation on process technology have been limited to a few statements regarding the routines of work (Hage and Aiken, 1969), levels of innovation (Child and Mansfield, 1972) and the degree of specialisation (Harvey, 1968), and the only safe generalisation to make is that process technology may relate to the importance which the organisation attaches to a plant, with headquarters plants being strategic and branch plants performing more routine functions.

Notwithstanding these limited conclusions, it is possible to propose other implications the structure of business organisations may have for plant technology by returning to some of the fundamental themes raised in earlier chapters. It was noted, for example, that the Aston studies, in which technology played a crucial part in determining the power of a sub-unit or plant, failed to address the issue of time and space, thereby overlooking the possibility that technology might diffuse within the organisation and so alter the structure of power relations. Admittedly, Burns and Stalker's (1961) classic study went part-way to recognising this influence, when they pointed out that organic organisations are more conducive to technological development than mechanistic organisations, because of the more profuse lateral and vertical contacts between personnel in different parts of the organisation. Apart from this exception, little or no recognition of spatial variation in organisational structure was made. There was even less attention given to the implications of spatial structure for technology.

Theoretically, therefore, it can be proposed that plant technology is not determined simply by the business organisation dividing up its total task and allocating the components as charters to individual sub-units. This situation may arise at first, but it is unlikely to persist for long as the business organisation develops, modifying its organisational and spatial structure in the process. As organisations respond to their cultural contexts, technological innovation must be seen within the environmental domain (Sutton, 1974; Normann, 1971), with product and process innovations representing forms of adaptation by an organisation to a differentiated environment (Steed, 1971; Rees, 1974). In simple terms, it seems reasonable to assume that uneven spatial and historical expansion by an organisation may have implications for the form of technology inside the plant, depending on the position it occupies within the corporate division of labour and the point in time at which it joined the organisation. As a result, the plants lower down the ownership hierarchy are more remote from the centre of the organisation, possibly with more rudimentary forms of technology caused by a lag-time between their innovation in central plants and their diffusion to plants at the periphery of the organisation. Thus, if central plants are the major centres of innovation in large corporations, it can be expected that different *mixes* of process technologies will be found in plants in contrasting positions. In addition, it is likely that technology in peripheral plants will consist of mixes of older technologies, compared to the central plants, where innovatory tendencies will maintain the existence of up-to-date production systems. Possibly the closest geographical research has come to pinpointing this issue is in the recognition that technology can vary within firms because of their uneven historical development (Le Heron, 1973; Freeman, 1974).

If plants which are part of the same business organisation do adopt technologies in sequence — as this reasoning implies — a final conceptual issue concerns the rationale of peripheral plants adopting 'outmoded' technologies when other more developed forms are available within the organisation. Do the less innovative establishments, for example, have a choice of technologies, or is the adoption of 'new' equipment dictated by local conditions? Established theory in industrial economics suggests that the early adopters are the most rational, so later adoption by peripheral plants is, apparently, less rational. Although a lack of information, or at least a lag in the flow of information within the business organisation, may provide an explanation for such an occurrence, Gold (1981) has also suggested that the plants which adopt later may, in fact, be more rational, because of the *progressive* nature of innovation. In other words, the net economic advantage of adopting a technological innovation is likely to vary between plants, even in the same business organisation, because innovations improve features, such as their reliability, quality, efficiency, capacity and cost-efficiency, over time. Consequently, Gold emphasises the importance of the pre-decision environment of the plant as the primary influence in determining adoption of an innovation. According to Gold, three considerations are integral to an understanding of the pre-decision environment:

1. prospective operational as well as economic benefits and burdens of the innovation over the period of expected utilisation;
2. availability of financial and technical resources required to adopt the innovation and to achieve effective functioning; and
3. assessment of the potential advantages and disadvantages of adoption at the present time, as against delaying such action and considering further improvements in the innovation and the costs of lagging behind competitors.

Evidently, these considerations reinforce the possibility of different mixes of technologies in plants within the business organisation, which may be influenced by both local domain characteristics as well as intra-organisational relations.

To summarise the discussion, a workable definition of technology as the equipment and organisation of processes operating inside the plant has been provided. Also, several key aspects of plant technology which may be influenced by the position the establishment occupies within the structure of the business organisation have been outlined. The most notable of these features is the need to compare plants within individual business organisations: to test whether or not there are different mixtures of technologies in plants of varying degrees of centrality and peripherality. This statement rests on the assumption that the central plants are the most significant centres of innovation, with technologies gradually diffusing within the business organisation towards the peripheral establishments. By comparison with central plants, therefore, peripheral plants are likely to embody mixtures of older process technologies, whilst central plants may have a mix of more recent process innovations. Several reasons were also suggested as a rationale for peripheral plants adopting older technologies, not the least of which are that they are tried and tested, and are likely to have been modified before reaching the periphery of the organisation. In addition, the adoption of technologies is probably influenced by the characteristics of the plant's environmental domain, which vary within the organisation, thereby altering the basis for adoption considerably, especially on the grounds of economics. In the following sections, these a priori assumptions are evaluated by a series of case studies of plants belonging to the paints division of ICI.

Case Studies of Plant Centrality and Process Technology

Technology was an integral component of the plant centrality framework developed in Chapter 5 and was shown to vary significantly in plants of varying degrees of peripherality in the business organisation. The technology and method of production used in central plants are a mixture of complex large batch and mass-production techniques, so that, overall, production is capital intensive. Conversely, the most peripheral plants use less complex, small-scale batch production methods, which are inherently more labour intensive. As such a level of analysis can only be indicative of broad changes in the structure of technology along the centrality continuum, there is a pressing need, if these generalisations are to be substantiated, to examine the form of process technology inside plants at different points within the organisation.

In examining technology within plants at different points in the structure of organisations, four plants were chosen from ICI's paints division — the same case studies used in the previous chapter. In order on the intra-organisational centrality index, these plants were the paints division headquarters at Slough (United Kingdom), Cabarita (Australia), Clayton (Australia) and Jurong (Singapore). As the range of functions of the plants varies, the product being produced was held 'constant'. Thus, the detailed analysis of process technology was restricted to that used to produce the main output of all four plants, domestic or decorative paints.

The technical assistance of works managers responsible for the running of each establishment was used in surveying the four plants.

Care was taken to focus on the four main aspects of technology — age, mixture, organisation and scale — to ensure the consistency of results between sites. The *age* of individual items of equipment was gauged by identifying the use of certain generations of machine types in each location. From these results it was also possible to summarise the *mixture* of technologies used at the four sites for each stage of the production process. Note was also taken of the method or *organisation* of production, the sequencing of events and, in particular, the characteristics of the interaction between equipment and shopfloor workers. The *scale* of production associated with the technologies used in each location was evaluated using three indicators: the total annual output of the plant; average batch size; and the proportion of the total output accounted for by each batch. This final indicator is regarded as critical because it is a measure of the output associated with the mix of technologies in individual establishments. Unfortunately, it was not possible to obtain figures for the output accounted for by individual process technologies as had been hoped, but the combined figure does provide at least preliminary information on which assessments of the effectiveness of the precise mix of technologies in each location can be made. However, before the results of the plant technology surveys are described, it is useful to outline briefly the main characteristics and stages involved in the production of paints. The remaining part of this section, therefore, provides a description of the 'machine' aspects of technology.

The Process of Paints Production

The production of paints can be viewed simply as a giant mixing process in which three classes of materials are combined:

1. a *resin* or resin mixture which forms the substance of the paint film. Resin is also known as 'binder' because of the cohesive property it imparts and, depending on which types of resins are incorporated, the final properties of the paint product can be regulated;
2. *pigments* which give colour to the paint and thereby increase its covering capacity and aesthetic properties; and
3. *solvents* to dissolve the resin and impart the required viscosity to the paint (as the solvents evaporate, the paint 'dries').

The order in which these elements are combined is shown schematically in Figure 7.1 which highlights the three basic stages of pigment dispersion, paint make-up and thinning. The pigment dispersion stage serves to distribute the pigment evenly throughout the resin and solvent,

Figure 7.1: Stages Involved in Paints Production

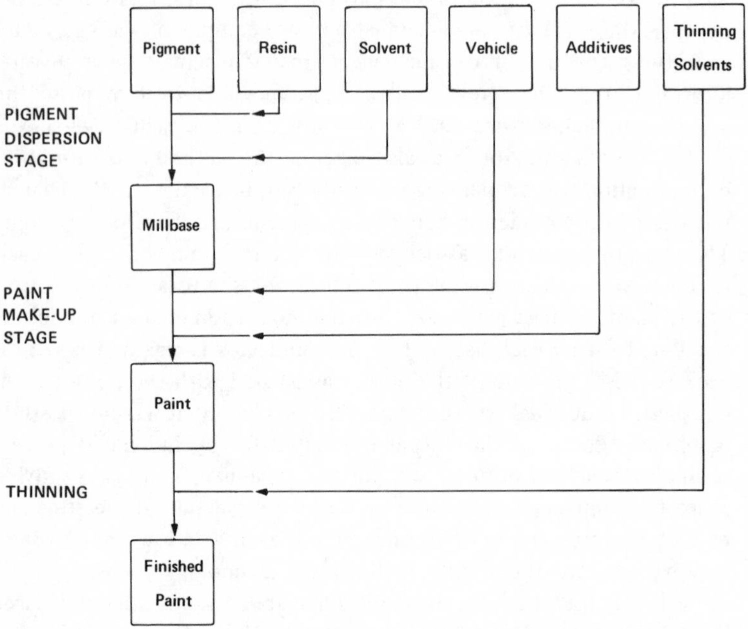

thus economising on the use of the pigment. In their combined form, the resin and solvent are known as the 'vehicle' and this is the medium into which the pigment 'premix' must be dispersed by the mixing process.

Once dispersed through the resin and solvent the pigment mixture is known as 'millbase' and contains a large proportion of pigment in relation to vehicle. Only a small amount of pigment is required in the final product, so different millbases are combined to produce the desired colour, and then thinned by adding additional vehicle and additives to give the paint its required viscosity and other properties.

Additional stages are required to the basic process in the commercial production of paints. For example, some plants prefer to produce their own resins and solvents, in whole or in part, rather than buying them from other producers. In-house testing for colour and other properties of each batch is a further stage. Packaging the paint in tins or drums and handling and storage on site are also integral to a full view of the process of paints production. The five basic stages of paints production which must be examined in the analysis, therefore, are the production of resins, mixing, testing, filling (or packaging) and handling.

Inter-plant Comparisons of Process Technology

A comparative study of the age, mixture, organisation and scale of process technologies used in each of the five stages of decorative paints production was made in the four chosen ICI plants (Slough, Cabarita, Clayton and Jurong). The various types of technology used in the plants deserve brief elaboration. Wherever possible, the equipment used is shown in chronological order, that is, the sequence in which various items have been developed. In the stage of resins production, the basic dichotomy is between the older forms of technology, where resins are produced in open 'kettles' with materials being loaded by hand, and the modern types of resin 'reactors' which are fully automatic. The capacity of individual kettles and reactors is also important and those characteristics have been noted.

In the mixing stage, five generations of technology were apparent in the plants (Figure 7.2). The oldest type of equipment found was the vestiges of roller mills, although these were no longer in use. Simple vertical mixers were the oldest mixing equipment in operation, and they are extremely flexible, normally being used where batches are small. Larger batches are dealt with using ball mills and bead mill attritors, but the latest fifth generation grinders can run continuously, lessening the need for benefits of economies of scale necessary in the other types of equipment. Once mixed, the batches are subjected to a testing stage, especially for colour tinting. Increasingly, the tinting and testing process is being undertaken by computerised spectrophotometers, highlighting the division between plants which utilise these more sophisticated methods and those which still rely on skilled manual testing methods.

Perhaps the most complex stage in the production process is the filling stage. The characteristics of the five generations of filling technology found are illustrated in Figure 7.3 and these are self-explanatory. However, it is important to note the main differences between, for instance, the advanced fast-line automated filler-packer, and the most rudimentary hand-filling equipment. These forms of equipment can be distinguished in terms of the size of batches handled; time of operation; degree of automation; and the role played by labour in the process.

In the final stage of handling the finished products, three methods

Figure 7.2: Generations of Mixing Equipment Used in Paints Production

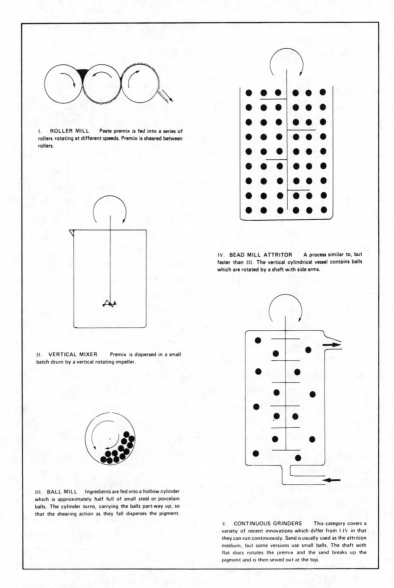

I. ROLLER MILL   Paste premix is fed into a series of rollers rotating at different speeds. Premix is sheared between rollers.

II. VERTICAL MIXER   Premix is dispersed in a small batch drum by a vertical rotating impeller.

III. BALL MILL   Ingredients are fed into a hollow cylinder which is approximately half full of small steel or porcelain balls. The cylinder turns, carrying the balls part-way up, so that the shearing action as they fall disperses the pigment.

IV. BEAD MILL ATTRITOR   A process similar to, but faster than III. The vertical cylindrical vessel contains balls which are rotated by a shaft with side arms.

V. CONTINUOUS GRINDERS   This category covers a variety of recent innovations which differ from I-IV in that they can run continuously. Sand is usually used as the attrition medium, but some versions use small balls. The shaft with flat discs rotates the premix and the sand breaks up the pigment and is then seived out at the top.

Source: Plant survey.

Figure 7.3: Generations of Filling Equipment Used in Paints Production

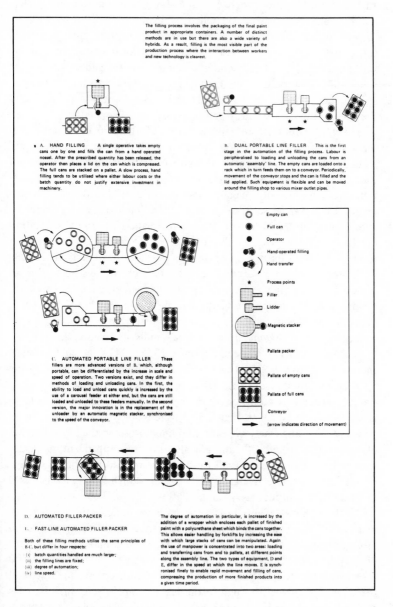

The filling process involves the packaging of the final paint product in appropriate containers. A number of distinct methods are in use but there are also a wide variety of hybrids. As a result, filling is the most visible part of the production process where the interaction between workers and new technology is clearest.

A. HAND FILLING   A single operative takes empty cans one by one and fills the can from a hand operated nossel. After the prescribed quantity has been released, the operator then places a lid on the can which is compressed. The full cans are stacked on a pallet. A slow process, hand filling tends to be utilised where either labour costs or the batch quantity do not justify extensive investment in machinery.

B. DUAL PORTABLE LINE FILLER   This is the first stage in the automation of the filling process. Labour is peripheralised to loading and unloading the cans from an automatic 'assembly' line. The empty cans are loaded onto a rack which in turn feeds them on to a conveyor. Periodically, movement of the conveyor stops and the can is filled and the lid applied. Such equipment is flexible and can be moved around the filling shop to various mixer outlet pipes.

C. AUTOMATED PORTABLE LINE FILLER   These fillers are more advanced versions of B, which, although portable, can be differentiated by the increase in scale and speed of operation. Two versions exist, and they differ in methods of loading and unloading cans. In the first, the ability to load and unload cans quickly is increased by the use of a carousel feeder at either end, but the cans are still loaded and unloaded to these feeders manually. In the second version, the major innovation is in the replacement of the unloader by an automatic magnetic stacker, synchronised to the speed of the conveyor.

	Empty can
	Full can
	Operator
	Hand-operated filling
	Hand transfer
	Process points
	Filler
	Lidder
	Magnetic stacker
	Pallate packer
	Pallate of empty cans
	Pallate of full cans
	Conveyor
	(arrow indicates direction of movement)

D. AUTOMATED FILLER-PACKER

E. FAST-LINE AUTOMATED FILLER-PACKER

Both of these filling methods utilise the same principles of B-C. but differ in four respects:

(i) batch quantities handled are much larger;
(ii) the filling lines are fixed;
(iii) degree of automation;
(iv) line speed.

The degree of automation in particular, is increased by the addition of a wrapper which encloses each pallet of finished paint with a polyurethane sheet which binds the cans together. This allows easier handling by forklifts by increasing the ease with which large stacks of cans can be manipulated. Again the use of manpower is concentrated into two areas: loading and transferring cans from and to pallets, at different points along the assembly line. The two types of equipment, D and E, differ in the speed at which the line moves. E is synchronised finely to enable rapid movement and filling of cans, compressing the production of more finished products into a given time period.

Source: Plant survey.

can be distinguished: manual; semi-automatic; and fully automatic. In the manual method, there is a liberal use of manpower, and pallets are moved either by trolley (pulled by hand or truck) or by forklift. Semi-automatic handling is characterised by forklifts running on fixed tracks between the warehouse storage racks, an operator moving the fork horizontally, vertically and laterally to store the pallet. Warehouses using fully automatic equipment are computer controlled, with the storage racks linked by conveyors and forks. Once the pallets enter the warehouse, they are fully controlled by a single operator.

These descriptions are representative of the structure of process technology found in the four plants overall, but when viewed individually there were marked differences in the technology in use in each location and these features are summarised in Table 7.1. Production at Slough, one of the paints plants most central to ICI, was characterised by the large scale of production technologies and a degree of automation unrivalled by the other three plants. The initial indication of this feature is given in the most recent forms of gas-heated resin reactors with a capacity of up to 30,000 litres per batch. This scale of resins production technology is unmatched anywhere else in ICI's paints division except, perhaps, at Stowmarket, which has recently opened a fully computerised resin facility (Product Finishing, 1983; Pigment and Resin Technology, 1983). Furthermore, the comprehensive installation of generation IV bead mills in the mixing stage — typical of equipment developed since 1975 — has served to reduce the need for large amounts of labour, a trend which is boosted by the scale of the equipment, well above other plants. Also, at the testing stage, procedures were fully computerised. The two latest filling technologies (see D and E in Figure 7.3) were employed at Slough, incorporating a fast and finely synchronised line for use on the larger batches of paint. The pallets of cans are also shrink-wrapped automatically with polyurethane sheet to aid forklift removal and warehouse storage by manual methods. Average batch size at Slough in 1980 was 5,500 litres and total output was 45 million litres.

At the Cabarita plant, resin reactors were under half the capacity of those at Slough and there was a larger variety of different generation mixing technologies, including vertical mixers, ball mills and bead mills of varying capacities. The much smaller average batch size of 3,500 litres is a reflection of this mixture of generations of technology, and the effect has flowed through to the testing stage where small batches are dealt with by hand-testing methods and are accompanied by hand-filling equipment. The portable versions of automated line fillers are

Table 7.1: Structure of Process Technology in ICI Paint Plants

ESTABLISHMENT	CAPACITY OF RESINS PRODUCTION (litres, '000)	GENERATIONS OF TECHNOLOGY USED AT STAGES OF PRODUCTION:*				AVERAGE BATCH SIZE (litres, '000)	TOTAL OUTPUT, 1980 (litres, millions)
		MIXING	TESTING	FILLING	HANDLING		
Slough (United Kingdom)	25-30, reactors	IV. Bead mill attritors	Computerised	D. Automated filler-packer E. Fast-line automated filler-packer	Manual	5.5	45.0
Cabarita (Australia)	16+5, reactors	II. Vertical mixers III. Ball mills IV. Bead mill attritors	Computerised and manual	A. Hand filling C. Automated portable line filler	Manual Semi-automatic Fully-automatic	3.5	14.5
Clayton (Australia)	7+7+3, reactors	II. Vertical mixers III. Ball mills IV. Bead mill attritors V. Continuous grinders	Computerised	A. Hand filling B. Dual portable line filler C. Automated portable line filler	Manual	3.5	15.0
Jurong (Singapore)	0.5-1, kettles	II. Vertical mixers IV. Bead mill attritors	Manual	A. Hand filling	Manual	1.0	3.0

Note: * For full explanation of process technologies see Figures 7.2 and 7.3.
Source: Plant survey.

more flexible than those fixed versions used at Slough, and can be moved around easily to cope with variations in production needs. One of the more advanced innovations at Cabarita is in the handling stage, with a fully automated warehouse. One of the reasons for this installation which was given by plant management was a response to the militancy of the storemen and packers. This type of technology is only recently being considered for installation at Slough, but overall, the scale of output of the plant is much smaller (14.5 million litres).

Production at the second Australian plant, Clayton, was roughly equivalent to that at Cabarita, with a similar resins capacity, mix of generations of technology, average batch size and total output. In contrast, several characteristics point to the plant as a centre of innovation and as the main site of research and development by ICI in Australia. These consist of a newly developed solvent recovery plant, which should save considerable costs generated by the loss of waste resins in production, and also an experimental fifth generation continuous grinder. Both of these innovations have generated considerable interest in ICI plants elsewhere in the world. In the stage of production, testing methods were computerised, contrasting with the manual techniques at the handling stage.

Process technology in ICI's Jurong plant in Singapore was, quite evidently, at the opposite end of the technology spectrum. Not only was production on a small scale with a total production of 3.0 million litres, but also the average batch size was only 1,000 litres. It was clear that older technologies, usually manually operated, were present in every stage of the production process. To illustrate this point, the capacity for the production of resins was only 500 to 1,000 litres, which was approximately 2-3 per cent of the capacity at Slough. Moreover, resins were produced in open kettles, first used at Slough in the 1940s. The apparent reason for the use of these small-scale technologies is the limited demand for a wide variety of products, with as many as 62 types of resin being produced at Jurong. The main characteristics of process technology at Jurong, however, were its simplicity, and the fact that the methods were labour-intensive to an extreme.

The above descriptions have demonstrated in a simple, largely qualitative way marked variations in the form of process technology used in four plants owned by ICI. Apart from the detailed differences in equipment, it is possible to deduce some more general statements concerning the structure of technology within the business organisation, by accepting that these plants are broadly indicative of the

Table 7.2: Characteristics of Process Technology and Plant Centrality

PLANT CENTRALITY	LEVEL OF INNOVATION	TECHNOLOGICAL MIX	AGE OF TECHNOLOGY	DEGREE OF AUTOMATION	BATCH SIZE	TOTAL OUTPUT
Central	high	concentrated	new	high	large	large
Semi-peripheral	medium	diverse	old and new	medium	medium	medium
Peripheral	low	concentrated	old	low	small	small

characteristics of plants along the intra-organisational centrality continuum. An attempt has been made in Table 7.2 to draw out the more fundamental features of variations in technology in central, semi-peripheral and peripheral plants.

The first feature which emerges from these case studies is the distinctions to be made in terms of the mix and age of technologies. At Slough, the most central plant examined, there was only a small range of technologies, with the latest generations of equipment in use at every stage except the handling process, and even changes to an automated warehouse at this stage of production were under consideration. By comparison, at the two Australian plants, there was a diverse mixture of old and new technologies at every stage of production, except perhaps in testing. In Jurong, a mix of technologies was not so evident and, in fact, they were concentrated largely on the older types of equipment. The only exception to this generalisation was in the mixing stage where bead mill attritors were in use, but only on a small scale to cope with the large-batch runs.

The indications are that there is very little process innovation in the peripheral plants and the limited evidence which was described appears to suggest a definite increase in innovatory capacity towards the more central plants. This preliminary conclusion would, therefore, seem to support the assertion that *in situ* variations in plant innovation are a feature of corporate organisation and there are direct outcomes in the form, age and mixture of technologies in use in individual locations, as Figure 7.4 illustrates schematically. Thus, a central plant, such as one in position A, is likely to be one of the main centres of innovation within the business organisation, developing and using the most recent forms or generations of technology. Through time, the organisation also acts as a conduit for the diffusion of established or proven and cost-effective innovations to other plants. Semi-peripheral plants (position B) will, therefore, have a mixture of old and new generations of equipment, but noticeably, not the most recent forms (e.g. generation V); whereas peripheral plants (position C) are likely to have only the older, tried-and-tested technologies with very little on-site innovation. Of course, this explanation does not preclude the possible overriding influence of local environmental forces, and it is probable that local conditions will affect which of the plants in the business organisation will adopt established forms of technology, and when. Further research would be needed to answer this question, however.

A second feature of the effects of plant centrality on technology which is highlighted by Table 7.2 is the scale and degree of automation

Figure 7.4: Technological Diffusion and Plant Centrality

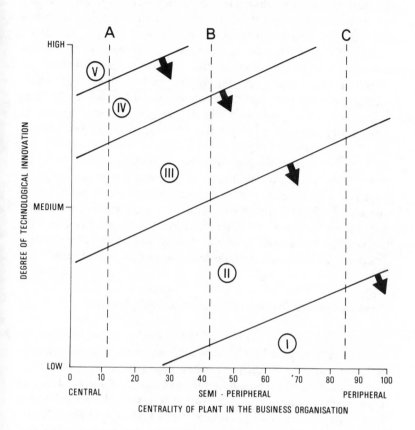

involved in production, which seems to vary considerably with plant centrality. Both total output and batch size are far larger in central plants than in peripheral plants. What is more, the proportion of total output accounted for by an individual batch is far greater in the latter than in the former. From the case studies, this figure was 0.033 per cent in Jurong, approximately 0.024 per cent in the two Australian plants and only 0.012 per cent in Slough. The implication is that there is a more rapid turnover of batches in the central plants compared to the peripheral plants, which is evidently enabled by the degree of automation in production. An understanding of both of these factors — variation in the scale and level of automation in production within the business organisation — helps to go some way to pinpointing the causes of the differences in the labour dynamics of individual plants. For instance, whereas labour is still an integral component of production in peripheral plants because of the low capital intensity of production, these proportions are drastically reduced in the central plants through the peripheralisation of labour within the production process. Consequently, differences in the technological basis of production which have been described are a vital explanatory component for patterns of labour dynamics (see Chapter 6).

It is less certain, however, what the underlying causes of the differences in the form of technology are between central and peripheral plants or, for that matter, how the dynamics of technological development are influenced by the position of a plant within the business organisation. In order to address these issues in a preliminary way, the final section describes and evaluates the attitudes displayed by the plant managers to the issue of technological development in production.

Plant Technology: Managerial Strategies and Peripherality

One of the interesting features of the discussion so far has been the marked difference in the structure of technology inside plants at different positions within the business organisation. As with the discussion of labour dynamics, however, the form of production described represented a culmination of historical forces, so the evaluation has been largely cross-sectional in nature. To provide a longitudinal element to the analysis, plant or works managers were interviewed with regard to whether or not, from their experience, they thought technological development in their plant had been influenced by its position within the organisational structure of ICI and how they sought to introduce new innovations. From these interviews, it was possible to glean reasons for contrasts in technology through the way in which managers perceived the operational environment of their plants. These issues will be discussed in turn.

Technology as a Response to Centrality or Peripherality

A characteristic which is integral to the centrality of a plant within organisational structure is the importance of the establishment in terms of size, but also in relation to its degree of dispensability or indispensability to the business organisation. It might be expected, for example, that management at Slough would react differently to those in Australian plants or at Jurong, depending on the way in which they perceived their position within ICI and the features of the local business environment.

In Britain, ICI dominates the commercial paints market, accounting for roughly 30 per cent of all paints consumed, and the bulk of the products are produced at the Slough and Stowmarket plants. This is, to say the least, a favourable position for Slough, which has been fortunate enough to have become responsible for brands with household names such as Dulux. Managerial attitudes reflected this situation, because as one manager noted:

> We don't have much contact with competitors' plants...I can't see us competing, you know, what productivity they have got up to in Crown — we'll never be on those terms...[within ICI and] ...within the different paint departments, once again, it is very difficult to compare. One is often looking for gross changes however, especially productivity. But generally speaking, this business is just too complicated...when you are making God knows how many products, and batch sizes, well, it's hard.

It is also significant that Slough is supervised closely by ICI's central management because of this importance, and there is a tendency to occasionally override decisions which have been made at the plant level with those handed down from above, such as those involved in wage cases. Having said this, the plant does display a considerable degree of autonomy, and it is a characteristic of the site that ICI has been willing to continue investing there. In the words of a plant manager:

> Certainly, on this site, I don't think, I haven't seen any starvation of capital. Certainly, there is a clamp-down. Where I think it is a little bit unsettling is when it is chopped and changed, but I handle capital for the works. Having said that, I think that if we stopped spending money entirely, that the place would go down hill, and I think part of the success of this site is the fact that money *has* been spent, and it is a vote of *confidence* in the site and it is always promoting further opportunities.

In fact, it could be suggested the confidence in the site is reflected in the up-to-date nature of the technology within the plant. As one of the few British establishments still open to investment, ICI is effectively committed both to the location and to Stowmarket, resulting in a heavy spatial concentration of resources. Thus, it is likely that the powerful position of the plant within the organisation and that site's investment inertia will be maintained, short of a drastic business downturn and ICI's decision to withdraw from the paints industry altogether. Given the steady profits the division has returned to the organisation over the last ten years this move seems very unlikely.

The operational environment of Slough bears similarities to that of Clayton and Cabarita, in the sense that historical precedents have laid the basis of the present strength of the two establishments. The link-up between British Australian Lead Manufacturers (BALM) and Du Pont was as important historically as the same relationship in Britain in establishing ICI brand names in the household, and the two sites emerged as the most important plants from this background, marketing 1300-1400 products under the Dulux banner and with only one major competitor, Berger. Though Clayton and Cabarita are, historically, and in current production terms, the most central of the Australian establishments − they are, in fact, the only plants with their own state managers − any similarity with the British plants diverges at this point. First, the total Australian paints market is, judging by the total volume of products produced by Dulux Australia, considerably smaller than that in Britain, probably less than half the size. Second, the market is greatly decentralised and has resulted in the setting up of five plants and a large number of warehouses. Cabarita and Clayton may be central to Dulux and ICI Australia, but taking these two factors into account reduces their order of merit within ICI on a global scale. The five plants now function as an integrated whole, which is demonstrated by the emphasis given to an inter-state telephone link-up between the managers at least once a week. One of the main features of peripherality − the ability, theoretically, for a plant to be substituted by other plants from within the subsidiary company − is, therefore, clearly evident in the case of Cabarita and Clayton. For example, in the succinct comment of one manager, it was noted that:

> The two biggest factories [Cabarita and Clayton] are located, obviously, in the two busiest centres. Queensland [Rocklea] is a very modern factory, on a much smaller scale, because it is the latest one, and it obviously make paints for other states. The other thing about Dulux, is that it is flexible, we supply each other. Somebody from above looks down and says 'which is the best plant to

make *this* in?', or 'is it cheaper to make it there?'. Labour is constant anyway, because we all pay the same rates but because of the *age* of the plants, obviously, there are benefits to be had by manufacturing in states other than New South Wales, or South Australia, or Western Australia, for example.

Judging by the reference to the age of plants, technology plays a large part in the functioning of the Australian establishments, with the capital funds having to be spread between five sites. As a result, it is not surprising that investment in new equipment is characterised by discontinuity, rather than continuity even, for instance, at the headquarters plant at Clayton, where the production manager stated that even though Dulux have 'spent a lot on new equipment, as the evidence shows. . .not much has been spent recently inside the factory in the last three years', a possible reason for which may be the investment in other plants within the company. Even so, because of the status of Cabarita and Clayton it is likely that they would be the last, rather than the first, sites to be hit by any ICI rationalisation in Australia, at least in terms of closure.

In comparison, the obvious peripherality of the Jurong plant illustrates some of the features and the structural context of the technological basis of peripherality. Paints manufacture only began in earnest in the new branch factory in 1971 under the brand name ICI rather than Dulux. As one of three plants owned by ICI Paints Malaysia in the region, Jurong displays some of the peripheral substitutability problems associated with the Australian plants, and this has apparently affected the propensity of ICI to invest in the location. Thus, in view of the marked recent 'success' of the site, a perplexed manager commented:

I feel as though a modern plant would increase productivity but the market situation dictates against installing new machinery. . . Business in the region is fairly restricted now, with ICI developing the Hong Kong market through the Taiwan factory, and also Indonesia.

The above description of the technology used in Jurong is testimony to the effects of a peripheral position and, in particular, to the inevitable effects of the relative lack of investment. As well as being restricted to expansion within the region by ICI, competition is also stiff within Singapore with twelve large national and multinational firms and forty or so small 'backyard' firms. Furthermore, the plant's contribution to profits is insignificant by comparison with Slough. None of this bodes well for the plant's future, with little likelihood of expansion, and it could even be suggested that the reluctance of ICI to invest in the site is related to this insecurity, with procrastination being the main feature of investment trends. Paradoxically, one plant manager was optimistic in this regard, emphasising that:

> Restriction of capital has not occurred from ICI, in fact the old machinery in the plant is seen as quite modern. Hopefully, 1984-85 should see a big expansion. New machinery should have been installed in 1982 but has been held back for a couple of years because of bad business. . .when the time is right, we will modernise.

These comments on the broader context of differences in plant technology serve to highlight the degree of interaction between organisational and environmental forces in determining the overall centrality of a plant within a business organisation, partly through the corporation's assessment of the potential of a state-level, national or regional market. In the words of one of the managers, continued investment in a plant does, very much, represent a 'vote of confidence' in the site and a spatial and financial commitment of corporate resources. If other empirical evidence is a guideline, therefore, it is the peripheral locations, where the size of the plant and market does not justify extensive investments, which are the sites most likely to be affected by corporate rationalisation, not the central plants.

Managing Technological Change

The preceding discussion helped to provide a basis for understanding variations in plant technology in addition to the more fundamental differences already described. The evidence also gives a strong indication of the inequalities in the dynamics of technology which underlie the dichotomy between plants within the business organisation. The purpose of this final section is to explore possible reasons for these contrasts in technology by referring to the emphases plant managers give to the role of technological change.

A Time of Opportunity. The effects of changing technology inside the plant had a significant bearing on the way in which new processes were introduced and these were influenced by the position of the plant within the business organisation. From interviews with plant managers the major reason that emerged to explain this pattern was the contrasting rates of technological change in different locations, caused by the degree of centrality or peripherality of the plants. A marked change in the emphases in production was thus brought about. At Slough, for example, where the structure of technology was recent — indicating a rapid rate of technological change — there was little doubt of the effects on plant employment levels in the minds of the managers. One manager emphasised this point clearly when he noted that:

> Change, where you have identifiable change, in my opinion, even though it can be a headache and is to be approached positively, is a time of opportunity. Because if you are installing new equipment, then as sure as hell, that is an excellent time to change your working methods. Whereas, if you go into a nice smooth-running plant, and you simply say, I want to increase productivity, and I want to chop and change it around, you are, by definition, inferring a lot of criticism, a lot of indictment. Whereas, if you take people to a new plant, and you say 'well, it is all different chaps, you've got to look at this now, we've got to really sort it out', then it is a lot more acceptable. It is a time of opportunity.

The fact that the introduction of new technology is seen as a time of opportunity to restructure working *methods* is indicative of the reduction in the employment at Slough over the last ten years, and also indicates how difficult it is to separate machines and working methods. Thus, a change in process as well as technology provides a chance to alter the organisation and sequence of production and provides a rationale for alterations to employment structure. Two examples can be used to illustrate this point. The big turnover rate of labour at Slough means, in the words of one manager:

> you very rarely actually have to get rid of people. . .you know that you just do not have to say to people 'I'm sorry, you're redundant'. We can *manage* it. That's not to say there is no problem. There is a problem, because you will be making fewer people do more work, *that's* your problem, rather than saying we need thirty redundancies.

Thus, judging by the way Slough has experienced changes in employment, the turnover of labour has provided one avenue for cutting the number of workers required, but there also seems to have been a second vital component, which is a change in the nature of work itself.

A manager emphasised that the effects of technological change depended on the 'traditions' of a job and the greatest impact had been experienced in the dirtier, heavier jobs. At the heart of these developments, however, has been a change in the skill content of some jobs caused by automation and computerisation. In conversation, one manager expressed the opinion that jobs have been made more interesting by automation and another noted 'you are looking for people of a higher intelligence level now than you probably could get away with before'. The first manager replied:

That's right. I think that it [work] is more interesting, the rather salutary thing though is that, generally speaking throughout ICI, computerising things and use of computer terminals is regarded as *degrading* a job, in terms of its marks. I have no doubt it does make their job a bit more interesting. . .[even though]. . .automation is going to increase the level of unemployment. I don't think there is any doubt about that, unless there is expansion again. Don't forget, since Crompton's mule, people have been expecting this to happen, and it hasn't happened yet. At the risk of sounding like a politician, I think it depends whether demand leads to lower prices, which leads to other products being required and therefore to a continued expansion of demand. . .[This allows]. . .the shedding of jobs and the benefits through the shedding of jobs, to come at the right pace to allow other things to be developed to replace them, I guess.

What is plain from these comments is the tendency to degrade jobs by introducing new technology, which in turn reduces the skills required of workers, but allows the organisation to search for more 'qualified' employees. The high turnover rate of labour at Slough thereby reduces the association between changes in technology and individual workers, making the transition smoother. In Australia, the situation was modified somewhat by the high real costs, and shortage of skilled labour. Here, the pace of technological change was evidently not so rapid, but there was still a tendency for new machinery to eliminate some labour needs. However, it is clear that 'most guys in the plant', to cite a manager, 'see new technology in a local sense, people losing their jobs are being employed elsewhere'.

On the surface at least, the marked difference in the pace of technological development at Cabarita and Clayton compared to Slough seems to have affected employment in two main ways. First, at Cabarita no difficulty was experienced in recruiting unskilled and semi-skilled labour, part of the reason being that there was a large Vietnamese population in and around the area. Second, there is a national shortage of skilled workers, to which the country has responded by attracting workers from overseas. The plant itself has responded by attempting to retain their valuable skilled employees. This situation is reflected in the history of employment at Cabarita, and as a plant manager said:

> There are two traditions on this site, one is longevity, and the other is for family associations. . .some of them came out with Cook! We've got a fellow who works in the store, whose family have worked for ICI for generations. . .not just in one factory, he's worked on all sorts of different sites for ICI.

At Jurong, a different emphasis was given to employees, probably because of the relatively slow rate of change in technology. The recent expansion of production has taken place largely through a growth in the workforce of the plant rather than by investment in new equipment. Ironically, the emphasis was given to increasing machine intensity which, as one manager explained, is:

> made necessary because of the high cost of and shortage of labour in Singapore. Competition for labour in Singapore is high, so many companies are now bringing in labour from Sri Lanka, Bangladesh, Indonesia and Malaysia. . .the Government is handing out work permits liberally, even 'block permits' for large numbers of workers.

Evidently, then, the conditions under which new technology is introduced and the reasons for changes, vary greatly between the four plants. In Slough, for example, it can be surmised that there is an attempt to reduce the magnitude and quality of labour involved in production in part because of its expense, and this is also the case in Cabarita and Clayton, although not to the same extent. In these plants, new technology is taken as an opportunity to change production and reduce employment. In Jurong the position of the plant is different, and production is heavily dependent on labour, so an attempt is being made to replace existing jobs with new equipment because of a labour shortage. The peripherality of the plant to ICI, however, militates against substantial investment, so the anachronism is likely to continue.

Preaching the Message. These fundamental differences in the technological basis of production between central and peripheral plants

also highlight significant variations in the emphasis given to technological change to improve production, particularly productivity. The
relative importance of Slough, Cabarita and Clayton compared to
Jurong, as shown in the structure of their technology, was contrasted
by the emphasis they give to improving productivity through non-
technical means, that is, other than by using new paint formulations
or by introducing new machinery. The more central plants are, therefore, alike in their stress on increasing the efficiency of manpower, and
as a manager at Slough commented:

> Things can always be improved by spending money, but as sure as
> hell, things can be improved by better management too, and better
> organisation. . .We take the view that the middle management and
> the senior management at my level — we are not paid to run things,
> we are paid to *change* things. If we don't change things then we
> don't really have a job, and the whole works can be run by foremen
> and supervisors.

In one sense, therefore, the advanced technological basis of production in central plants is mirrored by different management strategies,
compared to those in peripheral establishments. The characteristics
of this approach are social as well as technical. As production in central
plants is usually at the forefront of technological innovation, this means
managers have to orientate their efforts to improving and maintaining
the performance of labour, as improvements to productivity by technological means become extremely difficult to achieve. This issue is
illustrated well by one plant manager at Slough:

> What you do find out there is that when one is trying to preach a
> message like 'you realise chaps, that if we do make more paint,
> that the costs come down and that we are satisfying a demand', and
> so on and so forth, you inevitably get back the guy's gripes. It is
> very hard to preach a message to a guy to take it in the spirit that
> it is given, rather than getting at him and that you are not really
> appreciating his problems. . .I've never found a perfect way of
> solving this, and I don't think there is a perfect way. . .only by
> telling them so, and more importantly, by telling your supervisors
> so, and making sure that you are objective and that people have
> targets and they are monitored and that you know what will happen,
> and you monitor all things, like absence, like time-keeping, like
> productivity generally, accidents, everything. There is a plethora of

data and these have to be broken down plant by plant, shift by shift, and monitored, and people given objectives — objectives which they have to deliver or you have to go into why. It sounds very hard but there are no magic answers. . .All we can do is keep preaching the message, and to try and make sure that you have a very consistent approach to people, because if you don't, once again, they will pick you off. You've got to be fair, you've got to be firm, you can't blaze any trails, you just have to be professional and thorough and objective.

This emphasis is contrasted by the attitudes of management at Jurong, where lack of productivity improvements were accounted for largely in technological terms and preliminary attempts to improve productivity by other means. As a manager pointed out:

there are many limiting factors with the present machinery. For instance, if we increased batch size to 5000 litres, we would save a lot of money. Shop floor pressures to increase productivity are few, but a few methods are emerging such as the Works Excellence Committee under discussion with the National Productivity Board at present, which attempts to see what management and unions can do to increase productivity. We also use the Q.C. [Quality Control] Committee — a Japanese and American concept — but we've found only management take notice, so phase two now means trying to educate the workers in its principles. Workers on the whole have been receptive to increasing productivity, especially as a national goal.

The above comments act as initial pointers to explaining the dynamic aspects of technology within organisational structure, by emphasising the importance of plant centrality in three respects. First, the development of technology inside a plant is, at one and the same time, an acid test of the business organisation's commitment to a particular location, as well as a material response to locational constraints. By comparison with central plants, the proliferation of peripheral plants and their relatively small size act to negate continual investment. Second, the propensity to invest in technology in central plants itself appears to generate very different strategies to production with greater attention being placed on non-technical aspects of improving productivity. Third, the insights into plant technology gained from the attitudes of plant managers serve to reinforce and expand the conclusions that technology is an integral component of a plant's centrality within a business organisation.

Conclusions

Rather than by examining plants drawn from different enterprises, the discussion has illustrated the main dimensions of changes in the form of technology, in plants of varying degrees of centrality within a single business organisation. Perhaps, the major result has been the apparent influence of features of both the plant's environmental domain and intra-organisational relations in determining the form of technology inside the establishment. Often, these factors reinforce one another, thereby creating their own historical inertia. On the one hand, the established central plants, which are technologically advanced, draw in and determine the distribution of investment from the parent, centralising resources further. On the other hand, business uncertainties and the relative ephemerality of peripheral plants, normally, although not always, located in peripheral environments, do not justify extensive and continual investment. Consequently, this pattern suggests growing inequality in the technological structure of plants within large corporations.

The limited evidence from the four plant case studies used, however, also indicates an approximate conformity between plant centrality and other characteristics, such as the age and mixture of their technology, with the largest, newest and most recent assemblages of equipment and working methods being found in central locations. Overall, this pattern would appear to provide some evidence to support the contention that the business organisation acts as a channel for the diffusion of technology, as well as a centre of technological innovation, by 'transferring' processes outwards from the dynamic central establishments to the peripheral plants. Apart from this broad conclusion, it has not been possible to address the nature of structural mechanisms which might aid in this transfer process, and this issue must remain an avenue for future research. At least two other issues have been raised but not addressed. These are, first, the precise balance of environmental and organisational forces which may influence plant technology and, second, the way in which new technologies are developed, assimilated and withdrawn from production and, possibly, moved to other sites.

What the study has been able to do is sketch some of the relationships between centrality and technology and also to suggest some causal features for explaining unequal patterns of labour dynamics between plants. It is fairly clear, for example, that a fundamental cause of the disparity in labour patterns is the gradual peripheralisation and reduction in the amount of labour required in production in central plants, where, perhaps paradoxically, additional emphasis is placed on increasing productivity through labour rather than through new equipment, in which there is little scope for improvement. In peripheral plants, any pressure to increase productivity puts additional stress on the need for new equipment, which is unlikely to be acquired over the short term because of the small size of the market and the larger number of plants. All that is left to do is to integrate these conclusions on the processes operating inside the plant with those aspects of the structure of business organisations that have been discussed in preceding chapters.

8 Summary and Conclusions

The patterns of business organisation described in this study are historically specific. They represent the most advanced forms of international production arising during the 1970s and early 1980s. Undoubtedly, corporate restructuring will continue, and new processes and structures will emerge. In interpreting these evolving patterns the connection between corporate structure and the organisation of the space economy will have to be drawn more precisely (Wood, 1981). As Dicken and Hewings (1982, pp. 58-9) have noted:

> we are only beginning to grope for ways of articulating and understanding how the macro-processes and organisational processes work to produce particular forms of differentiation and integration in the space economy. . .it is a simple matter to assert that corporate organisation is a key element in an understanding of the way regional economies work: it is another matter to provide the necessary conceptual and empirically testable set of hypotheses and/or models to examine how corporate processes and structures operate to produce particular geographical configurations of activities.

It is to be hoped that this study has made a useful start towards this goal. The argument developed at the outset of this study sought to establish a preliminary relationship between spatial form and corporate organisation beginning with the concern that 'so few geographers have examined the corporation as a geographic phenomenon that the key problems are yet to be stated' (McNee, 1974, p. 50). It was emphasised that industrial geographers have, instead, been preoccupied with attempting to establish relationships between the spatial form and behaviour of enterprises, with the result that they have failed to examine in any depth how organisational structure acts as the primary mediating mechanism (e.g. McConnell, 1982). Thus, the more normally adopted approach in industrial geography which emphasises space as a set of causal factors was judged to be an inadequate means of tackling

248

this issue because such an approach concentrates on location-specific factors, such as the notion of comparative advantage, which though not invalid, cloak and mystify the processes of industrial change operating on and within business organisations (Fagan, 1981).

Corporate organisation, therefore, has formed the focus of this discussion, based on the supposition that the structure of organisations supplies us with analytical benchmarks against which our conclusions can be gauged, though it does not provide an explanation of firm behaviour (Massey and Meegan, 1979b). Consequently, a study of the organisational structure of business organisations in the chemicals industry was used as the pivot for examining the relationship between the internationalisation of production and the changing spatial division of labour. The principal unit of investigation was the individual business organisation so that an understanding of the processes shaping corporate form could be developed in a systematic rather than an anecdotal fashion.

In pursuing the business organisation approach three key questions were posed: what different forms of corporate organisation exist and what role does space play within these structures; what regularities can be identified in the operations of these multi-plant organisations; and how can the gap between these two aspects of organisational and multi-plant structures be bridged? These questions led to a review of some of the more useful concepts relating to the organisational and spatial structure of business organisations that could be derived from organisation theory and industrial geography and integrated them within an a priori model of the spatial organisation of corporations (Chapter 2).

Clearly, this generalised model could not be comprehensively developed and tested within the limits of this study. Instead, the empirical analysis was designed to investigate the principal dimensions of corporate structure in a selective way, to answer the three key questions posed above. For example, the essential features of the production, performance, organisational structure and geographical structure of major business organisations were explored within the context of the chemicals industry (Chapter 3). This analysis demonstrated the distinct pattern of business organisation segmentation that existed in 1980; it also highlighted the significance of large business organisations in this industry. Thus, different forms of corporate organisation were identified and different spatial components of organisational structure were highlighted. In a bid to overcome some of the limitations of this cross-sectional approach, spatial processes were emphasised by evaluating the restructuring initiatives of one global corporation, ICI, between 1970 and 1980 (Chapter 4). Within this case study, the integral role of space in corporate organisation was illustrated and, in particular, the repercussions of restructuring for the workforce of ICI were discussed.

The regularities within the multi-plant structure of corporations were then investigated. In particular, an attempt was made using plants in ICI's paints division to develop a deeper understanding of the relationship between the plant at a micro-scale and the business organisation at a macro-scale (Chapter 5). After notions of plant structure were derived from industrial geography and organisation theory, a preliminary attempt was made to operationalise the concept of *plant centrality* within business organisations. This objective was achieved by defining and calibrating the national environmental domains and intra-organisational relations of individual plants within the paints division of ICI. The centrality concept thus provided an explanatory framework within which plant features and characteristics could be examined through a combination of organisational and locational parameters.

The resolution of this problem led to an examination of plant employment by developing a set of measures of labour dynamics, which were then explained in relation to the main characteristics of each plant's location and position within the larger business organisation. Together with selected plant case studies, these insights underlined the effects on labour of the technological foundations of plant centrality and peripherality within corporate structures (Chapter 6). The critical dimensions of technology were then explored to illustrate the complexity of organisation-environment relationships (Chapter 7).

Once these results relating to the role of space in corporate organisation were established, the principal focus of the study could be addressed — the relationship between changes in the structure of business organisations and the internationalisation of production. Then, the secondary focus concerning the implications of structural change in corporations for the changing spatial division of labour can be discussed. Finally, some of the implications of the study can be detailed by outlining some directions for future research.

Organisations, Space and Power

The results of this study have demonstrated that important insights into the functioning of the international space economy can be gained by adopting a business organisation approach rather than the environment-centred approach normally adopted in industrial geography, which has emphasised space as a set of autonomous processes (McDermott and Taylor, 1982). A business organisation perspective isolates the corporation as a discrete unit of investigation, operating within its *own* space economy − a corporate space rather than a geographic space. Such a perspective, which views corporate structure as a force unifying otherwise separate geographical areas, consequently draws a direct link between industrial change in local or regional economies and a primary causal mechanism − the corporation. By examining large business organisations, it is possible to see that not only are corporations constrained by interaction with their environments, but that they also make strategic choices (Child, 1972a; Thomas, 1980) in a way which is *spatially* selective. Indeed, McDermott and Taylor (1982, p. 201) have commented that 'this finding raises the possibility that spatial monopoly is an important mechanism which is used by all types of organisation to achieve external effectiveness and internal efficiency in relation to a physically constrained and therefore more certain external environment'.

What is more, the specific spatial configuration of business organisation is vital in initiating, maintaining and increasing dependencies of power both between and within corporations. Organisational form is, therefore, central to an understanding of the dynamics of enterprise and the formulation of a theory of 'structuration' of corporate space, the significance of which has been stressed by a large number of authors recently (e.g. March, 1981; Hage, 1980). In particular, Ranson, Hinings and Greenwood (1980, p. 4) have pointed out that:

If. . .we are to establish clearly the degree to which actors in fact construct their worlds, if we are to provide a causal explanation that goes beyond statistical uniformities, we must conserve but transcend. . .the previous levels of analysis, and lock our explanation into a *temporal* mode which focusses on the historical development of structures. The derived propositions at this level are neither day-to-day negotiated practices nor reified uniformities, but the discovery through time of underlying structures of social relationships whose constitutive political processes account for the structural arrangements that we wish to explain.

Couched in these terms, the present study has been partial in its approach

Figure 8.1: Conceptualising the Relationship between Business Organisation and Plant Structures

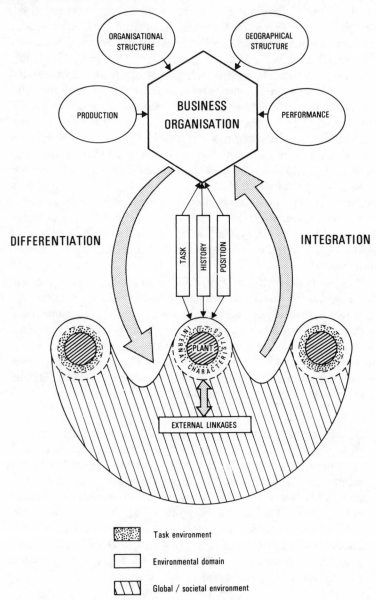

to the dynamic aspects of corporate structure. Nevertheless, it has provided some insights into the relationships between organisational form and the environment in several ways (Figure 8.1). A debate that continues to flourish in the literature on organisations, for instance, relates to the association between differentiation and other structural features in business organisations (see for example, Donaldson, 1982; Grinyer, 1982; Child, 1982). The 'divisionalisation' measure of differentiation has been tentatively related to attributes of corporate size and the degree of diversification of an organisation.

A result of this study, however, has been to demonstrate relationships between the geographical decentralisation of a corporation, and the degree of structural differentiation and integration. It is likely that the identification of this association reflects a significant response to the spatial differentiation of an organisation's environment.

The four types of large business organisation operating in the chemicals industry which have been identified at an international scale displayed very different degrees of decentralisation, multinationality and the spatial extent of their operations. Furthermore, contrasting organisational forms appeared to operate in different environments with those environments measured here by the characteristics of their relevant host countries. At one extreme, the global and global restructuring corporations were highly decentralised from their home countries and were extensively multinational. At the other extreme, multinational corporations and especially large national business organisations were more centralised and dependent upon the home countries. These very different spatial structures underline the significance of global corporations compared to multinational and large national business organisations respectively. The sheer size and geographical spread of global corporations makes them the dominant partners in an industry characterised by highly unequal inter-organisational power relations.

Also, the results have demonstrated that the more developed forms of corporate organisation are not necessarily superior. Although structure can and does form the basis of unequal power relations, it does not guarantee high performance. The disparities in the performance of the business organisations identified testify to this conclusion. Indeed, other recent evidence has questioned the earlier view (Stopford and Wells, 1972; Franko, 1976) that the global and multinational structures are best suited to dealing with global environments. Bartlett (1983) has asserted that there is, in fact, no ideal international structure because of the consolidation of two tendencies: the emergence of global competitors in many industries, which has resulted in a battle for global rather than national markets (Levitte, 1983); and the rising demands placed on corporations by host country governments, which have acted to reduce the advantages of internationalised production. *Flexibility* instead is now held to be the key to success, a function of the nature of the decision process characteristic of an organisation, rather than simply a change in structural design, which can divert attention away from business and have traumatic effects on organisational success (Bartlett, 1983). The frictions of space still felt in more nascent forms of business organisation, therefore, coupled with the existence of large oligopolistic global and multinational corporations, reinforce the conclusion that this unevenness between enterprises will continue. Indeed, 'the time when a firm is born and the cohort of firms it is born into is extremely important for its growth potential and the development sequence it can have in the future' (Taylor and Thrift, 1982a, p. 31).

An interesting theoretical corollary which arises from this conclusion is the need to understand factors which influence the evolution of structures in motion. For instance, Astley and Van de Ven (1983) have recently suggested that there is a need to determine whether organisational forms are actions or reactions; the outcome of, first, internal adaptation or selection of environments, and second, whether or not they are created by management choice alone. The idea that one-way relationships can be identified, however, is altogether too simplistic. As a remedy, Ranson, Hinings and Greenwood (1980) have put forward the proposition that structural evolution must be seen as being both defined *and* mediated by existing conditions. They defined the main elements as:

1. provinces of meaning, such as the beliefs and values of managers in positions of influence in organisations;
2. the availability of alternative schemes and the dependencies of power between these choices; and
3. the existence of contextual constraints, including the existing structure, features of the environment and capital resources available for change.

The two-way relationship between organisation and environment over time was illustrated by the case study of restructuring within ICI. It showed how organisational changes in the mid-1970s arose out of a shift in the geographical and functional emphases of the corporation, and a changing business environment. This interrelationship between organisation and environment is important, because as Meyer (1982, p. 535) forcefully noted, 'by plunging organisations into unfamiliar circumstances, jolts can legitimate unorthodox experiments that revitalize them, teach lessons that reacquaint them with their environments'. ICI's decentralisation of production facilities out of the United Kingdom during the 1970s was a simultaneous reaction to over-reliance on the British economy and the potential offered by expanding into new regions overseas. Indeed, this strategy emphasises the vital role that spatial aspects of corporate structure have played in maintaining and increasing ICI's position as one of the most powerful global corporations in the chemicals industry.

At a more specific level, this study has also shown that space plays an important role *within* the multi-plant structure of business organisations (Figure 8.1). The result of large corporations cutting across international boundaries, uniting quite separate and different establishments under ties of common ownership, creates a structural basis for the promotion of intra-organisational power relations. Although the tasks of individual plants, as allocated to them by the organisation, are critical in determining the initial centrality of an establishment, as the Aston studies showed (Pugh *et al.*, 1969; Hinings *et al.*, 1974), this analysis has also highlighted and emphasised the significance of the combined influence of the spatial and historical development of the corporation in determining plant centrality or peripherality. Specifically, the centrality framework advocated here underlined the importance of the position of a plant in the ownership hierarchy of a corporation, because this is more or less synonymous with the history of that establishment as part of the organisation. What this means is that the overall centrifugal tendency which is characteristic of the process of the internationalisation of production in large corporations carries with it a direct structural corollary, simply because expansion is uneven in time and space.

Put simply, the plants which are set up or acquired earliest by the business organisation are likely to be the establishments which survive because they have been able to accumulate and consolidate their power *vis à vis* others in the corporation, in the form, for example, of larger outputs and administrative functions. Further, the characteristic of a plant's environmental domain will frequently reinforce its intra-organisational centrality or peripherality. Hence, new plants will enter the multi-plant structure on an unequal footing because of a self-perpetuating historical inertia, caused by the on-site accumulation of fixed capital assets (e.g. Massey and Meegan, 1979b). This usually implies that large plants will be located in larger markets and small plants in smaller markets. By inference, therefore, the functional position of a plant within an enterprise as a whole will be more significant than branch plant or subsidiary status per se in determining the likely impacts on the local economy (Dicken, 1982).

Structural inertia will add to intra-organisational inequalities as the most central plants, unlike their peripheral counterparts, tend to draw investment into the organisation and to mediate its distribution and allocation throughout the whole enterprise. Furthermore, the gap between central and peripheral establishments will be highlighted because there are fewer central establishments. Hence, increased spatial concentration of resources will occur in these locations. The greater number and relative ephemerality of peripheral plants, in contrast, will produce a spatial decentralisation of corporate resources. A significant upshot of this process is present in the form of production technology used in different plants, with the newest mixtures of equipment and advanced working methods generally being found in the central establishments. According to these results, therefore, the technologies used within the plants of multinational corporations will not necessarily represent the most recent forms available within the organisation, because techniques will be adjusted to local working conditions.

This study has, therefore, demonstrated some of the main effects that space can exert on corporate structure. At one level, these effects can be viewed in terms of the way the organisation differentiates and integrates its structure in response to environmental pressures. At another level, they can be recognised in the way that inherently hierarchical structures are mapped out in space through the disposition of individual plants (Figure 8.1). Whichever level of analysis is chosen, more attention must be given to this aspect of organisational structure in the future.

Structural Dynamics and the Changing Spatial Division of Labour

At the outset it was noted that the major problem of Fröbel, Heinrichs and Kreye's (1980) concept of a 'new international division of labour' was the lack of a suitable analytical framework through which to study it, rather than any intrinsic faults associated with the concept itself. Thus, the secondary focus of the study was to explore the utility of a business organisation framework in obtaining an additional perspective on the changing spatial division of labour. Insights have been gained from the analysis into aspects of labour dynamics at three main levels: between different types of business organisation operating in the chemicals industry; geographically, within the divisions of a single corporation, ICI; and between plants within the paints division of ICI.

In examining different types of business organisation, it was evident that the dynamics of corporate workforces were related to the structure and performance of enterprises. The two groups of global corporations − global and global restructuring − displayed similar structural characteristics, and were performing very differently, with direct repercussions on their workforces. Although both the global and global restructuring groups of corporations employed between 80,000 to 100,000 workers, changes in their business environments overall resulted in the former expanding its workforce rapidly and the latter contracting − both in the order of several thousand workers annually. However, the multinational corporations and the large national business organisations, with workforces averaging 20,000 and 13,000 respectively, were performing reasonably well, with the result that their workforces were growing slightly. This result suggests that the type of organisational structure is critical in evaluating both the *magnitude* and the *rate of change* of the workforce of a corporation.

The geographical implications of the structural dynamics of corporations can only be addressed through a detailed analysis of individual organisations, such as the one undertaken for ICI. It was possible, for example, to explain the changing spatial division of labour within ICI, within the context of the organisation's diversification of its geographical base. In effect, this resulted in a rapid contraction of the United Kingdom workforce because of the parallel processes of domestic rationalisation and extension of overseas facilities. Changes in the nature of production and products produced, alongside this geographical restructuring, were additional components central to an explanation of the new spatial division of labour, which was characterised by a much smaller and spatially decentralised workforce (albeit unevenly) at an international level. Having established these general patterns, however, the changes described for ICI as a whole, were not mirrored uniformly through the organisation's individual divisions. Also, the aggregate analysis of the corporate workforce examined only the major changes that arose from alterations to the number, size and locations of plants; it did not include in situ changes to production that contributed to the changing spatial division of labour.

As a complement to these broader perspectives, the survey of labour dynamics specific to individual plants in ICI's paints division was made to investigate the effects of on-site restructuring in a single product area. Three aspects of employment — job mix, job stability and production efficiency — were found to vary significantly with the characteristics of a plant's environmental domain and intra-organisational relations — the centrality of its position in a corporate power network. The size of a plant's workforce and the degree of instability of jobs were shown, for example, to increase with domain and plant centrality. Similarly, the mix of jobs, as indicated by the administrative ratio, increased in proportion to the size and age of an establishment and the centrality of its domain. The causes of these various labour patterns were shown to be variations in the nature and efficiency of production between plants, including the variable nature of their technologies and working methods.

Highly capital-intensive production in central plants, for instance, was a product of the age of the plant (reflecting the advanced technological development and high innovative capacity) and the competitive environment in which they were located. These facts reinforced the need to offset rapidly rising labour costs in these locations. The distinct labour dynamics of these establishments are, therefore, to be explained through the interaction between plant and environment characteristics which affect technology, more than any single factor. In central plants, the highly developed state of technology results in more advanced working methods and a reduction in the amount of labour required because of the adoption of mass production processes. This peripheralisation of labour in production in central establishments is contrasted by the integral nature of labour to production in some peripheral plants. Over time, therefore, it is suggested that the labour dynamics experienced in a plant reflect the structural centrality or peripherality of the establishment itself.

The major problem associated with Fröbel, Heinrichs and Kreye's exposition of a new international division of labour, as outlined at the beginning of this book, is the lack of a theoretical perspective and, in particular, the underplaying of the process of capital accumulation itself (Castles, 1979; Thrift, 1980). As accumulation is an inherently historical process, the division of labour can only be explained within these limits, as the outcome of the current stage of corporate development. However, Fröbel, Heinrichs and Kreye begin their analysis with types of countries, rather than organisations, as the basic building blocks, which are arranged in a simple hierarchy arising through the vertical division of labour. This analytical strategy is inappropriate since it fails to explain the continuation of uneven accumulation with changing geographical 'centres' and international interpenetration (Jacobson, Wickham and Wickham, 1979; Thrift, 1980).

A related weakness is the study's 'uncritical acceptance of the entire tradition of dependency theory, a theory which is basically useless to explain current changes in capitalism, for it cannot actually explain change at all' (Jacobson, Wickham and Wickham, 1979, p. 128), such as the development of new labour processes and technological and organisational innovation. The view that changes in the spatial division of labour can be divorced from the stage of an organisation's development is, quite clearly, erroneous.

By adopting the business organisation as the prime analytical focus, this study has focused attention on the role played by changes in corporate strategy and organisation in the evolution of the spatial division of labour. It would be shortsighted to make studies of this phenomenon, therefore, without reference to the corporation, or simply by referring to employment figures alone. Such an approach would reveal nothing of the causes and changes in the methods of production which undoubtedly underlie the formation of the changing spatial division of labour (Fagan, 1980). In other words, the new international division of labour is not simply, as Fröbel, Heinrichs and Kreye (1980, p. 15) claim, the product of 'the relocation of production to new industrial sites, where labour-power is cheap to buy, abundant and well disciplined; in short, through the transnational reorganisation of production'. Although this assertion may hold true for certain industries − especially the textile and clothing sector on which their conclusions were based − not all production is internationally hyper-mobile, tied as some industries are in varying degrees to markets and sources of labour, capital and materials. Thus, a business organisation perspective of the spatial division of labour serves to highlight the distinction between *in situ* labour dynamics and changes affected by the *relocation* of production sites. The type of analysis used in this study shows how the restructuring of multinational corporations can, in fact, be used to *derive* a new international division of labour. However, a significant qualification to this thesis is that some large business organisations, such as ICI, are still practising an *old* international division of labour by predominantly using wage labour in the main industrial centres to serve local economies; as well as a *new* international division of labour − by incorporating developing countries into their structure − the *raison d'être* of which is export-led industrialisation directed at world markets. In retrospect, this finding is not surprising, given the well-recorded historical evolution of these business organisations.

Future Directions

Space is an intrinsic aspect of corporate organisation, the structure of which cannot be considered independently of geographical configuration. The business organisation approach has been used in this study to examine some of the principal dimensions of the organisation of corporate space, by attempting to develop the relationship between theories of organisational structure and industrial geography's conceptions of organisation-environment interaction. Through this analysis, it has also been possible to throw some light on the corporation as an important mechanism bringing about the formation of a new international division of labour, one of the primary geographical reflections of economic activity. By focusing upon the importance of corporate structure for the space economy, a basis has been established for future work. Several such research avenues can be charted.

First, there is a need for studies of geographical variations in the form of labour processes within individual corporations, so that the link between labour's characteristics and social reproduction and multinational enterprise can be more fully developed (Sayer, 1980; Clark and Massey, 1982; Clarke, 1982). Indeed, the centrality framework which has been developed to conceptualise the intra-organisational positions of plants offers a potential context within which such comparative studies could be operationalised. This conclusion, however, emphasises the need to know a great deal more about technology and the organisation of production involved in locational processes (Dicken and Hewings, 1982), especially the role of the state in formulating unequal contexts for industrial relations and work organisation. Future work in these and other areas such as comparisons of labour costs could be profitably pursued within the centrality framework. Indeed, this call for research into the organisation of production within the context of corporate organisation demonstrates how far geographical thinking has progressed since Ullman (1953, p. 55) noted that:

> We have no more interest in the production process inside a factory than has an economic theorist. What we are mainly interested in, as Professor Tower noted years ago, is what comes in the back door

and what goes out the front door of a plant, so that we may know why it is located where it is and what its effect on the area under study is. The effects of changes in internal processes, however, are relevant in so far as they affect these external relations.

Second, as this study has only examined the structure of business organisations operating in the chemicals industry, several questions are raised with regard to the degree of universality of characteristics of the spatial and organisational structure of large corporations. For instance, are global corporations more or less evident in other industries; how do these characteristics affect the functioning of these industries compared to the chemicals industry; what are the spatial implications of such structural contrasts; and how do these patterns of power relations between large business organisations influence the operations of smaller firms which operate alongside them?

A third research field is related to the nature of theoretical and methodological approaches to the dynamics of industries and firms. As has been shown, there are significant structural corollaries of the historical development of organisational structure, not the least of which are the intra-organisational as well as inter-organisational power relations which such evolutionary processes initiate, maintain and increase. Not only do firms evolve unevenly over time and space, but also the environment of the organisation itself is highly variable, and this holds potential implications for corporate structures and strategies which need to be more fully explored. For example, recession in one region in which a business organisation operates may not affect its operations in other regions. Future studies would do well to examine whether or not various types of corporate organisation can act as strategic mechanisms to resist or adapt to such inequalities and changes in their environments. Related to this emphasis is the need to investigate the influence exerted by individual managers in positions of power within organisations on redirecting corporate structural and spatial strategies.

Finally, the need for an overall research thrust into the geography of business organisations has been reinforced by Dicken and Hewings's (1982, p. 75) argument that 'if we are to contribute to the continued understanding of the evolution of the space economy, it is clear that longitudinal analysis and monitoring are going to have to assume a far more visible and generally accepted role than hitherto assigned to them'. This long-term objective of obtaining a more detailed understanding of the organisation of corporate space can only be achieved by a much deeper probing into the ideas and concepts of the organisational sciences, coupled with a willingness and capacity to develop these theoretical guidelines within industrial geography.

References

Adrian, C. and Evans, C. (1984) 'Borg-Warner (Albury Wodonga): A Lead Firm in a Regional Economy?' in M.J. Taylor (ed.), *The Geography of Australian Corporate Power*, Croom Helm, Sydney, pp. 159-71

Aglietta, M. (1979) *A Theory of Capitalist Regulation: the US Experience*, New Left Books, London

Aldrich, H.E. and Mindlin, S.E. (1978) 'Uncertainty and Dependence: Two Perspectives on Environment' in L. Karpik (ed.), *Organization and Environment*, Sage, London, pp. 149-70

Alford, J. (1979) 'Australian Labour, Multinationals and the Asian-Pacific Region', *Journal of Australian Political Economy*, 6, 4-23

Aliber, R.Z. (1970) 'A Theory of Direct Investment' in C.P. Kindleberger (ed.), *The International Corporation*, MIT Press, Cambridge, Mass.

Aliber, R.Z. (1971) 'The Multinational Enterprise in a Changing World' in J.H. Dunning (ed.), *The Multinational Enterprise*, Croom Helm, London, pp. 49-56

Allan, J. (1981) 'When ICI's Front Doorstep Moved a Thousand Kilometres South', *ICI Magazine*, 59, 74-9

Allen, T.J. (1977) *Managing the Flow of Technology*, MIT Press, Cambridge, Mass.

Allen, T.J. and Cohen, S.I. (1969) 'Information Flow in Research and Development Laboratories', *Administrative Science Quarterly*, 14, 12-19

Amin, A. (1984) 'Restructuring and Spatial Decentralisation in Fiat' in R. Hudson and J. Lewis (eds.), *Dependent Development in Southern Europe*, Methuen, London

Ansoff, H.I. (1965) *Corporate Strategy*, McGraw-Hill, New York

Ashcroft, B. and Ingham, K.P.D. (1979) 'Company Adaptation and the Response to Regional Policy: a Comparative Analysis of the MNC Subsidiaries and Indigenous Companies', *Regional Studies*, 13, 25-37

Astley, W.G. and Van de Ven, A.H. (1983) 'Central Perspectives and Debates in Organization Theory', *Administrative Science Quarterly*, 28, 245-73

The Australian (1981) 22 October, p. 1

Averitt, R.T. (1968) *The Dual Economy: the Dynamics of American Industry Structure*, Norton, New York

Banaji, J. (1977) 'Modes of Production in a Materialist Conception of History', *Capital and Class, 3*, 1-44

Baran, J.N. and Bielby, W.T. (1980) 'Bringing the Firms back in: Stratification, Segmentation and the Organisation of Work', *American Sociological Review, 45*, 737-65

Bartlett, C.A. (1983) 'MNCs: Get off the Reorganization Merry-go-round', *Harvard Business Review, 83*, 138-46

Bassett, K. (1984) 'Corporate Structure and Corporate Change in a Local Economy: The Case of Bristol', *Environment and Planning A, 16*, pp. 879-900

Bennett, S. and Bowers, D. (1976) *An Introduction to Multivariate Techniques for Social and Behavioural Sciences*, Macmillan, London

Benson, J.K. (1975) 'The Interorganizational Network as a Political Economy', *Administrative Science Quarterly, 20*, 229-48

Berger, S. and Piore, M.J. (1980) *Dualism and Discontinuity in Industrial Societies*, Cambridge University Press, Cambridge

Beynon, H. (1975) *Working for Ford*, EP Publishing, Wakefield

Blackbourn, A. (1974) 'The Spatial Behaviour of American Firms in Western Europe' in F.E.I. Hamilton (ed.), *Spatial Perspectives on Industrial Organization and Decision-making*, John Wiley, Chichester, pp. 245-64

Blackbourn, A. (1982) 'The Impact of Multinational Corporations on the Spatial Organisation of Developed Nations' in M.J. Taylor and N.J. Thrift (eds.), *The Geography of Multinationals*, Croom Helm, London, pp. 147-57

Blackburn, R.M. and Mann, M. (1979) *The Working Class in the Labour Market*, Cambridge Studies in Sociology, Macmillan, London

Blalock, H.M. (1972) *Social Statistics*, McGraw-Hill, New York

Blau, P.M. (1970) 'A Formal Theory of Differentiation in Organisations', *American Sociological Review, 35*, 201-18

Blau, P.M., McHugh-Falbe, C., McKinley, W. and Tracy, P.K. (1976) 'Technology and Organization in Manufacturing', *Administrative Science Quarterly, 21*, 20-40

Bloomfield, G.T. (1981) 'The Changing Spatial Organisation of Multinational Corporations in the World Automotive Industry' in F.E.I. Hamilton and G.J.R. Linge (eds.), *Spatial Analysis, Industry and the Industrial Environment, Volume II: International Industrial Systems*, John Wiley, London, pp. 357-94

BLPG (Brighton Labour Process Group) (1977) 'The Capitalist Labour Process', *Capital and Class, 7*, 3-26

Bluestone, B. and Harrison, B. (1982) *The Deindustrialisation of America*, Basic Books, New York

Boehm, W.T., Menkhaus, D.J. and Penn, J.B. (1976) 'Accuracy of Least Squares Computer Programs: Another Reminder', *American Journal of Agricultural Economics, 58*, 757-60

Braverman, H. (1974) *Labour and Monopoly Capital*, Monthly Review Press, New York

Brooke, M.Z. and Remmers, H.L. (1970) *The Strategy of Multinational Enterprise: Organizational and Finance*, American Elsevier, New York

Buckley, P.J. and Casson, M. (1976) *The Future of Multinational Enterprise*, Macmillan, London

Burawoy, M. (1979) *Manufacturing Consent*, University of Chicago Press, Chicago

Burns, T. and Stalker, G.M. (1961) *The Management of Innovation*, Tavistock, London

Burton, F.N. and Inoue, H. (1983) 'Country Risk Evaluation Methods: A Survey of Systems in Use', *The Banker, 133*, 41-3

Cardoso, F.H. (1972) 'Dependency and Development in Latin America' *New Left Review, 74*, 83-95

Carmichael, C.L. (1977) 'Employer Labour-force Adjustment to Changing Market Conditions, with Special Respect to Declining Demand', *Working Paper 2*, Department of Geography, London School of Economics

Carney, J., Hudson, R. and Lewis, J. (1980) *Regions in Crisis: New Perspectives on European Regional Theory*, St Martin's Press, New York

Castles, S. (1979) 'Review Article: Die neue internationale Arbeitsteilung (The New International Division of Labour)', *Capital and Class, 7*, 122-5

Cattrell, R.B. (1966) 'Factor Analysis: An Introduction to Essentials', *Biometrics, 21*, 190-215

Caves, R.E. (1983) 'Multinational Enterprise and Economic Analysis', Cambridge University Press, Cambridge

Chandler, A.D. (1962) *Strategy and Structure: the History of the American Industrial Enterprise*, MIT Press, Cambridge, Mass.

Chapman, K. (1973) 'Agglomeration and Linkage in the United Kingdom Petro-chemical Industry', *Transactions, Institute of British Geographers, 60*, 33-68

Chapman, K. (1974) 'Corporate Systems in the United Kingdom Petrochemical Industry', *Annals, Association of American Geographers, 64*, 126-37

Chemical Age (1979) 27 July, pp. 20-1

Chemical Age (1980a) 14 March, pp. 16-20

Chemical Age (1980b) 5 January, pp. 16-19

Chemical Age (1980c) 7 November, p. 3

Chemical Age (1980d) 20 June, p. 4

Chemical Age (1980e) 18 July, p. 10

Chemical Age (1981) 29 May, pp. 12-13

Chemical Business (1981) 27 July, pp. 9-16

Chemical Week (1980a) 19 March, pp. 32-8

Chemical Week (1980b) 22 October, p. 19

Chemical Week (1981) 9 September, pp. 59-60

Child, J. (1972a) 'Organization Structure and Strategies of Control: A Replication of the Aston Study, *Administrative Science Quarterly, 17*, 163-77

Child, J. (1972b) 'Organizational Structure, Environment and Performance: the Role of Strategic Choice', *Sociology, 6*, 1-22

Child, J. (1973) 'Parkinson's Progress: Accounting for the Number of

Specialists in Organizations', *Administrative Science Quarterly*, *18*, 328-48

Child, J. (1982) Discussion Note: Divisionalization and Size: a Comment on the Donaldson/Grinyer Debate, *Organization Studies*, *3/4*, 351-3

Child, J. and Mansfield, R. (1972) 'Technology, Size and Organization Structure', *Sociology*, *8*, 369-93

Clark, G.L. (1981) 'The Employment Relation and the Spatial Division of Labour: a Hypothesis', *Annals, Association of American Geographers*, *71*, 412-24

Clark, G.L. and Massey, D. (1982) 'A Research Agenda on Multinational Enterprises and the Spatial Division of Labour' in B.T. Robson and J. Rees (eds.), *Geographical Agenda for a Changing World*, SSRC, London, pp. 78-85

Clarke, I.M. (1981) 'The Labour Process in the New International Division of Labour', unpublished seminar paper, Department of Human Geography, Australian National University

Clarke, I.M. (1982) 'The Changing International Division of Labour within ICI' in M.J. Taylor and N.J. Thrift (eds.), *The Geography of Multinationals*, Croom Helm, London, pp. 90-116

Clarke, I.M. (1984) 'The Chemicals Industry and ICI: The Form and Impact of Global Corporations in Australia' in M.J. Taylor (ed.), *The Geography of Australian Corporate Power*, Croom Helm, pp. 125-55

Clegg, S. (1980) 'Restructuring the Semi-peripheral Labour Process' in P. Boreham and G. Dow (eds.), *Work and Inequality. Volume One: Workers, Economic Crisis and the State*, Macmillan, Melbourne, pp. 28-53

Cohen, J. (1977) *Statistical Power Analysis for the Behavioral Sciences*, Academic Press, New York

Comstock, D.E. and Scott, W.R. (1977) 'Technology and the Structure of Sub-units: Distinguishing Individual and Workgroup Effects', *Administrative Science Quarterly*, *22*, 177-202

Coriot, B. (1980) 'The Restructuring of the Assembly Line: a New Economy of Time and Control', *Capital and Class*, *11*, 34-43

Coulter, P.B. (1979) 'Organizational Effectiveness in the Public Sector: The Example of Municipal Fire Protection', *Administrative Science Quarterly*, *24*, 65-82

Crum, R. and Gudgin, R. (1978) *Non-production Activities in UK Manufacturing Industry*, European Commission, Brussels

CSE (Conference of Socialist Economists) (1976) 'The Labour Process and Class Strategies', *CSE Pamphlet No. 1*, London

Dahl, R.A. (1957) 'The Concept of Power', *Behavioral Science, 2*, 201-15

Daily Telegraph (1980) 29 August, p. 7

Daily Telegraph (1981) 9 November, p. 14

Danson, M.W. (1982) 'The Industrial Structure and Labour Market Segmentation: Urban and Regional Implications', *Regional Studies*, *16*, 255-65

Daultrey, S. (1976) 'Principal Components Analysis', *Concepts and*

Techniques in Modern Geography (CATMOG), No.8, Geo Abstracts, Norwich

Davidson, W.H. and Haspeslagh, P. (1982) 'Shaping a Global Product Organization', *Harvard Business Review*, *60*, 125-32

Davies, W.K.D. (1971) 'Varimax and the Destruction of Generality – A Methodological Note', *Area*, *3*, 112-18

Davis, S.M. (1979a) 'Basic Structures of Multinational Corporations' in S.M. Davis (ed.), *Managing and Organizing Multinational Corporations*, Pergamon Press, Oxford, pp. 193-211

Davis, S.M. (1979b) 'Trends in the Organization of Multinational Corporations' in S.M. Davis (ed.), *Managing and Organizing Multinational Corporations*, Pergamon Press, Oxford, pp. 231-48

Dewar, R. and Hage, J. (1978) 'Size, Technology, Complexity, and Structural Differentation: Towards a Theoretical Synthesis', *Administrative Science Quarterly*, *23*, 111-36

Diamond Company Handbook (1981), Tokyo

Dicken, P. (1976) 'The Multiplant Business Enterprise and Geographical Space: Some Issues on the Study of External Control and Regional Development', *Regional Studies*, *10*, 401-12

Dicken, P. (1977) 'A Note on Location Theory and the Large Business Enterprise', *Area*, *9*, 138-43

Dicken, P. (1982) 'Recent Trends in International Direct Investment, with Particular Reference to the United States and the United Kingdom' in B.T. Robson and J. Rees (eds.), *Geographical Agenda for a Changing World*, SSRC, London, pp. 118-61

Dicken, P. and Hewings, G. (1982) 'The Changing Organisational Structure of Regional Economies and the Role of Transnational Corporations: Some Research Issues' in B.T. Robson and J. Rees (eds.), *Geographical Agenda for a Changing World*, SSRC, London, pp. 57-77

Dicken, P. and Lloyd, P.E. (1976) 'Geographical Perspectives on United States Investment in the United Kingdom', *Environment and Planning A*, *8*, 685-705

Dicken, P. and Lloyd, P.E. (1979) 'The Corporate Dimension of Employment Change in the Inner City' in C. Jones (ed.), *Urban Deprivation and the Inner City*, Croom Helm, London, pp. 32-62

Dill, W.R. (1958) 'Environment as an Influence on Managerial Autonomy', *Administrative Science Quarterly*, *2*, 409-43

Doehringer, P.B. and Piore, M.J. (1971) *Internal Labour Markets and Manpower Analysis*, D.C. Heath, Lexington, Mass.

Donaldson, L. (1982) 'Divisionalization and Size: a Theoretical and Empirical Critique', *Organization Studies*, *3/4*, 321-37

Donaldson, L., Child, J. and Aldrich, H. (1975) 'The Aston Findings on Centralization: Further Discussion', *Administrative Science Quarterly*, *20*, 453-59

Draper, N. and Smith, H. (1966) *Applied Regression Analysis*, John Wiley, New York

Dun and Bradstreet (1981-82) *Who Owns Whom* (various volumes), London

Dunning, J.H. (1979) 'Explaining Changing Patterns of International

Production: in Defence of the Eclectic Theory', *Oxford Bulletin of Economics and Statistics*, *41*, 269-95

Duvall, R., Jackson, S., Russett, B., Snidal, D. and Sylvan, D. (1981) 'A Formal Model of 'Dependencia' Theory' in R. Merritt and B. Russett (eds.), *From National Development to Global Community*, Allen and Unwin, London, pp. 47-62

The Economist (1980a) 19 April, pp. 70-1

The Economist (1980b) 15 March, p. 75

The Economist (1980c) 18 October, pp. 95-6

The Economist (1980d) 24 May, pp. 96-8

The Economist (1980e) 17 August, pp. 76-7

The Economist (1980f) 26 January, pp. 100-1

The Economist (1981a) 15 August, pp. 57-8

The Economist (1981b) 4 July, pp. 73-6

The Economist (1981c) 26 September, pp. 82-3

The Economist (1981d) 6 June, pp. 73-4

The Economist (1981e) 3 January, pp. 48-9

The Economist (1981f) 21 March, p. 88

The Economist (1981g) 1 August, p. 55

The Economist (1981h) 4 July, p. 23

The Economist (1981i) 4 April, p. 83

The Economist (1981j) 31 October, pp. 69-70

The Economist (1982a) 11 September, pp. 66-7

The Economist (1982b) 28 August, p. 51

The Economist (1982c) 10 July, pp. 64-5

The Economist (1982d) 9 October, pp. 69-70

The Economist (1982e) 13 February, p. 92

The Economist (1983a) 21 May, p. 76

The Economist (1983b) 18 June, p. 72

Edwards, R. (1979) *Contested Terrain: the Transformation of the Workplace in the Twentieth Century*, Basic Books, New York

Edwards, R.C., Reich, M. and Gordon, D.M. (eds.) (1975) *Labour Market Segmentation*, D.C. Heath, Lexington, Mass.

European Chemical News (1980) 18 August, p. 12

Evan, W.M. (1963) 'The Organization-set: Toward a Theory of Inter-organizational Relations' in J.D. Thompson (ed.), *Approaches to Organizational Design*, University of Pittsburgh Press, Pittsburgh, pp. 173-91

Evans, P.B. (1975) 'Multiple Hierarchies and Organizational Control', *Administrative Science Quarterly*, *20*, 250-9

Evans, P.B. (1981) 'Recent Research on Multinational Corporations', *Annual Reveiw of Sociology*, *7*, 199-223

Fagan, R.H. (1980) 'The Internationalisation of Capital: A Perspective on Stephen Hymer's Work on Transnational Corporations' in R. Peet (ed.), *An Introduction to Marxist Theories of Underdevelopment*, Department of Human Geography Monograph, Publication HG14, Australian National University, Canberra, pp. 175-80

Fagan, R.H. (1981) 'Geographically Uneven Development: Restructuring of the Australian Aluminium Industry', *Australian Geographical*

Studies, 19, 141-60

Ferguson, R. (1977) 'Linear Regression in Geography', *Concepts and Techniques in Modern Geography (CATMOG), No.15,* Geo Abstracts, Norwich

Fiedler, F. (1965) 'Engineer the Job to Fit the Manager', *Harvard Business Review, 43,* 37-48

Financial Times (1980a) 19 October, p. 19

Financial Times (1980b) 15 October, p. 1

Financial Times (1980c) 28 January, p. 24

Financial Times (1981) 1 December, p. 35

Firn, J.R. (1975) 'External Control and Regional Development: the Case of Scotland', *Environment and Planning A, 7,* 393-414

Forbes, D.K. (1982) 'Energy Imperialism and a New International Division of Resources: the Case of Indonesia', *Tijdschrift voor Economische en Sociale Geografie, 73,* 94-108

Fortune Magazine, (1970-1982), New York

Fothergill, S. and Gudgin, G. (1982) *Unequal Growth: Urban and Regional Employment Change in the UK,* Heinemann, London

Frank, A.G. (1967) *Capitalism and Underdevelopment in Latin America,* Monthly Review Press, New York

Franklin, J.L. (1975) 'Down the Organization: Influence Processes Across Levels of Hierarchy', *Administrative Science Quarterly, 20,* 153-64

Franko, L.G. (1976) *The European Multinationals,* Harper and Row, London

Freeman, C. (1974) *The Economics of Industrial Innovation,* Penguin, Harmondsworth

Freeman, J.H. (1973) 'Environment, Technology, and the Administrative Intensity of Manufacturing Organizations', *American Sociological Review, 38,* 750-63

Friedlander, F. and Pickle, H. (1968) 'Components of Effectiveness in Small Organizations', *Administrative Science Quarterly, 13,* 289-304

Friedman, A. (1977a) *Industry and Labour: Class Struggle at Work and Monopoly Capitalism,* Macmillan, London

Friedman, A. (1977b) 'Responsible Autonomy versus Direct Control of the Labour Process', *Capital and Class, 1,* 43-57

Friedman, H. and Meredeen, S. (1980) *The Dynamics of Industrial Conflict: Lessons from Ford,* Croom Helm, London

Fröbel, F., Heinrichs, J. and Kreye, O. (1980) *The New International Division of Labour,* Cambridge University Press, Cambridge

Galbraith, J.K. (1972) *The New Industrial State,* Andre Deutsch, London

Gallie, D. (1978) *In Search of the New Working Class: Automation and Social Integration within the Capitalist Enterprise, Studies in Sociology, 9,* Cambridge University Press, Cambridge

Geddicks, A. (1977) 'Raw Materials: The Achilles' Heel of American Imperialism?', *The Insurgent Sociologist, 7,* 3-13

Gibson, K. (1980) 'The Internationalisation of Capital and Uneven Development within Capitalist Countries' in R. Peet (ed.), *An*

Introduction to Marxist Theories of Underdevelopment, Department of Human Geography Monograph, Publication HG14, Australian National University, Canberra, pp. 169-73

Gillespie, A.E. and Owen, D.W. (1981) 'Unemployment Trends in the Current Recession', *Area*, 2, 189-96

Goddard, J. and Kirby, A. (1976) 'An Introduction to Factor Analysis', *Concepts and Techniques in Modern Geography (CATMOG), No.8*, Geo Abstracts, Norwich

Gold, B. (1981) 'Technological Diffusion in Industry: Research Needs and Shortcomings', *Journal of Industrial Economics*, 29, 247-69

Goodman, P.S., Pennings, J.M. and Associates (1977) *New Perspectives on Organizational Effectiveness*, Jossey-Bass, San Francisco

Gorz, A. (ed.) (1976) *The Division of Labor: the Labor Process and Class Struggle in Modern Capitalism*, New Jersey Humanities Press, Atlantic Highlands

Grinyer, P.H. (1982) 'Discussion Note: Divisionalization and Size: a Rejoinder', *Organization Studies*, 3/4, 339-50

Grunberg, L. (1981) *Failed Multinational Ventures*, Lexington, Toronto

Hage, J. (1980) *Theories of Organizations: Form, Process, and Transformation*, John Wiley, New York

Hage, J. and Aiken, M. (1969) 'Routine Technology, Social Structure and Organization Goals', *Administrative Science Quarterly*, 14, 366-76

Håkanson, L. (1979) 'Towards a Theory of Location and Corporate Growth' in F.E.I. Hamilton and G.J.R. Linge (eds.), *Spatial Analysis, Industry and the Industrial Environment, Volume I: Industrial Systems*, John Wiley, Chichester, pp. 115-38

Hamilton, F.E.I. and Linge, G.J.R. (eds.) (1979) *Spatial Analysis, Industry and the Industrial Environment, Volume 1: Industrial Systems*, John Wiley, Chichester

Harrison, E.F. (1978) *Management and Organizations*, Houghton Mifflin, Boston

Harvey, D. (1982) *The Limits to Capital*, Blackwell, Oxford

Harvey, E. (1968) 'Technology and the Structure of Organizations', *American Sociological Review*, 33, 247-59

Hayter, R. (1982) 'Truncation, the International Firm and Regional Policy', *Area*, 14, 277-82

Hayter, R. and Watts, H.D. (1983) 'The Geography of Enterprise: a Reappraisal', *Progress in Human Geography*, 7, 157-81

Healey, M.J. (1982) 'Plant Closures in Multi-plant Enterprises – the Case of a Declining Industrial Sector', *Regional Studies*, 16, 37-51

Hickson, D.J., Pugh, D.S. and Pheysey, D.C. (1969) 'Operations Technology and Organization Structure: An Empirical Reappraisal'. *Administrative Science Quarterly*, 14, 378-97

Hickson, D.J., Hinings, C.R., Lee, C.A., Schneck, R.E. and Pennings, J.M. (1971) 'A Strategic Contingencies Theory of Intra-organizational Power', *Administrative Science Quarterly*, 16, 216-29

Hinings, C.R., Hickson, D.J., Pennings, J.M. and Schneck, R.E. (1974) 'Structural Conditions of Intra-Organizational Power', *Admin-*

istrative Science Quarterly, *19*, 22-44

Hirsch, P.M. (1975) 'Organizational Effectiveness and the Institutional Environment', *Administrative Science Quarterly*, *20*, 327-44

Holland, S. (1976a) *The Regional Problem*, Macmillan, London

Holland, S. (1976b) *Capital Versus the Regions*, Macmillan, London

Hood, N. and Young, S. (1982) *Multinationals in Retreat: The Scottish Experience*, Edinburgh University Press, Edinburgh

Hout, T., Porter, M.E. and Rudden, E. (1982) 'How Global Companies Win Out', *Harvard Business Review*, *60*, 98-108

Howells, J.R.L. (1983) 'Filter-down Theory: Location and Technology in the UK Pharmaceutical Industry', *Environment and Planning A*, *15*, 147-64

Hower, R.M. and Lorsch, J.W. (1967) 'Organizational Inputs' in J.A. Seiler (ed.), *Systems Analysis in Organizational Behaviour*, Irwin and Dorsey Press, Homewood, Illinois, pp. 157-76

Hudson, R. (1981) 'The Development of Chemicals Production in Western Europe in the Post-War Period', unpublished paper presented to XXI Annual Congress of the European Regional Science Association, Barcelona, 25-28 August

Hymer, S. (1960) 'The International Operations of International Firms: A Study of Direct Investment', unpublished PhD dissertation, Massachusetts Institute of Technology, Boston

Hymer, S. (1972) 'The Multinational Corporation and the Law of Uneven Development' in H. Radice (ed.), *International Firms and Modern Imperialism*, Penguin, Harmondsworth, pp. 39-62

ICI (Imperial Chemical Industries Limited) (1970-82) *Annual Reports*, London

ICI (Imperial Chemical Industries Limited) (1971) *Information Handbook*, London

ICI (Imperial Chemical Industries Limited) (1980) *The Financial Record of ICI*, London

ICI (Imperial Chemical Industries Limited) (1981) *ICI Worldwide*, London

IMF (1982) *International Financial Statistics*, IMF, Geneva

Ireland, D. (1982) *The Unknown Industrial Prisoner*, Sirius, Sydney

Isard, W. (1956) *Location and Space Economy*, MIT Press, Cambridge, Mass.

Jacobs, D. (1974) 'Dependency and Vulnerability: an Exchange Approach to the Control of Organizations', *Administrative Science Quarterly*, *19*, 45-59

Jacobson, D., Wickham, A. and Wickham, J. (1979) 'Review Article: Die neue internationale Arbeitsteilung (The New International Division of Labour)', *Capital and Class*, *7*, 125-30

The Japanese Economic Yearbook (1981), Tokyo

Jurkovich, R. (1974) 'A Core Typology of Organisational Environments', *Administrative Science Quarterly*, *19*, 380-94

Kahl, J. (1976) *Modernization, Exploitation and Dependency*, Transactions Press, New Jersey

Kanter, R.M. and Brinkerhoff, D. (1981) 'Organizational Performance:

Recent Developments in Measurement', *Annual Review of Sociology*, 7, 321-49

Kaplan, A. (1964) 'Power in Perspective' in R.L. Kahn and E. Boulding (eds.), *Power and Conflict in Organizations*, Tavistock, London, pp. 11-32

Kast, F.E. and Rosenzweig, J.C. (1974) *Organization and Management: A Systems Approach*, McGraw-Hill, Tokyo

Katz, D. and Kahn, R.L. (1966) *The Social Psychology of Organizations*, John Wiley, New York

Kaufman, R.L., Hodson, R. and Fligstein, N.D. (1981) 'Defrocking Dualism: A New Approach to Defining Industrial Sectors', *Social Science Research*, 10, 1-31

Keeble, D. (1976) *Industrial Location and Planning in the United Kingdom*, Methuen, London

Khandwalla, P.N. (1974) 'Mass Output Orientation of Operations Technology and Organizational Structure', *Administrative Science Quarterly*, 19, 74-97

King, L.J. (1969) *Statistical Analysis in Geography*, Prentice-Hall, Englewood Cliffs

Knickerbocker, F.T. (1973) *Oligopolistic Reaction and Multinational Enterprise*, MIT Press, Cambridge, Mass.

Krümme, G. (1969) 'Towards a Geography of Enterprise', *Economic Geography*, 45, 30-40

Krümme, G. (1981) 'Making it Abroad: the Evolution of Volkswagen's North American Production Plans' in F.E.I. Hamilton and G.J.R. Linge (eds.), *Spatial Analysis, Industry and the Industrial Environment, Volume II: International Industrial Systems*, John Wiley, Chichester, pp. 329-56

Lawrence, P.R. and Lorsch, J.W. (1967) 'Differentiation and Integration in Complex Organizations', *Administrative Science Quarterly*, 12, 1-47

Le Heron, R.B. (1973) 'Best Practice Technology, Technical Leadership and Regional Economic Development', *Environment and Planning*, 5, 735-49

Le Heron, R.B. (1978) 'R & D in New Zealand Manufacturing Firms and the Goal of the Efficient and Flexible Economy', *Pacific Viewpoint*, 18, 58-78

Levine, S. and White, P.E. (1961) 'Exchange as a Conceptual Framework for the Study of Interorganisational Relationships', *Administrative Science Quarterly*, 5, 583-601

Levitte, T. (1983) 'The Globalization of Markets', *Harvard Business Review*, 83, 92-102

Litterer, J. (1965) *The Analysis of Organizations*, John Wiley, New York

Lloyd, P.E. and Reeve, D.E. (1982) 'North West England 1971-1977: a Study in Industrial Decline and Economic Re-structuring', *Regional Studies*, 16, 345-59

Longley, J.W. (1967) 'An Appraisal of Least Squares Programs for the Electronic Computer from the Point of View of the User',

Journal of the American Statistical Association, 62, 819-41

McAleese, D. and Counahan, M. (1979) '"Stickers" or "Snatchers"? Employment in the Multinational Corporations During the Recession', *Oxford Bulletin of Economics and Statistics, 41,* 345-58

McConnell, J.E. (1982) 'The Internationalisation Process and Spatial Form: Research Problems and Prospects', *Environment and Planning A, 14,* 1633-44

McDermott, P.J. (1976) 'Ownership, Organisation and Regional Dependence in the Scottish Electronics Industry', *Regional Studies, 10,* 319-35

McDermott, P.J. and Keeble, D. (1978) 'Manufacturing Organisation and Regional Employment Change', *Regional Studies, 12,* 247-66

McDermott, P.J. and Taylor, M.J. (1976) 'Attitudes, Images, and Location: The Subjective Context of Decision Making in New Zealand Manufacturing', *Economic Geography, 52,* 325-47

McDermott, P.J. and Taylor, M.J. (1982) *Industrial Organisation and Location,* Cambridge University Press, Cambridge

McNee, R.B. (1958) 'Functional Geography of the Firm, with an Illustrative Case Study From the Petroleum Industry', *Economic Geography, 34,* 321-37

McNee, R.B. (1960) 'Towards a More Humanistic Economic Geography: the Geography of Enterprise', *Tijdschrift voor Economische en Sociale Geografie, 51,* 201-6

McNee, R.B. (1974) 'A Systems Approach to Understanding the Geographic Behavior of Organizations, especially Large Corporations' in F.E.I. Hamilton (ed.), *Spatial Perspectives on Industrial Organization and Decision-making,* John Wiley, Chichester, pp. 47-75

Malecki, E.J. (1979) 'Agglomeration and Intrafirm Linkage in R & D Locations in the United States', *Tijdschrift voor Economische en Sociale Geografie, 70,* 322-32

Malecki, E.J. (1980a) 'Technological Change: British and American Research Themes', *Area, 12,* 253-9

Malecki, E.J. (1980b) 'Corporate Organization of R & D and the Location of Technological Activities', *Regional Studies, 14,* 219-34

Malecki, E.J. (1982) 'Industrial Geography: Introduction to the Special Issue', *Environment and Planning A, 14,* 1571-5

Mandel, E. (1978) *The Second Slump,* New Left Books, London

March, J.G. (1981) 'Footnotes to Organizational Change', *Administrative Science Quarterly, 26,* 563-77

Marshall, J.N. (1979) 'Corporate Organization and Regional Office Employment', *Environment and Planning A, 11,* 553-63

Marshall, J.N. (1982) 'Organisational Theory and Industrial Location', *Environment and Planning A, 14,* 1667-83

Marx, K. (1967) *Capital,* International Publishers Edition, New York

Mason, C. (1982) 'Foreign-owned Manufacturing Firms in the United Kingdom: some Evidence from South Hampshire', *Area, 14,* 7-17

Massey, D.B. (1979) 'In What Sense a Regional Problem?', *Regional Studies, 13,* 233-44

Massey, D. and Meegan, R.A. (1979a) 'Labour Productivity and Regional Employment Change', *Area, 11,* 137-45

Massey, D. and Meegan, R.A. (1979b) 'The Geography of Industrial Reorganisation', *Progress in Planning, 10,* 155-237

Massey, D. and Meegan, R.A. (1982) *The Anatomy of Job Loss,* Methuen, London

Mather, P.M. (1976) *Computational Methods of Multivariate Analysis in Physical Geography,* John Wiley, Chichester

Merkle, J.A. (1980) *Management and Ideology: the Legacy of the International Scientific Management Movement,* University of California Press, Berkeley

Meyer, A.D. (1982) 'Adapting to Environmental Jolts', *Administrative Science Quarterly, 27,* 515-37

Mizruchi, M.S. and Bunting, D. (1981) 'Influences in Corporate Networks: an Examination of Four Measures', *Administrative Science Quarterly, 26,* 475-89

Nakase, T. (1981) 'Some Characteristics of Japanese-type Multinationals Today', *Capital and Class, 13,* 61-98

National Times (1983) 13-19 May, pp. 41-2

Negandhi, A.R. and Reimann, B.C. (1973) 'Task Environment, Decentralization and Organizational Effectiveness', *Human Relations, 26,* 203-14

Newfarmer, R.S. and Topik, S. (1982) 'Testing Dependency Theory: a Case Study of Brazil's Electrical Industry' in M.J. Taylor and N.J. Thrift (eds.), *The Geography of Multinationals,* Croom Helm, London, pp. 33-60

Neville, W. and Taylor, M.J. (1980) 'The Impact of Government on Managerial Attitudes: a Singapore Example', *Tijdschrift voor Economische en Sociale Geografie, 71,* 223-37

Nichols, T. and Beynon, H. (1977) *Living with Capitalism: Class Relations and the Modern Factory,* Routledge and Kegan Paul, London

Norcliffe, G.B. (1975) 'A Theory of Manufacturing Places' in L. Collins and D.F. Walker (eds.), *Locational Dynamics of Manufacturing Activity,* John Wiley, Chichester, pp. 19-57

Normann, R. (1971) 'Organizational Innovativeness: Product Variation and Reorientation', *Administrative Science Quarterly, 16,* 203-15

Oakey, R.P., Thwaites, A.T. and Nash, P.A. (1980) 'The Regional Distribution of Innovative Manufacturing Establishments in Britain', *Regional Studies, 14,* 235-53

Oakey, R.P., Thwaites, A.T. and Nash, P.A. (1982) 'Technological Change and Regional Development: Some Evidence on Regional Variations in Product and Process Innovation', *Environment and Planning A, 14,* 1073-86

OECD (1982a) *Financial Statistics Monthly,* December, No. 12, Paris

OECD (1982b) *Development Co-operation: Efforts and Policies of the Members of the Development Assistance Committee,* OECD, Paris

Olle, W. and Schoeller, W. (1982) 'Direct Investment and Monopoly Theories of Imperialism', *Capital and Class, 16,* 41-60

Oster, G. (1979) 'A Factor Analytic Test of the Theory of the Dual

Economy', *Review of Economics and Statistics, 61*, 33-9

Ouchi, W.G. (1977) 'The Relationship Between Organizational Structure and Organizational Control', *Administrative Science Quarterly, 22*, 95-113

Ouchi, W.G. and Maguire, M.A. (1975) 'Organizational Control: Two Functions', *Administrative Science Quarterly, 20*, 559-68

Palloix, C. (1976) 'The Labour Process: from Fordism to Neo-Fordism' in Conference of Socialist Economists, *The Labour Process and Class Strategies*, CSE Pamphlet No. 1, London, pp. 46-67

Palloix, C. (1977) 'The Self-expansion of Capital on a World Scale', *Review of Radical Political Economics, 9*, 1-28

Pennings, J.M. (1975) 'The Relevance of the Structural-contingency Model for Organizational Effectiveness', *Administrative Science Quarterly, 20*, 393-410

Perlmutter, H.V. (1969) 'A Drama in Three Acts...the Tortuous Evolution of the Multinational Corporation', *Columbia Journal of World Business*, Jan-Feb, pp. 9-18

Perrons, D.C. (1981) 'The Role of Ireland in the New International Division of Labour: a Proposed Framework for Regional Analysis', *Regional Studies, 15*, 81-100

Perrow, C. (1967) 'A Framework for the Comparative Analysis of Complex Organizations', *American Sociological Review, 32*, 194-208

Petit, T.A. (1967) 'A Behavioural Theory of Management', *Journal of Academic Management*, pp. 341-50

The Petroleum Economist (1982) July, pp. 286-90

Pfeffer, J. (1972) 'Merger as a Response to Organizational Interdependence', *Administrative Science Quarterly, 17*, 382-94

Pfeffer, J. (1981) *Power in Organizations*, Pitman, London

Pfeffer, J. and Salancik, G.R. (1978) *The External Control of Organizations: A Resource Dependence Perspective*, Harper and Row, London

Pick's Currency Yearbook (1980) Pick Publishing Corporation, New York

Pigment and Resin Technology (1983) May, *12*, 4-5

Poole, M.A. and O'Farrell, P.N. (1971) 'The Assumptions of the Linear Regression Model', *Transactions, Institute of British Geographers, 53*, 145-58

Product Finishing (1983) May, *36*, 6

Pugh, D.S., Hickson, D.J., Hinings, C.R. and Turner, C. (1968) 'Dimensions of Organization Structure', *Administrative Science Quarterly, 13*, 63-105

Pugh, D.S., Hickson, D.J., Hinings, C.R. and Turner, C. (1969) 'The Context of Organization Structures', *Administrative Science Quarterly, 14*, 91-114

Rabey, G.F. (1977) 'Contraction Poles: an Exploratory Study of Traditional Industry Decline within a Regional Industrial Complex', *Discussion Paper 3, Centre for Urban and Regional Development Studies*, University of Newcastle-upon-Tyne

Ranson, S., Hinings, B. and Greenwood, R. (1980) 'The Structuring of Organizational Structures', *Administrative Science Quarterly*, *25*, 1-17

Reader, W.J. (1970) *Imperial Chemical Industries: A History. Volume 1: The Forerunners, 1870-1926*, Oxford University Press, London

Reader, W.J. (1977) 'Imperial Chemical Industries and the State, 1926-1945' in B. Supple (ed.), *Essays in British Business History*, Clarendon Press, Oxford, pp. 227-43

Rees, J. (1972) 'The Industrial Corporation and Location Decision Analysis', *Area*, *4*, 199-205

Rees, J. (1974) 'Decision-making, the Growth of the Firm and the Business Environment' in F.E.I. Hamilton (ed.), *Spatial Perspectives on Industrial Organization and Decision-making*, John Wiley, Chichester, pp. 189-211

Rees, J. (1978) 'On the Spatial Spread and Oligopolistic Behaviour of Large Rubber Companies', *Geoforum*, *9*, 319-30

Reeves, T.K. and Turner, B.A. (1972) 'A Theory of Organisation and Behaviour in Batch Production Factories', *Administrative Science Quarterly*, *17*, 81-98

Richardson, K. (1981) 'Poised for Attack', *ICI Magazine*, *59*, 84-7

Rimmer, P.J. and Black, J. (1983) 'Global Financiers, Consultants and Contractors in the Southwest Pacific Since 1970', *Pacific Viewpoint*, *24*, 112-39

Robinson, J.N. (1981) 'Is it Possible to Assess Country Risk?', *The Banker*, *131*, 71-9

Rose, M. (1975) *Industrial Behaviour: Theoretical Developments since Taylor*, Allen Lane, London

Rugman, A.M. (ed.) (1982) *New Theories of the Multinational Enterprise*, Croom Helm, London

Sayer, R.A. (1980) 'Some Methodological Problems in Industrial Location Studies', paper delivered to the IBG Industrial Geography and Economic Activity Group, 9 May

Schmenner, R.W. (1982) *Making Business Location Decisions*, Prentice-Hall, Engelwood Cliffs

Schmenner, R.W. (1983) 'Every Factory has a Life Cycle', *Harvard Business Review*, *83*, 121-9

Siegel, S. (1956) *Non-parametric Statistics for the Behavioural Sciences*, McGraw-Hill, London

Simon, H.A. (1957) *Models of Man*, John Wiley, New York

Sinclair, R. and Walker, D.F. (1983) 'Industrial Development via the Multinational Corporation: General Motors in Vienna, *Regional Studies*, *16*, 433-42

Singh, A. (1977) 'UK Industry and the World Economy: a Case of Deindustrialisation?', *Cambridge Journal of Economics*, *1*, 113-36

Smith, I.J. (1979) 'The Effects of External Takeovers on Manufacturing Employment Change in the Northern Region between 1963 and 1973', *Regional Studies*, *13*, 421-37

Smith, I.J. and Taylor, M.J. (1983) 'Takeovers, Closures and the Restructuring of the UK Ironfoundry Industry', *Environment and Planning A*, *15*, 639-61

Sohn-Rethel, A. (1976) 'The Dual Economics of Transition' in Conference of Socialist Economists, *The Labour Process and Class Strategies*, CSE Pamphlet No. 1, London, pp. 26-45

Stanfield, G.G. (1976) 'Technology and Organisation Structure as Theoretical Categories', *Administrative Science Quarterly, 21*, 489-93

Steed, G.P.F. (1970) 'Changing Linkages and Internal Multiplier of an Industrial Complex', *Canadian Geographer, 14*, 229-42

Steed, G.P.F. (1971) 'Changing Processes of Corporate Environment Relations', *Area, 3*, 207-11

Stobaugh, R. and Telesio, P. (1983) 'Match Manufacturing Policies and Product Strategy', *Harvard Business Review, 83*, 113-20

Stopford, J.M., Dunning, J.H. and Haberich, K.O. (1980) *The World Directory of Multinational Enterprises*, Sijthoff and Noordhoff, Netherlands

Stopford, J.M. and Wells, L.T. (1972) *Managing the Multinational Enterprise: Organisation of the Firm and Ownership of the Subsidiaries*, Longman, London

Storper, M. (1982) 'Technology, the Labour Process and the Location of Industries', unpublished PhD dissertation, University of California, Berkeley

Storper, M. and Walker, R. (1983) 'The Theory of Labour and the Theory of Location', *International Journal of Urban and Regional Research, 7*, 1-41

Sunday Times (1980a) 2 March, p. 47

Sunday Times (1980b) 26 October, p. 36

Sunday Times (1983) 24 July, p. 25

Sutton, R.L. (1974) 'Cultural Context and Change–agent Organizations', *Administrative Science Quarterly, 19*, 547-62

Taylor, M.J. (1975) 'Organisational Growth, Spatial Interaction and Location Decision-making', *Regional Studies, 9*, 313-23

Taylor, M.J. (1983) 'Technological Change and the Segmented Economy' in A. Gillespie (ed.), *Technological Change and Regional Development*, *London Papers in Regional Science 12*, Pion, London, pp. 104-17

Taylor, M.J. and Thrift, N.J. (1979) 'Guest Editorial', *Environment and Planning A, 11*, 973-5

Taylor, M.J. and Thrift, N.J. (1981a) 'Organisation, Location and Political Economy: Towards a Geography of Business Organisations', *Centre for Urban and Regional Studies Working Paper 38*, University of Newcastle-upon-Tyne

Taylor, M.J. and Thrift, N.J. (1981b) 'Some Geographical Implications of Foreign Investment in the Semi-periphery: the case of Australia', *Tijdschrift voor Economische en Sociale Geografie, 72*, 194-213

Taylor, M.J. and Thrift, N.J. (1982a) 'Models of Corporate Development and the Multinational Corporation' in M.J. Taylor and N.J. Thrift (eds.), *The Geography of Multinationals*, Croom Helm, London, pp. 14-32

Taylor, M.J. and Thrift, N.J. (1982b) 'Industrial Linkage and the

Segmented Economy: 1. Some Theoretical Proposals', *Environment and Planning A, 14,* 1601-13

Taylor, M.J. and Thrift, N.J. (1982c) 'Industrial Linkage and the Segmented Economy: 2. An Empirical Reinterpretation', *Environment and Planning A, 14,* 1615-32

Taylor, M.J. and Thrift, N.J. (eds.) (1982d) *The Geography of Multinationals,* Croom Helm, London

Taylor, M.J. and Thrift, N.J. (1983) 'Business Organization, Segmentation and Location', *Regional Studies, 17,* 445-65

Taylor, M.J. and Thrift, N.J. (1984) 'The Regional Consequences of a Dualistic Industrial Structure: the Case of Australia', *Australian Geographical Studies, 22*

Taylor, P.J. (1981) 'Factor Analysis in Geographical Research' in R.J. Bennett (ed.), *European Progress in Spatial Analysis,* Pion, London, pp. 251-67

Teulings, A.W.M. (1984) 'The Internationalisation Squeeze: Double Capital Movement and Job Transfer within Philips-Worldwide', *Environment and Planning A, 16,* 597-614

Thirwall, A.P. (1982) 'Deindustrialisation in the United Kingdom', *Lloyds Bank Review, 144,* 22-37

Thomas, M.D. (1980) 'Explanatory Frameworks for Growth and Change in Multiregional Firms', *Economic Geography, 56,* 1-17

Thomas, W.A. (1978) *The Financing of British Industry 1918-1976,* Methuen, London

Thompson, J.D. (1967) *Organizations in Action,* McGraw-Hill, New York

Thrift, N.J. (1980) 'Fröbel and the New International Division of Labour' in R. Peet (ed.), *An Introduction to Marxist Theories of Underdevelopment,* Department of Human Geography Monograph, Publication HG14, Australian National University, Canberra, pp. 181-9

Thwaites, A.T. (1978) 'Technological Change, Mobile Plants and Regional Development', *Regional Studies, 12,* 445-61

The Times (1980) 15 December, p. 19

The Times (1981a) 27 February, p. 17

The Times (1981b) 14 April, p. 23

The Times (1982) 21 January, p. 15

The Times (1983a) 26 May, p. 25

The Times (1983b) 18 March, p. 5

The Times (1983c) 29 July, p. 43

Tinkler, K.J. (1971) 'A Coefficient of Association for Binary Data', *Area, 3,* 31-5

Tolbert, C., Horan, P. and Beck, E.M. (1980) 'The Structure of Economic Segmentation: A Dual Economy Approach', *American Journal of Sociology, 85,* 1095-116

Törnqvist, G. (1968) 'Flows of Information and the Location of Economic Activities', *Geografiska Annaler, 50B,* 99-107

Törnqvist, G. (1970) 'Contact Systems and Regional Development', *Lund Studies in Geography, Series B,* Human Geography, 35,

University of Lund

Törnqvist, G. (1979) 'On Fragmentation and Coherence in Regional Research', *Lund Studies in Geography, Series B*, Human Geography, 45, University of Lund

Townsend, A.R. (1981) 'Geographical Perspectives on Major Job Losses in the UK 1977-80', *Area, 13*, 31-8

Townsend, A.R. (1982a) 'Recession and the Regions in Great Britain, 1976-1980: Analyses of Redundancy Data', *Environment and Planning A, 14*, 1389-1404

Townsend, A.R. (1982b) *The Impact of Recession: on Industry, Employment and the Regions, 1976-1981*, Croom Helm, London

Tukey, J.W. (1969) 'Analyzing Data — Sanctification or Detective Work?', *American Pscyhologist, 24*, 83-91

Tushman, M.L. (1979) 'Work Characteristics and Subunit Communications Structure: A Contingency Analysis', *Administrative Science Quarterly, 24*, 89-97

Ullman, E.L. (1953) 'Human Geography and Area Research', *Annals, Association of American Geographers, 43*, 54-66

UN (1980) *Yearbook of Industrial Statistics, Volume 1: General Industrial Statistics*, UN, New York

UN (1981) *Yearbook of International Trade Statistics, Volume 1: Trade by Commodity, 1980*, UN, New York

UN (1983) *Monthly Bulletin of Statistics*, February, 37, UN, New York

UNESCO (1978) *Transnational Corporations in World Development: a Re-examination*, United Nations, New York

Utrecht, E. (1978) 'The Political Economy of ASEAN', *Journal of Australian Political Economy, 2*, 46-66

Van de Ven, A.H. and Delbecq, A.L. (1974) 'A Task-contingent Model of Work-unit Structure', *Administrative Science Quarterly, 19*, 183-97

Van den Bulcke, D., Boddewyn, J.J., Martens, B. and Klemmer, P. (1979) 'Investment and Divestment Policies of Multinational Corporations in Europe', Saxon House, Farnborough

Vernon, R. (1966) 'International Investment and International Trade in the Product Cycle', *Quarterly Journal of Economics 80*, 190-207

Vernon, R. (1979) 'The Product Cycle Hypothesis in a New International Environment, *Oxford Bulletin of Economics and Statistics, 41*, 255-67

Walker, R. and Storper, M. (1980) 'Technological Innovation, the Labour Process, and the Location of Industries: a Research Progress Report', Department of Geography and Institute of Urban and Regional Development, University of California, Berkeley

Walker, R. and Storper, M. (1981) 'Capital and Industrial Location', *Progress in Human Geography, 5*, 473-509

Wallerstein, I. (1979) *The Capitalist World Economy*, Cambridge University Press, Cambridge

Watts, H.D. (1974) 'Spatial Rationalisation in Multi-plant Enterprises', *Geoforum, 17*, 69-76

Watts, H.D. (1978) 'Inter-organisational Relations and the Location of Industry', *Regional Studies, 12*, 215-25

Watts, H.D. (1979) 'Large Firms, Multinationals and Regional Development: Some New Evidence from the United Kingdom', *Environment and Planning A, 11*, 71-81

Watts, H.D. (1980a) *The Large Industrial Enterprise*, Croom Helm, London

Watts, H.D. (1980b) 'The Location of European Direct Investment in the United Kingdom', *Tijdschrift voor Economische en Sociale Geografie, 71*, 3-14

Watts, H.D. (1981) *The Branch Plant Economy: a Study of External Control*, Topics in Applied Geography, Longman, London

Watts, H.D. (1982) 'The Inter-regional Distribution of West German Multinationals in the United Kingdom' in M.J. Taylor and N.J. Thrift (eds.), *The Geography of Multinationals*, Croom Helm, London, pp. 61-89

Wertheimer, H.N. (1971) 'The International Firm and International Aspects of Policies on Mergers' in J.B. Heath (ed.), *International Conference on Monopolies, Mergers and Restrictive Practices*, HMSO, London, pp. 171-206

Wishart, D. (1975) *'Clustan'*, University College, London

Wood, P.A. (1978) 'Industrial Organisation, Location and Planning', *Regional Studies, 12*, 143-52

Wood, P.A. (1980) 'Industrial Geography', *Progress in Human Geography, 4*, 406-16

Wood, P.A. (1981) 'Industrial Geography', *Progress in Human Geography, 5*, 414-19

Wood, P.A. (1984) 'Industrial Geography', *Progress in Human Geography, 6*, 576-83

Woodward, S. (1965) *Industrial Organization: Theory and Practice*, Oxford University Press, Oxford

World Bank (1982) *World Development Report*, Oxford University Press, New York

Yannopoulos, G.M. and Dunning, J.H. (1976) 'Multinational Enterprises and Regional Development: an Exploratory Paper', *Regional Studies, 10*, 389-99

Zimbalist,. A. (ed.) (1979) *Case Studies on the Labour Process*, Monthly Review Press, New York

Subject Index

281

Author Index